Milestones of History

8 Age of Optimism

1803

1803

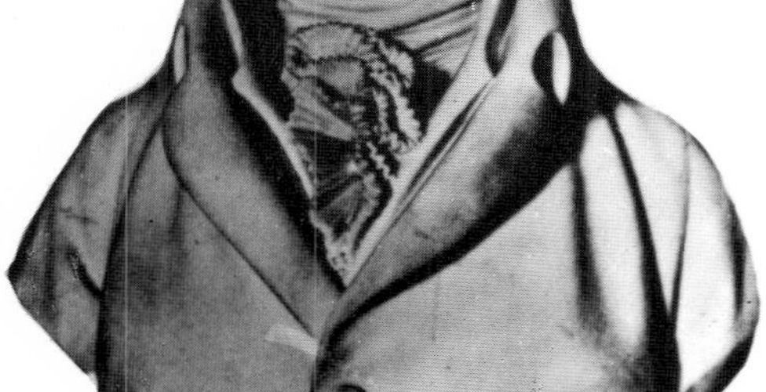

1807

1811

Newsweek Books New York

Editor Alan Palmer

1812

1815

1824

Milestones of History

8 Age of Optimism

1824

1829

1830

ISBN: Clothbound edition 0-88225-072-8
ISBN: Deluxe edition 0-88225-073-6
Library of Congress Catalog Card No. 73-81690

First published 1970. Revised and expanded edition 1974

Printed and bound in Italy by
Arnoldo Mondadori Editore – Verona

1834

1836

1848

1850

1851

1854

Contents

Introduction

The coming of the French Revolution, symbolized by the fall of the Bastille, was celebrated throughout Europe as the beginning of a new age. "Bliss was it that dawn to be alive, but to be young was very heaven," wrote Wordsworth looking back on the year 1789 after the turn of the new century. To a reading public whose intellect had been sharpened by Rousseau and whose imagination had been stirred by Herder and Goethe it appeared natural, in that summer of 1789, for mankind to shake off the restraints of political absolutism by such a supreme gesture of defiance. Ahead there seemed to lie a world in which democratic rule and fraternal understanding would ensure eternal peace. The eighteenth century had taught and sought the perfectibility of man. Now at last had come the opportunity for self discovery, the moment for casting aside the dynastic wars of princes and the interminable squabbles of religion. Good sense, allied to popular enthusiasm, would establish a society in which men would live in harmony with one another, willing to harness the benefits of science for bettering life alike in the towns and the country. At the start of this last decade of the Age of Reason a whole range of theories and ideals, of artistry and invention, proclaimed a consciousness of change and a faith in the future.

Ten years later, when the new century began, much of this optimism had evaporated. The reality of revolution fell far short of expectation. What had seemed to many in 1789 the first streaks of day was no more than the romantic glow of a false dawn. "The red fool-fury of the Seine" (to use Burke's vivid phrase) swept aside tradition and convention but imposed in their place a new rigidity of belief. The brotherhood of peoples sounded a hollow ideal when exported behind the cannon and bayonets of an invading army. Nor were these disappointments limited to political change. The technological revolution, which had seemed to promise more food and more clothing for more people, was placed at the service of war, and the growth of industry was hampered by the artificial barriers imposed on trade by the long conflict. Men who had at first admired the French Revolution and looked for prosperity from the Industrial Revolution were left bewildered and confused by the contradictions and frustrations that followed in their wake. Wordsworth regretted a Europe "yet in bonds" and William Blake wrote of English laborers condemned to "spend the days of wisdom in sorrowful drudgery to obtain a scanty pittance of bread."

Yet there remained in continental Europe—and in Britain, too—a residue of hope during these opening years of the nineteenth century. Napoleon's progression through the forms of a Consulate to the dignity of Empire may have offended true champions of liberty, but at least he swept aside the accumulated dust of feudal institutions: there could never be a return to the privilege and bigotry of the old order. Moreover, even when forced to serve in the new mass armies, the young felt their spirit freer than it had been in the campaigns of the fallen dynasties—there was a Romanticism of action as well as a Romanticism of creativity. Writers of verse and novels, artists and composers were no longer bound to subjugate their inspiration to a fixed order of discipline. This was the mood, not only of the later Beethoven, but of the patriot poets who, having found first their own personalities, went on to evoke a collective spirit from an idealized past and thereby held out hope for peoples seeking to realize their national identity. When Napoleon fell in 1814 the Romantic spirit became the principal source of creative energy in Europe for the Age of Optimism.

Across the Atlantic, life moved at a different pace. In 1778 the French statesman, Turgot, sent a famous letter, published seven years later, to Dr. Richard Price: "This people," he wrote, "is the hope of the human race. It may become the model. It ought to show the World by facts that men can be free and yet peaceful." Turgot's concept of the thirteen American states proving an inspiration for a troubled world added a stamp of nobility to the often fractious struggles of the four million ex-colonists in their search for a durable union. He did not, however, enunciate a new principle. Pioneer settlers had always hoped they were establishing a saner society than existed in the Europe they had left; and the belief that the American Union was giving shape to this design filled the young nation with confidence under the administrations of the first seven or eight presidents. Yet, in one sense, this was a limited ideal. The real motive force in the growth of America eluded Turgot: the earliest English, Dutch and Swedish emigrants were aware that along the rivers and behind the hills there was free land calling for settlement; and, during the passage of more than two hundred years, this desire for expansion intensified until it became a secular mission, and sometimes a spiritual one, too. Throughout the first half of the nineteenth century—and, indeed, for several decades more—the principal task of the American people, in their own eyes, was to advance the line of settlement westward across "the continent allotted by Providence for the free development of our yearly multiplying millions." Although this sense of Manifest Destiny was not put into words until 1845, it was present from the beginning of the century, when President Jefferson sent Meriwether Lewis and William Clark to blaze a trail across the territories he had newly purchased from Napoleonic France. The American Ideal remained rich in hope and promise, for the white man, even if it was not for the Indians or the Negroes on the plantations.

It was otherwise in the Europe of the Vienna Congress. The new political map completed in 1815 denied fulfillment to almost every liberal aspiration of the age. There was, on that map, no unified Germany and no unified Italy; the wrong committed against the Poles by the three partitions of their old elective kingdom was not rectified; and no one at the Congress responded to the stirrings of the Greeks as they sought recognition of their independent nationhood. The furious pen of Byron, roused to bitter contempt by the slow and pompous deliberations of the statesmen, continued to castigate them until his death in 1824. He made little distinction between the leaders of his own country and of Europe—"They're alike," he railed, "As common coin as ever mint could strike." And a people disappointed that the New Europe was not so very different from the Old echoed the Romantic Hero's scorn long after his remains were interred in a Nottinghamshire grave.

Today it is clear the conservative statesmen and sovereigns themselves hoped for a better world after the downfall of Napoleon. Metternich and Castlereagh believed they had devised a diplomatic system that would save the Continent from the tragedies of war and upheaval. Tsar Alexander I thought it possible, through religious sentiment, to bind the rulers of Europe in a union of virtue so as to elevate international conduct to a new moral plane. But throughout the Continent both the Metternich System and Alexander's "Holy Alliance" were seen by Romantic liberals as instruments of repression—sterile and therefore bound to fail. Hope for the future gave the politically oppressed remarkable resilience. The fortress prison of the Spielberg towered over the town of Brno and the fertile valleys of Moravia, a hundred and forty miles north of Vienna. Throughout the Metternich era Italian patriots were confined there, in the dark cells of a medieval castle. One of them, Silvio Pellico, committed his thoughts to paper, showing not merely a rare patience and charity of spirit but an utter confidence in the final triumph of the liberal and national cause. A similar faith, sorrow-resigned but optimistic, sustained the Polish prophet-poet, Adam Mickiewicz, in exile and many other political dissidents, whether imprisoned by their governments or forced to seek sanctuary abroad. Some were ready to fight for freedom elsewhere than in their own lands. The great Garibaldi recruited an Italian legion in Uruguay, designing for it a black flag for his country's mourning but decorating it with a volcano beginning to erupt, a symbol of the constant flame of hope.

By the end of the 1830s, liberals and conservatives in Europe were living once more in expectation of revolution. When at last it came, in the year 1848, the liberals won easy successes but suffered swift disaster. The revolutionaries of 1848, though differing in so many ways from one nation to another and even from town to town, were all children of the Romantic imagination. For the most part they came from the urban middle classes and they responded, all too readily, to the seductively irrational thrill of political make-believe. The revolutions were not a total failure; they shattered many dreams but they also gave rise to new legends that provided inspiration for the future. Basically, however, the character of the political contest was never the same after 1848. The new generation was less concerned with striking fine gestures on the barricades of revolt and more interested in the mechanics of political power. By the middle of the 1850s, in broad terms, Realism was triumphing over Romanticism: hope for the future came to rest on the achievements of science and industry rather than on forms of government.

There was good reason for this changed sense of optimism. During the politically arid years of Metternich's primacy, the Industrial Revolution spread to the mainland of Europe, forcing old methods of production to make way for the new factories. In Germany alone, industrial production doubled in the thirty years after the Napoleonic Wars, though in some countries, notably France, progress was much slower because of a relative shortage of coal deposits. More factories inevitably meant much human degradation, but they also gave more people than ever before the opportunity to make—or lose—money. Socially and economically the most startling change was the development of railways, conveying not only people but goods and raw materials between regions previously separated by distance and the contours of geography. The linking of Liverpool and Manchester by rail in 1830 was followed by twenty years of rapid growth in Europe and America. By midcentury there were 2,000 miles of railway in France, 4,000 in Germany, 7,000 in Britain and 9,000 in the United States. If the iron rail held out the prospect of new fortunes in Europe, across the Atlantic it promised a way of girdling the continent from ocean to ocean, from the sprawling cities of the eastern seaboard to the stream beds of the Sierra Nevada where men sought gold in the sand of a washbowl. It is one of the ironies of American history that the decade that preceded the Civil War should have been marked by a sense of prosperity and optimism that was greater than any known before.

The Age of Steam meant, of course, far more than cumbersome locomotives puffing their way westward to Pittsburgh or Chicago. The Dutch vessel *Curaçao* had made the first all-steam crossing of the Atlantic as early as 1826, and by midcentury Samuel Cunard's transatlantic steamship company already had ten years of experience behind it. Advances in technological science were contracting world society with remarkable speed; less than half a century after Fulton's *Clermont* made the first thirty-hour steam voyage up the Hudson to Albany, steam frigates of the United States Navy were anchored below Mount Fuji, ready to "open up" Japan. While steam was changing the character of communications, other inventions—less dramatic in form—were revolutionizing agriculture. Cyrus McCormick's reaping machine of 1834, followed three years later by the introduction to the American and Canadian prairies of John Deere's steel plough, ensured that at least the Industrial Revolution would be able to promise the grain that the new urban centers required for their expanding population. When, in 1851, Victorian England celebrated the material achievements of science in the Great Exhibition, pride of place went naturally to British manufacturers, but it was the new labor-saving devices from America that excited the most wonder. The Age of Optimism, it seemed, was making way for an Age of Plenty.

ALAN PALMER

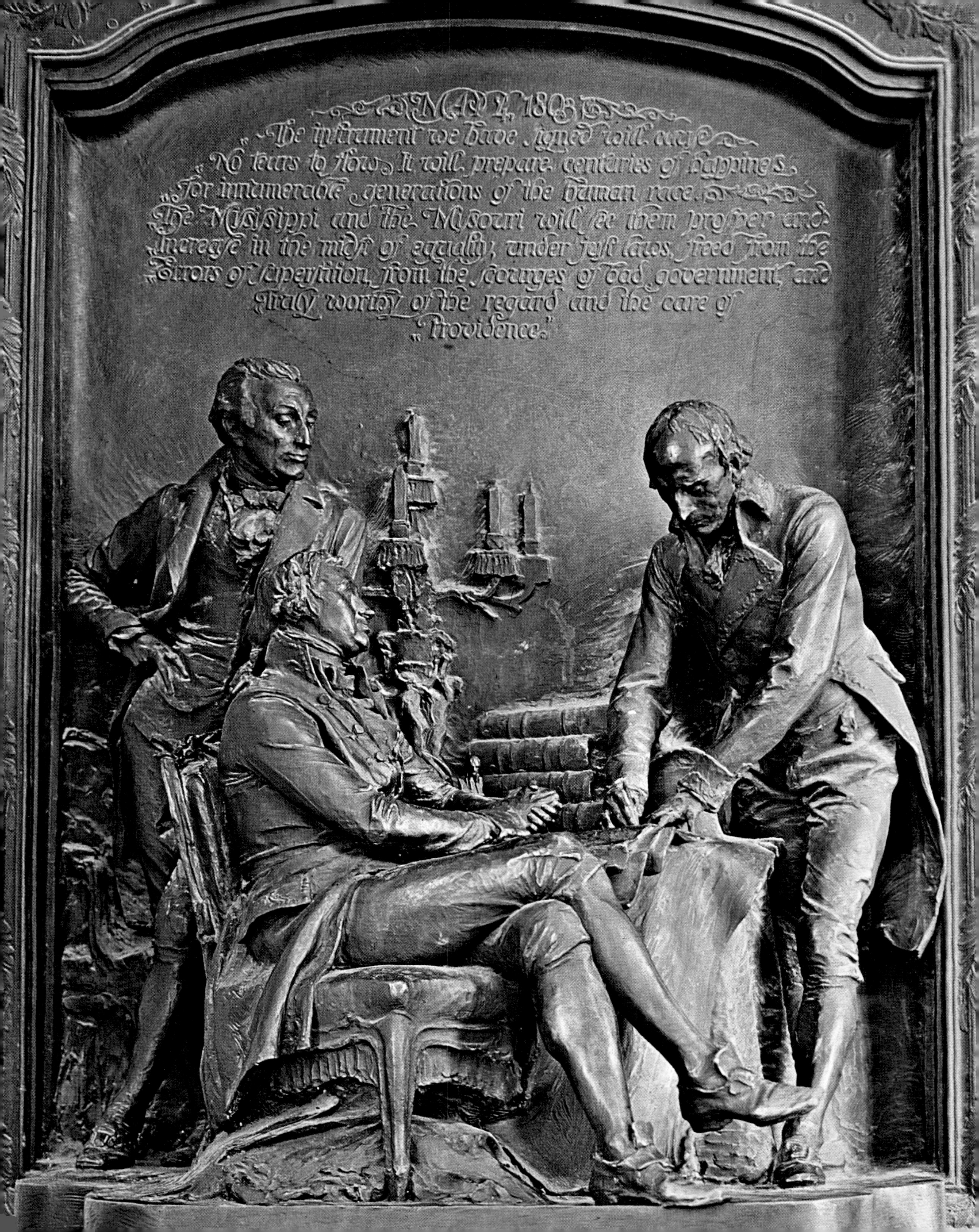
MAY 4, 1803
"The instrument we have signed will cause
No tears to flow. It will prepare centuries of happiness
For innumerable generations of the human race.
The Mississippi and the Missouri will see them prosper and
increase in the midst of equality, under just laws, freed from the
errors of superstition, from the scourges of bad government, and
truly worthy of the regard and the care of
Providence."

The Louisiana Purchase 1803

In 1803, President Thomas Jefferson sent James Monroe to Paris to assist Ambassador Robert Livingston in his attempt to buy from France the then-French port of New Orleans. To their astonishment, they were offered the entire "Louisiana Territory" of more than 800,000 square miles. Although lacking the authority to do so, Livingston and Monroe made the purchase and were backed later by Jefferson and finally the Congress. In so doing they had practically doubled the size of the United States at the rock-bottom cost of roughly five cents per acre.

In 1800, Napoleon Bonaparte, First Consul of the French Republic, forced Spain to cede back to France the vast Louisiana territory west of the Mississippi River, which had been under Spanish sovereignty since the Peace of Paris of 1763. Europe was just then enjoying the lull in the Napoleonic Wars that the Peace of Amiens had brought, but everyone knew that the renewal of hostilities was merely a question of time. In America the War Hawks clamored for action against France before Napoleon could mount a campaign in America. But the young American Republic had been neutral since the start of the Wars in 1793, and President Thomas Jefferson had a better idea. Why not, he asked himself, block a future French attack by buying the port at the mouth of the Mississippi, the island town of New Orleans, from the French government?

It was a bold idea and its outcome surprised even Jefferson. In April, 1803, the American negotiators at Paris pulled off one of the most astounding bargains in history. For just over $27,000,000 they had purchased, not just New Orleans, but the whole vast wilderness—more than 800,000 square miles—of Louisiana. As he was about to sign the deed to complete the sale, the American minister in Paris, Robert Livingston, paused and said: "We have lived long, but this is the noblest work of our whole lives. . . . From this day the United States take their place among the powers of the first rank."

Only a quarter of a century earlier, the thirteen American colonies had been scarcely able to submerge their bickering and mutual suspicion in the effort to throw off British imperial rule. Now, just two decades after becoming a nation, their central government had by a flourish of the pen nearly doubled the area of the country and set America on its expansionist course. It was an astonishing mark of the speed with which America was growing up. And not the least astonishing aspect of the affair was that Thomas Jefferson was responsible for it.

Thomas Jefferson was born into an eminent place in the planter aristocracy of Virginia, the elite of colonial America. At the age of fourteen he inherited nearly three thousand acres of land and a large number of slaves. During most of his adult life he owned ten thousand acres and from one to two hundred slaves. As a young man he easily took on the political leadership that was expected of the Virginian gentry. After being admitted to the bar, he was elected to Virginia's House of Burgesses at the age of twenty-six. By 1790, he had risen to become Secretary of State in George Washington's cabinet.

When Washington began his presidency in 1789, political parties in the United States had not yet been born. But the partisan activities of his Secretary of the Treasury, Alexander Hamilton, soon divided the nation into two camps: Federalists and Republicans. Hamilton was the leader of the Federalists and the mantle of Republican leadership fell inevitably upon the shoulders of his greatest rival, Jefferson.

The main obstacle to union among the American colonies had been the jealous concern of each new state for its independent powers of legislation. For that reason the Constitution of 1787 had placed all powers not specifically granted to the central, federal government in the hands of the state governments—the origin of the doctrine that was to bedevil American politics for much of her history, the doctrine of "states' rights." Nevertheless, under Hamilton, the federal government acted unashamedly in the services of the mercantile and investing classes. By funding the national debt, by establishing a national bank and by other subsidiary policies, Hamilton subsidized those people who invested in manufacture, commerce and the public securities. And in doing so he stretched the authority of the federal government beyond what most

Thomas Jefferson, third President of the United States. Leader of the traditional agricultural interest and a champion of states' rights, he envisaged the westward expansion of "an Empire for liberty."

Opposite The signing of the Louisiana Treaty; a monumental plaque by Karl Bitter. By the purchase the United States extended her frontiers to the Rocky Mountains, thereby becoming a territorial power of the first rank.

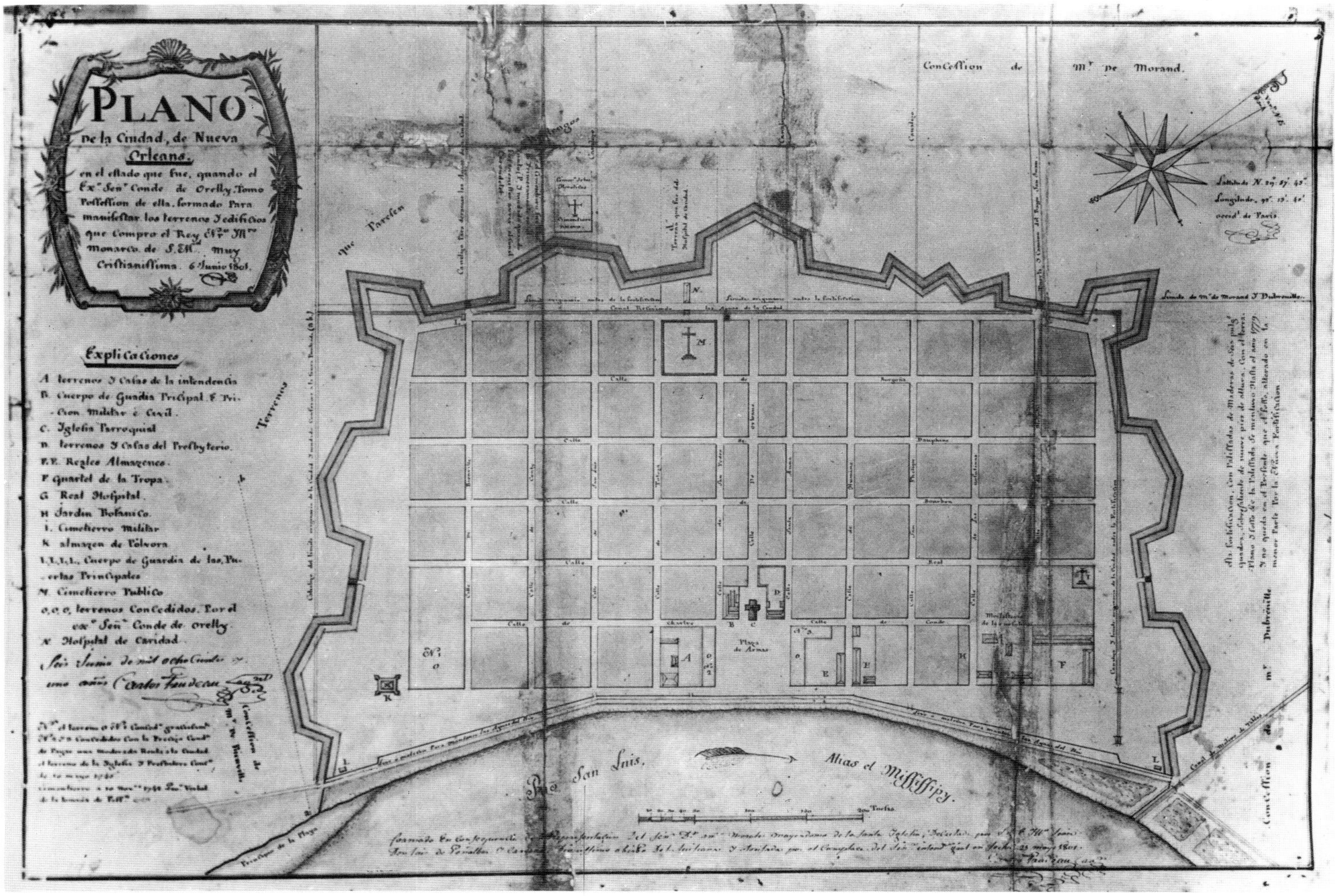

A Spanish plan of New Orleans, 1801. Wary of Napoleon's imperial ambitions, Jefferson offered to buy the city. The French decision to sell the whole of Louisiana surpassed his greatest expectations.

lawyers considered were its constitutional limits. It was because of Hamilton's wide interpretation of the powers of the federal government that his party became known as the Federalists and Jefferson fought a losing battle inside the government against Hamilton's policies. And yet, in 1803, Jefferson, in a blatant extension of presidential power, purchased Louisiana even though the Constitution makes no provision whatsoever for the acquisition of foreign territory.

The Louisiana Purchase seemed to make a mockery of Jefferson's long-standing quarrel with Hamilton. But there was another side to the question. Jefferson had opposed Hamilton, not simply because of the constitutional implications of Hamilton's policies—the creation of a huge central authority at Washington, remote from the people—but also because Hamilton was favoring the commercial and manufacturing classes and throwing as much of the tax burden as he could on farmers and Southern planters. During the 1790s the landed interest drew together and organized the Republican party in opposition to the Federalists. The landed interest was the majority of the nation, and it was with their votes that Jefferson won the presidential election of 1800.

Jefferson and the Republicans, then, stood for the traditional interest of America as an agricultural country against the rising commercial and manufacturing interests of the northeast. Throughout the colonial period America had supplied raw materials for British industry to manufacture, and Jefferson wished the workshops of America to remain in Europe. Partly, he was concerned about protecting the future of those people whose property was invested in the land. But more important, he wished to preserve an agrarian way of life, because he believed that it was morally superior to an urban way of life. "Those who labor in the earth," he said, "are the chosen people of God, if ever he had a chosen people. Corruption of morals in the mass of cultivators is a phenomenon of which no age or nation has furnished an example." Farmers were therefore "the true representatives of the great American interest . . . alone to be relied upon for expressing the proper American sentiments." Free land, and plenty of it, was the essential requirement for the United States. "I think our governments will remain virtuous for many centuries," Jefferson prophesied, "as long as they remain chiefly agricultural; and this will be as long as there shall be vacant lands in any part of America. When they get piled upon one another in large cities, as in Europe, they will become corrupt."

Long before the Louisiana Purchase, the lure of the West had proved irresistible to frontiersmen. The British government's closing of the West to colonial settlers and traders had been one of the major disputes leading to the War of Independence. Edmund Burke, in a famous speech to the House of Commons in 1775 advising conciliation with America, had warned the government that its policy was a futile attempt to stem the future course of history. It was silly, Burke said, "to forbid as a crime, and to suppress as an evil, the command and blessing of Providence, 'Increase and multiply,' " and "to keep as a lair of wild beasts that earth which God, by an express Charter, has given to the children of men."

In the agreement that went into effect in 1783, Benjamin Franklin and John Jay, the American peace negotiators, had secured as the boundary of the new nation the Mississippi River from its source (wherever that was) to the southern extremity of Georgia at the line of 31° latitude: the eastern half of the Mississippi Valley had been secured for the American democracy. And before the ink was dry on the peace treaty, settlers were flooding through the Cumberland Gap into the territories of Kentucky and Tennessee, where they joined those pioneers who had been taken through illegally by Daniel Boone in and after 1775. By the late 1780s flatboats were beginning to float down the Ohio River; by the late 1790s the great pioneer cart track, shortcutting the winding Ohio River route, was being made into the Indiana and Illinois country, right up to the old French settlement of St. Louis, since 1763 in Spanish hands.

Jefferson had made his reputation as a reformer, and there were some people who conceived the building of a western empire and the precepts of political liberty to be incompatible. Not so Jefferson. Louisiana was an area that, apart from a few trappers and *voyageurs*, and forty thousand Creoles and their slaves on the banks of the Mississippi, remained unexploited—a vast wilderness going to waste. To Jefferson, born on the frontier within sight of the Blue Ridge of the Alleghenies, it was a challenge. He pictured the spread to the west coast of "free and independent Americans, unconnected with us but by ties of blood and interest, and employing like us the rights of self-government." The West was to be "an Empire for liberty," a wilderness that America was "destined to fill with arts, with science, with freedom and happiness."

And while that vision danced in Jefferson's head, his roving imagination sensed the danger to the United States that would result if the decaying and effete Spanish monarchy were to give the Louisiana Territory back to the aggressive and rejuvenated French Republic under Napoleon. France had been the ally of America against Britain during the War of Independence, and although the violence of the French Revolution had turned some Americans—mostly Federalists—against her, Jefferson and his followers had continued to defend the French revolutionaries' pursuit of liberty and had thus earned themselves the name of Republicans. By the mid-1790s, however, Franco-American relations had become severely strained. When the United States refused to allow French privateers to use American harbors as refuges from the British, while at the same time allowing the British to capture French provision ships in American waters, French anger exploded. In 1796, the Revolutionary government unloosed a swarm of privateers upon American shipping heading for Britain, and by the summer of 1797 they had captured more than three hundred American vessels. It was then that the merchants and manufacturers of New England began to scream for war. But although an undeclared war at sea continued throughout 1798–99, open war was averted.

In 1800, Napoleon forced the Spanish to give Louisiana back to the French. But since France did not take immediate possession of the territory, the treaty of retrocession was kept secret for more than a year. In May, 1801, Jefferson got wind of it, and at the same time Bonaparte's ambition to reestablish a French empire on the Mississippi in compensation for the loss of Canada in 1763 was revealed. A

Charles Maurice de Talleyrand, Napoleon's skillful Foreign Minister. For months he kept Livingston, the American ambassador, at bay until a firm decision to jettison the French role in the Caribbean had been reached.

Right John Jay, who together with Benjamin Franklin had negotiated the borders of 1783, securing the eastern half of the Mississippi Valley for the new Republic and marking the first stage in America's westward expansion.

French expedition was sent to the island of Santo Domingo to put down a slave insurrection there, with instructions to continue on to Louisiana via New Orleans. That was an alarming prospect for America, which had only partial control over the new states of Kentucky and Tennessee, both of which had shown signs of separatist ambitions almost as soon as they had entered the Union in 1792 and 1796 respectively. Napoleon's army had therefore to be kept from America's back door.

On April 18, 1802, Jefferson wrote to the American minister in Paris, Robert Livingston: "The day that France takes possession of New Orleans fixes the sentence which is to restrain her forever within her low-water mark. It seals the union of two nations, who, in conjunction, can maintain exclusive possession of the ocean. From that moment, we must marry ourselves to the British fleet and nation." It was an extraordinary letter, ignoring Washington's farewell warning to the United States to avoid foreign entanglements and alliances, and going counter to the pattern of American foreign relations of the previous quarter of a century.

Jefferson instructed Livingston to approach Napoleon's Foreign Minister, Charles Maurice de Talleyrand, and to ascertain whether the retrocession of Louisiana had actually taken place. If not, he was to try to prevent it. If it had, then he was to offer to buy New Orleans. Livingston was unable to gain a personal audience with Talleyrand and for months he had to be content with tantalizing rumors of a possible deal. Then, when war broke out again in Europe early in 1803, Jefferson seized his opportunity. By that time the transfer of Louisiana to France had openly taken place and Napoleon had hinted that he might be prepared to sell New Orleans to the United States, which was neutral, in order to prevent the possibility of its being captured by the British navy. In March, Jefferson commissioned James Monroe to go to Paris as a special envoy to negotiate with Livingston for the purchase of New Orleans.

They were instructed to offer any price up to $10,000,000 for New Orleans and the Floridas, thus adding to the United States the entire east bank of the Mississippi River and the Gulf of Mexico coast to the east. If that offer were rejected, then three-quarters the amount was to be offered for New Orleans alone. If even that failed, they were to insist upon a guarantee that the right of free navigation on the Mississippi would be preserved and that American traders would be allowed the right of deposit, or temporary storage, of their goods at New Orleans. That final ultimatum was to be backed by a threat of a closer American connection with Great Britain—a connection France would never tolerate.

Livingston began the negotiations before Monroe sailed from America. For a time he made little progress. Then, on April 11, 1803, Livingston went to the Foreign Minister's offices to repeat his offer to buy New Orleans. To his surprise Talleyrand suddenly blurted to him one question: "What will you give for the whole of Louisiana?" The American negotiators possessed neither the instructions nor the authority to purchase the whole of Louisiana; nevertheless they decided to act on their own. By April 30 the bargaining was finished. America had bought Louisiana for a song. The agreement was to pay $11,250,000 outright and to assume claims of its citizens against France in the amount of $3,750,000. Interest payments incidental to the final settlement made the total price $27,267,622—or about five cents per acre.

Why did Napoleon do it? The answer can be only conjecture, but there are a number of reasonable explanations. One was the failure of the Santo Domingo expedition. Napoleon poured 35,000 troops into the venture and lost them all, either to the enemy or to yellow fever. Without Santo Domingo, Louisiana lost most of its value to France. In addition, Jefferson's letter to Livingston, hinting at an Anglo-American alliance, had been deliberately leaked to Napoleon by Pierre Samuel Du Pont de Nemours, and may have influenced him. Most important of all was Napoleon's decision to renew the war with Great Britain, whose navy would certainly blockade and probably capture New Orleans. It must therefore have seemed sensible to Napoleon to surrender the whole territory and fatten his war coffers.

By twenty-four votes to seven the American Senate ratified the purchase. A few of the Federalists gnashed their teeth at Jefferson's high-handed action, but not Alexander Hamilton. Unlike some

The United States of America, 1803

Packing cotton in the American South. The burgeoning cotton industry spilled over into the adjacent Louisiana Territory. Thus the southermost states west of the Mississippi River—Louisiana, Missouri and Arkansas—eventually developed cotton-based economies.

Eastern financiers, he had never been in doubt about the value of the West and he parted company with some members of his party in order to advocate strenuously that the purchase be accepted. On December 20, 1803, the French prefect at New Orleans formally transferred Louisiana to the United States, and at New Orleans the tricolor was brought down and the Star-Spangled Banner hoisted in its place.

As early as 1787, John Adams, one of the signatories to the peace treaty of 1783, had predicted that his country was "destined" to spread over "the entire north part of this quarter of the globe." That early reference to the Manifest Destiny of America—one of the great preoccupying themes of nineteenth-century American history—was then hardly taken seriously. America was still an uneasy confederation of states, which were nearly bankrupt and militarily exhausted after their long struggle with Great Britain, and barely able to maintain in the west the boundaries gained in 1783. Now, in 1803, America had extended her frontiers to the Rocky Mountains in the west, to the headwaters of the Missouri River in the northwest, and to the Sabine River in the southwest. In the next two decades, six new states joined the Union: Louisiana (1812), Indiana (1816), Mississippi (1817), Illinois (1818), Alabama (1819), and Missouri (1821). And in 1819, one leftover of the purchase—the protracted dispute with Spain over the ownership of West Florida and Texas—was at last settled by the purchase of the Floridas from Spain and the establishment of a fixed southwestern boundary line. The northern boundary had a year earlier been confirmed by an Anglo-American convention as the 49th parallel running between the Lake of the Woods and the Rocky Mountains.

The Louisiana Purchase transformed America and brought her a new place in the eyes of the world. "This accession of territory [by the Americans]," remarked Napoleon, "affirms forever the power of the United States, and I have just given England a maritime rival that sooner or later will lay low her pride." ROBERT STEWART

Above James Monroe, co-signatory of the Louisiana Treaty. Jefferson's special envoy, he was sent to Paris to purchase New Orleans.

Left Robert R. Livingston, U.S. ambassador to Paris. On receiving Talleyrand's offer he and Monroe negotiated the purchase of all Louisiana despite the fact that they had no authorization to do so. In the event, a Senate majority ratified the purchase.

Opposite Raising the flag. Louisiana is formally transferred to the United States in a ceremony at New Orleans on December 20, 1803.

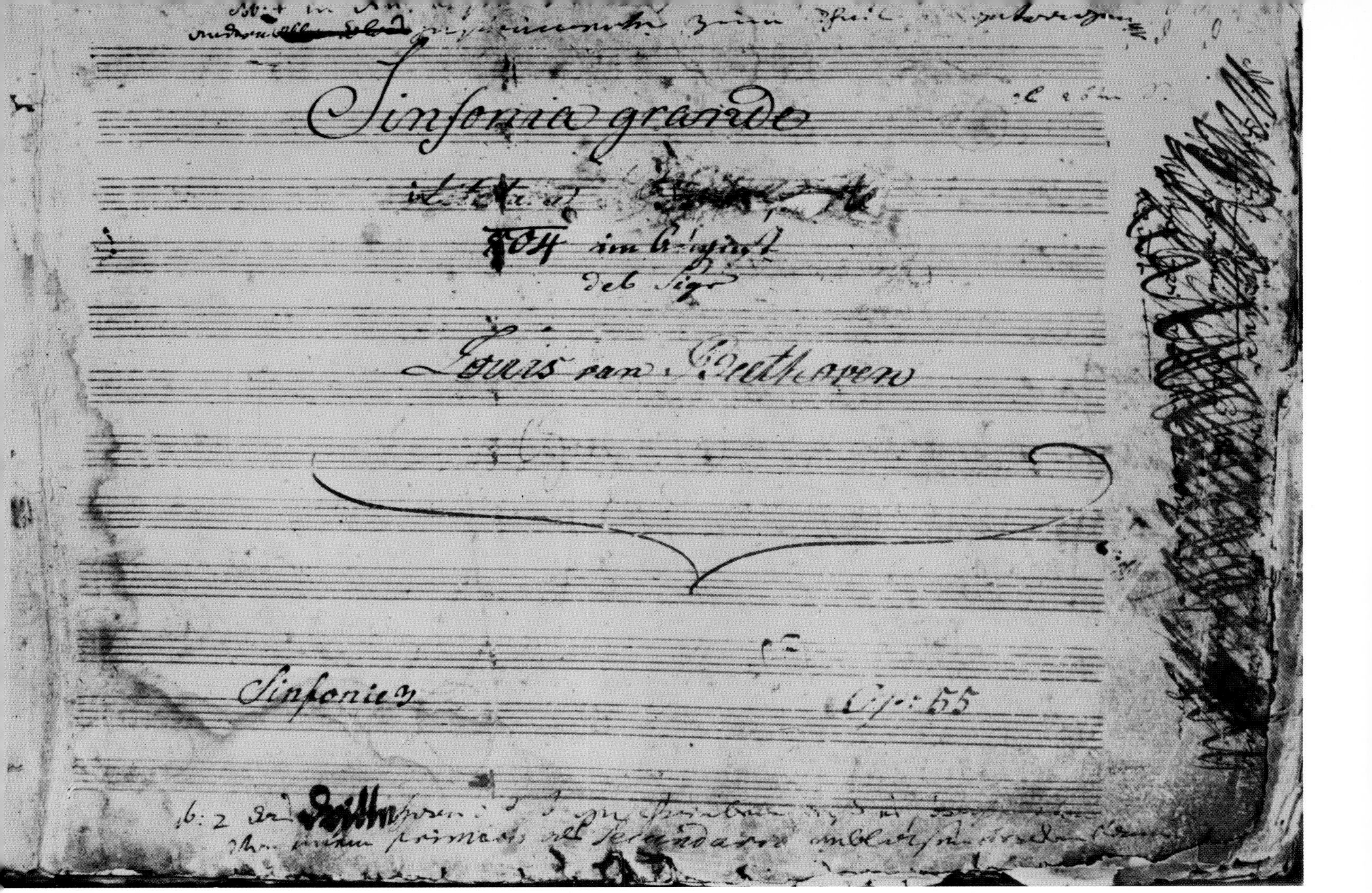
Sinfonia grande
1804 im August
del Sigr
Louis van Beethoven
Sinfonie
Op: 55

Allegro molto

Beethoven's Rededicated Masterpiece

1803

On December 2, 1804, Napoleon Bonaparte crowned himself Emperor of France. His action incensed the young German composer Ludwig van Beethoven, who had recently added a dedication to Napoleon to the written score of his newest symphony. Declaring that Napoleon had become "a tyrant," the thirty-four-year-old composer ripped the dedicatory page in half and discarded it. Later that same year, Beethoven's rededicated symphony—which he called the Eroica*—was performed for the composer's patron, Prince Franz Josef von Lobkowitz. The fascinating but bewildering new work was altered slightly in the next two years (in response to critical appraisals), and a final, authorized score was published in 1806. The vast scale of the* Eroica*—which was twice the length of Beethoven's earlier compositions—dwarfed the works of Beethoven's contemporaries and set a new standard for future composers.*

Ludwig van Beethoven was thirty-three when he began to sketch out a new symphony in E flat major, the *Eroica*, in 1803. Throughout his life he had been interested in politics, and thus it was natural that the activities of Napoleon Bonaparte should have occupied the composer's thoughts. Several contemporaries tell us that Beethoven intended the new symphony to center on the fascinating and controversial Corsican.

Beethoven's attitude changed, however, when Bonaparte crowned himself Emperor in 1804. The composer's pupil, Ferdinand Ries, gives us an interesting description of his teacher's reaction:

> Not only I but several other intimate friends saw this symphony, already written down in score, lying on his table, and on the title-page there was the word "Bonaparte" way at the top and way at the bottom "Luigi van Beethoven," not a word more. If and how the gap was supposed to be filled, I do not know. I was the first to bring him the news that Bonaparte had declared himself Emperor, whereupon he was enraged and cried, "He is not anything but a man like the rest of us! Now he will trample all the rights of man and only indulge his own ambitions; now he will put himself above everyone else and will become a tyrant!" Beethoven went to the table, took the title-page at the top and tore it in half, throwing it on the floor. The first page was written again, and now the symphony got its title: *Sinfonia eroica.*

This autograph manuscript has disappeared, but we do have a nineteenth-century manuscript score with many corrections and additions in Beethoven's own hand. The title-page of this score contains Beethoven's autograph and the dedication to Napoleon, which has been vigorously scratched out. This early copy, now owned by the Gesellschaft der Musikfreunde in Vienna, is dated 1804, the year in which Beethoven probably completed the first version of the symphony. When the symphony was published the title-page read, *Sinfonia eroica composta per festeggiar il sovvenire d'un grand uomo* (*Heroic symphony composed to celebrate the memory of a great man*).

As always, Beethoven worked long and hard before arriving at the final form of his new composition. In recent years a big sketchbook containing many pages of *Eroica* sketches has been discovered in the Soviet Union and published in facsimile. Many of the principal themes and other parts of the work are contained in these Russian sketchbooks, but not all appear for the first time. Beethoven constantly reshaped his material to make it more telling and very often more concise. One of the principal themes in the *Eroica*'s finale turns up in two other Beethoven compositions produced in 1801: a set of contredanses and the ballet *Die Geschöpfe des Prometheus* (*The Creatures of Prometheus*). Beethoven also used the theme as a subject for piano variations. But interesting though the use of the theme in these other works is, the *Eroica* seems to place it in a new context, which gives it a new dimension.

Because this was a period in which the composer was most inadequately protected by copyright laws, Beethoven conceived a scheme whereby he gave the exclusive right of performance of large-scale works to some wealthy patron for a year or two. In the case of the *Eroica*, the patron was Prince Franz Josef von Lobkowitz, a talented amateur musician (a contemporary newspaper describes him as having a "bass voice of rare beauty") at whose beautiful winter palace in Vienna the first performances of the *Eroica* took place sometime in 1804.

We have only very fragmentary reports of the symphony's reception at these semiprivate performances, but two contemporary reports illustrate something of the shock with which this new,

A sketch of Beethoven.

Opposite above The title-page of a contemporary manuscript of the *Eroica*, signed by Beethoven. *Below* A page of the score from the same manuscript.

Jacques Louis David, court painter of the Napoleonic Empire.

towering masterpiece was received. One is related to us by Ferdinand Ries. He tells us of the horn dissonance just before the recapitulation in the first movement, wherein the horn announces the beginning of the theme in the tonic while the tremolo strings are still in the dominant. It is even now a terrific dissonance. Ries reports: "At the first rehearsal of this symphony, which was ghastly, the horn player came in correctly. I was standing next to Beethoven and I thought he [the horn player] made a mistake and said: 'That damned horn player! Can't he count? It sounds monstrously wrong!' I think I was very near getting my ears boxed. Beethoven did not forgive me for a long time."

Another reaction came from the cultivated and charming Prince Louis Ferdinand of Prussia, who visited Vienna about this time and was at a concert given by Lobkowitz's private orchestra, at which the *Eroica* was performed. The Prince, himself a virtuoso pianist and a talented composer, was stunned by Beethoven's new composition and at the end asked to have the whole thing repeated.

The new symphony fascinated but also bewildered contemporaries. Georg August Griesinger, the friend and biographer of Joseph Haydn, who was Saxonian legation secretary at Vienna and who was in constant correspondence with the publishers Breitkopf & Härtel in Leipzig, wrote on February 13, 1805, from Vienna: "This much I can tell you, that the symphony was given in two concerts, one held at Prince Lobkowitz's and the other by a hard-working amateur called Wirth, and was received with much success. I hear both admirers and opponents of Beethoven praising it as a work of genius. The one group says, here is more than Haydn and Mozart, the symphonic ideal has been brought to a higher plane! The others [opponents] miss a certain overall roundness, they object to the piling-up of colossal ideas."

The first public performance took place on April 7, 1805, at a benefit concert by the violinist Franz Clement in the Theater an der Wien. (It was for Clement, a child prodigy who had played with Haydn in England, that Beethoven later composed his violin Concerto in D, Op. 61.) The critic of the *Allgemeine Musikalische Zeitung* must have summed up the general opinion when he wrote about the work as follows:

> This long, highly difficult composition is actually a very widely conceived, bold and wild fantasy. In it we do not miss original and beautiful passages in which one must recognize the energetic, talented spirit of its creator. . . . . The reviewer certainly belongs to Beethoven's sincerest admirers; but with this work he must admit that he finds all too many harsh and bizarre effects as a result of which it is difficult to preserve an overall view and its unity almost entirely disappears.

In a review after the second performance of the *Eroica*, the same correspondent tells his readers that the symphony lasted a whole hour. In those days, the first part of the opening movement's exposition was repeated, an idea that Beethoven later abandoned. The correspondent suggests:

> . . . the Symphony would greatly gain . . . if Beethoven could bring himself to shorten it and to introduce more light, clarity and unity into the whole . . . instead of the *Andante* there is a Funeral March in C minor which later receives fugal treatment. But that fugal section sinks from organized order into apparent confusion: and if after repeated hearing one misses an overall conceptual line even when one listens most attentively, this fact must appear curious to any unprejudiced lover of music. Also there is much missing in order that the symphony could please generally.

As was frequently the case with his most important compositions, Beethoven took his time about the *Eroica*'s first publication. No doubt many of the changes in the Gesellschaft der Musikfreunde copy of the score were made as a result of early performances.

Napoleon's coronation at Notre Dame, painted by David. When Napoleon became Emperor, Beethoven, furious that his hero had proved himself ambitious and fallible, changed the inscription of his third symphony.

It was not in fact until the autumn of 1806 that Beethoven allowed the work to be published. As was the custom in those days, the first edition was not of the score but of the individual parts. The work was dedicated to Prince Lobkowitz and contained the following interesting note on one of the pages of the first violin part:

This Symphony, having been expressly conceived as longer than customary, should be performed rather at the beginning than at the end of a concert, shortly after an overture, an aria, or a concerto; for if it is placed on the program later it will lose its proper and intended effect for the listener, who will have been tired by the previous numbers. The part of the third horn has been so conceived that it may be executed at will either by a first or second horn player.

Beethoven himself held the *Eroica* in high esteem. After he had written the Fifth Symphony, but before he had written the Ninth, he and a friend went to Nussdorf to dine at a favorite restaurant. Beethoven was in a particularly good mood, and the friend asked the composer which of his symphonies he preferred. "Ha, ha, the *Eroica*," said Beethoven in great good humor. His friend: "I would have thought the C minor [No. 5]." Beethoven: "No, the *Eroica*."

The symphony as Beethoven found it was a highly developed and beautifully symmetrical work of art. It had begun in Italy in the early eighteenth century as a *sinfonia* or operatic overture with three movements: fast-slow-fast. Then the Austrians and Germans had taken over the form and turned it into a concert symphony.

In 1740 a minor Austrian composer, G. M. Monn (1717–50), added a minuet as a penultimate movement. After some vacillation as to whether the minuet should be the second or third movement, and after some indecision as to whether it should be included at all, the minuet soon became an integral part of the symphonic structure.

Some of the early Austro-German productions were large-scale affairs with trumpets and drums, but others, particularly the Austrian, were chamber symphonies with a small orchestra generally consisting of oboes, horns and strings. By the middle of the century the symphony was a well-developed art form flourishing all over Europe, particularly in Paris, which was then one of the centers of the musical world and also the center for music publishing.

Although the early eighteenth-century symphony had much to recommend it—it was a highly civilized, formally subtle and neatly orchestrated affair—it could not be said that it plumbed the emotional depths. Audiences expected to hear bright and gay music, and such melancholy as there might be was generally confined to the slow movements and had a mild benevolence about it, rather like the Italian winter. Obviously this lack of emotional depth must have struck more than one composer, and it is interesting to observe that in the second part of the 1760s there seems to have been a kind of musical revolution all over Europe. Suddenly elegance was simply not enough. In

Above Beethoven in middle age. Despite his growing deafness, Beethoven continued to compose.

Below left The courtyard of the house in Bonn in which Beethoven was born.

Below right The organ on which Beethoven played from an early age. One of his first posts was as a court organist.

The Old Court Theater in the Michaelerplatz in Vienna. Beethoven studied under Haydn at Vienna, center of the musical world.

Paris, we find Franz Beck, a contemporary of Haydn and a pupil of Johann Stamitz, writing symphonies with a new spiritual depth and a strength that often borders on real violence. The minor key now assumed a different emotional character. Before, Italians such as Vivaldi had often treated minor keys in much the same manner as major ones. In this new revolutionary language, the minor key became the vehicle for an agonizing reappraisal.

In Vienna a whole group of interesting young composers, foremost among them Joseph Haydn, began to experiment with turbulent symphonies in the minor key. We find G minor symphonies by Haydn, Johann Christian Bach and the impressionable young Mozart, whose so-called Little G minor Symphony (K. 183) was composed as a result of a trip to Vienna in 1773. Some of the Haydn symphonies of this period achieve a disturbed emotional violence that is unique not only in Haydn's oeuvre but also in the whole eighteenth century. And not only symphonies were affected by this new and forceful language: we find it in sonatas, operas, and especially in the new string quartet form, such as Haydn's Opus 20 quartets of 1772. (These Haydn quartets also reintroduce large contrapuntal forms, including full-fledged fugues, into the sonata form. Beethoven was much impressed by the fugal finales in Haydn's Opus 20 and copied at least one entire movement for study.)

This musical movement has been allied to a similar movement in German literary circles known as the *Sturm und Drang* (Storm and Stress)—a philosophic concept that took its name from a now nearly forgotten play by Friedrich von Klinger written in 1776. The musical revolution, however, took place a few years before this German literary movement of the 1770s, which included Goethe and Schiller among its members. In any case Haydn himself to some extent repudiated his *Sturm und Drang* style, and his later symphonies returned to a better balanced, if emotionally less exciting, world.

Meanwhile Mozart had burst upon the scene, and while he did not write very many symphonies after his arrival in Vienna in 1781, those he did write caused a profound impression on thinking musical people. In particular the last four Mozart symphonies—the *Prague* in D, K. 504 (1787); in E flat, K. 543 (1788); in G minor, K. 550 (1788); in C, K. 551 (1788)—created a new atmosphere that was in part just as emotionally disturbed as the *Sturm und Drang* symphonies composed twenty years earlier. The G minor, K. 550, pushes the eighteenth-century symphony as close as possible to a frightening new world in which the ordered scheme of things sometimes appears almost to disintegrate: at the beginning of the second section in the symphony's finale, Mozart grimly flirts with what would in future be known as the twelve-note system.

Haydn's last twelve symphonies, written between 1791 and 1795, followed Mozart's, and in some respects they go even further formally and in pure brilliant force than Mozart's. Beethoven felt very much in awe of this grandiose symphonic tradition when he came to Vienna to study with Haydn in 1792, and although it would have been an expected move for Beethoven to write a symphony, he did not do so until 1799.

Beethoven's First Symphony was dedicated to Gottfried van Swieten, Haydn's and Mozart's patron and the author of the librettos for Haydn's *The Creation* and *The Seasons*. Chronologically, the symphony crosses the bridge to the nineteenth century but it is still very much an eighteenth-century work. Although it is beautifully executed and orchestrated by a master, it nevertheless does not penetrate into any new world. Nor does Beethoven's Second Symphony, a work of great brilliance and effect composed in 1802. The fast scherzos that Beethoven inserted in place of the traditional minuet derive from Haydn's late quartets of Opus 76 and especially Opus 77, in which are found the one-in-the-bar fast scherzo archetype that from then on was to become standard. Beethoven's orchestration is also that of late Haydn and Mozart: pairs of woodwinds, brass and kettledrums.

It is significant that after 1795 Haydn himself never wrote another symphony and even resisted attractive offers from Paris and elsewhere to do so. Obviously, he considered his concept of the symphony to be completed with his last three works of 1795. In a sense there was nothing other composers could do, if they were to remain within the boundaries established and perfected by Haydn and Mozart, except to write variants of what already had been done so brilliantly.

When Haydn returned from London in 1795, he turned his attention to large-scale choral music and produced the six last masses and the enormous oratorios *The Creation* (1798) and *The Seasons* (1801). Obviously Haydn had become interested in large-scale forms for which he felt the symphony was not fitted. We know from Beethoven's own words that he assiduously studied Haydn's late masses, and the complicated broad forms found in Haydn's *Schöpfungsmesse* (1801) and *Harmoniemesse* (1802) must have excited Beethoven's attention. Such a movement as the *Kyrie* in the *Harmoniemesse*—a long and involved slow movement that formally opens up a whole new world to conquer—may have suggested to Beethoven that a symphony might well be composed along similar lines.

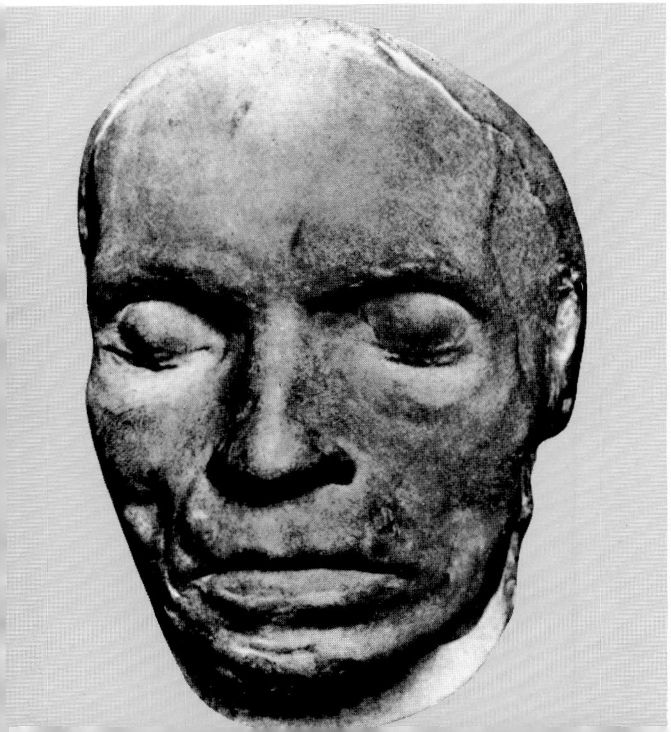

It is interesting that the *Eroica* is twice the length of not only Haydn's and Mozart's symphonies but also Beethoven's earlier efforts in the form. Quite simply, there are ideas on a vast scale that are better suited to grandiose movements. After all, no one had laid down the rule that it was necessary to write symphonies with Haydn's conciseness; and indeed, one of the very principles of Haydn's symphonic art is the at times violent telescoping of ideas such as that found in the first movement of Symphony No. 102. And if Haydn himself turned in his old age to broader ideas and larger form, it was clear that the symphony might be reorganized along such lines.

There has been much discussion as to whether Beethoven was a Classicist or a Romanticist. Nowadays we tend to think of him as the culmination of the Classical period. After all, Beethoven was deaf after about 1810 and can hardly have heard many of the new works of the budding German Romantic composers. There is one point, nevertheless, in connection with the *Eroica* that is worth making. Hitherto, composers' personalities to a certain extent tended to be subordinate to the concept and form of the art work they produced. If there is anything Romantic in Beethoven's treatment of the symphony, it is that the force of his towering personality is felt throughout the four movements. Here the listener feels that the personality has absolute command over form and content.

As far as the finale is concerned, this was perhaps the movement of the eighteenth century that was the most stereotyped. Naturally Haydn and Mozart wrote all sorts of different finales, some rondos, some in sonata form, and some in a brilliant combination of sonata and rondo. In one of the biggest Haydn finales, Symphony No. 101 (1794), there is a brilliant double fugue that enters in the middle of a sonata-rondo. And Mozart's fabulous *Jupiter* finale (K. 551, 1788) pointed the way to the finale's becoming much more than a witty and sophisticated conclusion. There is one characteristic insert in the *Eroica* finale that serves greatly to enlarge the horizon: the slow section that comes just before the final coda, and that not only broadens the size of the movement but introduces us to the innermost secrets of Beethoven's heart. Here was a man larger than life—here indeed was a soul expanded to greatness; here was one of the major milestones in the history of music.

From this point, indeed, the symphony never was the same; it never could go back to its eighteenth-century size and scope. Just as nothing in painting was ever the same after Masaccio and nothing in literature after Shakespeare, music was now ruled by the Beethoven stamp. Future composers would measure their efforts against his mighty ones. Johannes Brahms, composing his First Symphony in C minor, was to say: "I feel his giant steps behind me." Schubert, Dvořák, César Franck, Bruckner, Mahler—all looked back to 1803, when, in a peaceful suburb of Vienna, the symphony was reborn.

H. C. ROBBINS LANDON

Mozart as a child. Mozart's influence, like Haydn's, is apparent in much of Beethoven's work.

Beethoven's death mask.

Napoleon's Empire

On May 18, 1804, the senators of France issued an official proclamation which declared that, subject to the verdict of a later plebiscite, "the Government of the Republic is entrusted to a hereditary Emperor." Within the space of a few weeks the French people gave their all-but-unanimous assent to establishment of the Empire, and on December 2, 1804, Napoleon assumed the imperial crown in a dramatic ceremony in the Cathedral of Notre Dame. Lest any devout legitimist mock the credentials of the revolutionary dynasty, the Pope himself had been induced to travel to Paris to sanctify the solemn pageant by his presence and benediction, although he was not allowed to place the crown on the Emperor's head. Napoleon thus became symbolic successor to Charlemagne, who had received his crown from Pope Leo III in A.D. 800. The young lieutenant who had watched a republican mob batter down the Tuileries gates in August, 1792, had come a long way in the intervening years.

Napoleon's coronation finally alienated many of his earlier admirers—it seemed to Beethoven to stultify the revolutionary spirit. Yet in essence it corresponded with the mood of the times. The Romantic revolt against the Age of Reason had begun by evoking Greco-Roman themes, and, appropriately, Napoleon wore the laurels of a Roman conqueror during the ceremony at Notre Dame. By 1804, however, the Romantics had fully "discovered" an idealized medieval past as well. Therefore it was no surprise that Napoleon's coronation ceremony also consciously echoed the ritual of the "Empire of the West"—the heroic age of the epic twelfth-century *chansons de geste*.

In 1805—and as late as the summer of 1812—the Emperor seemed to be a man of destiny. Romantic ideas stirred the imagination of young conscripts with the thrill of a great adventure. "We are going to Greater India. It is three thousand miles from Paris," wrote a nineteen-year-old fusilier, as he set out for Moscow and the agony of the battle at the Berezina River. The rhetoric of the imperial bulletins, which identified the armies of the present with the victorious hosts of the past, encouraged a sense of marching with destiny. So long as Napoleon himself could hail "the God of War and the God of Success" as comrades-in-arms, the peoples of his Empire felt no need of a nostalgic quest through the centuries for national identity

The early years of the Empire were a long cavalcade of victory. During the fall of 1805, Napoleon marched against the most powerful of his enemies—Russia and Austria. On November 13, his troops entered Vienna, and one week later the first performance of Beethoven's *Fidelio*, an opera passionately exalting the ideals of 1789, was attended by an audience consisting exclusively of the Emperor's officers. On the first anniversary of his coronation, Napoleon routed the combined armies of Austria and Russia at Austerlitz. In the following October he humbled the Prussians at Jena, and in June, 1807, he wiped out another Russian army at Friedland. Tsar Alexander I of Russia, for two years France's implacable foe, sued for peace. He and Napoleon met on a raft in the Neman River at Tilsit, and the Tsar was soon flattered into friendship and alliance. A grandiose plan for partitioning Europe into a western sphere of influence (under the domination of France) and an eastern sphere (under the domination of Russia) made Tilsit the apogee of Napoleon's career. The Grand Army would gain other triumphs—it was to take Vienna a second time in May, 1809, and it was to see the golden cupolas of Moscow glinting under the September sun of 1812—but only at Tilsit did Napoleon hold the map of Europe in the palm of his hand. "The world begged me to govern it," he was to say amid the uncertainties of later years.

The meeting of Napoleon and Tsar Alexander I at Tilsit in 1807.

England's war effort

The British remained obstinately disinclined to make peace from the breakdown of the Peace of Amiens in 1802 until the final collapse of the Empire in 1814. Their military contribution to the campaigns of those years was slight, however. In the summer of 1808 a force of 15,000 men under General Sir Arthur Wellesley (1769–1852) landed in Portugal to check the inroads of General Junot's army in the Iberian Peninsula. For six years Wellesley's men tied down the French in the dusty red hills of Cantabria and Castile, thereby succoring the insurgent Spanish guerrillas, whose national insurrection was the first to challenge Napoleon's *imperium*. The fighting in Spain was to be immortalized by the engravings of Goya (1746–1828), but despite the fact that Wellesley (who became Earl of Wellington in 1812 and Duke in 1814) crossed the Pyrenees and reached Toulouse before the Emperor abdicated, the Peninsular Campaign remained essentially a sideshow, a second front that never became a decisive arena of battle. The "Spanish ulcer" may have weakened Napoleon, but it did not destroy him.

The principal British war effort was at sea. French mastery of the English Channel was essential if the soldiers of Napoleon's

The H.M.S. *Agamemnon, Captain, Vanguard, Elephant* and *Victory*—vessels in which Nelson won distinction as Captain, Commodore and Admiral.

that Britannia rules the waves

Grand Army were ever to land in southern England. The French naval squadrons were divided between the bases of Brest and Rochefort in the Atlantic and Toulon in the Mediterranean, and for two years after the resumption of war in 1803, the Royal Navy kept a close watch on each of those bases. Three-decker ships of the line—floating batteries of a hundred cannon—and single-decked frigates mounted with two or three dozen guns braved gales in the Bay of Biscay and squalls in the Mediterranean to batten down the Franco-Spanish squadrons.

Despite the British navy's vigilance, the Count of Missiessy managed to slip out of Rochefort, and Admiral Pierre de Villeneuve (1763–1806) managed to evade the blockade of Toulon early in 1805. The French admirals sought to carry the war to the West Indies, where they hoped to evade the British patrols and double back along an unguarded channel. Missiessy successfully raided Martinique, but he was eventually forced to return to Rochefort; Villeneuve was chased by Admiral Horatio Nelson (1758–1805) for five months before he finally found refuge at Cadiz.

Trafalgar

On October 21, 1805, Villeneuve put to sea again. He was intercepted by the British off Cape Trafalgar and lost eighteen of his thirty-three ships. Some 4,408 French and Spanish sailors perished in that battle and the storm that followed it; the British lost 449 officers and seamen, among them Nelson himself. Consequently, the news of Britain's greatest naval victory was received not with jubilation but with mourning.

Detail from the *Death of Nelson*, by Denis Dighton.

The battle at Trafalgar confirmed the supremacy of British sea power, and although Napoleon rapidly rebuilt his fleet (he did more for the French navy than any administrator since Colbert), British command of the high seas was never seriously challenged until the end of the nineteenth century. Naval maneuvers in the decade following Trafalgar consisted primarily of blockade operations and the interception of commercial shipping. It was a war of attrition, expensive and exhausting. Conditions of service in the Royal Navy were grim; more than twelve times as many British seamen died from disease in the Napoleonic Wars as were killed in battle. Since numbers could be kept up only by impressment, it is hardly surprising that there were 10,000 more desertions than deaths. The hardy veterans who survived were famous for their jollity and good cheer; with two shillings and sixpence a week in pay, a diet of salt beef and maggoty biscuit, and the threat of fifty or more lashes for disobedience, they certainly needed a merry temperament if they were to remain sane!

Once the danger of invasion receded in 1805, the Napoleonic Wars made little direct impact on the people of the British Isles. The novels of Jane Austen (1775–1817), most of which were written in that period (while her brothers were serving as naval officers in the Mediterranean and the Atlantic), are vignettes of a comfortably peaceful society. The wars did not constitute a serious drain on manpower. Wellington's total casualties in the Iberian Peninsula were lower than those lost by the Russian General Mikhail Kutuzov (1745–1813) in ten hours at Borodino in 1812. Indeed, fewer than 54,000 British sailors and soldiers died from enemy action in the eleven years between the resumption of hostilities and the abdication of Napoleon—6,000 fewer than were killed on the first day of the Battle of the Somme in 1916.

Movement for the abolition of slavery

The deaths in the Napoleonic Wars were so few that during the years of the wars Europe's population continued to rise rapidly. At the same time increasing mechanization of manufacturing processes meant that with little or no increase in the labor force it was possible for production to rise enormously. This was the background against which the issue of slavery and the slave trade began to be questioned. From the middle of the eighteenth century there had been attacks on slavery, mostly on egalitarian grounds based on Enlightenment ideas. In 1788 the

Clapham Rectory, spiritual home of the Clapham Sect.

Société des Amis des Noires was founded in France and soon became an influential pressure group, and in 1794 the Constituent Assembly declared that all slaves in France's colonies were French citizens.

Some of the American states—led by Delaware in 1776—abolished slavery before the end of the eighteenth century. But although Britain had led the way by effectively abolishing slavery within the United Kingdom itself in 1772, this did not apply in the colonies. Nor did it prevent British ships from carrying slaves, and Britain continued to dominate the world slave trade. The abolition of the British slave trade, which was quickly to be followed in most of the other European states, was largely due to a group of evangelical Christians, who were known as the Clapham Sect. The most influential members of the Sect were Henry Thornton (1760–1815) and Zachary Macaulay (1768–1838), who brought the issue before a wide public for the first time. But it was William Wilberforce (1759–1833), another member of the Clapham Sect, who persistently raised the issue in Parliament and attempted to introduce legislation. Although many members of Parliament regarded anti-slavery legislation as "a shred of the accursed web of Jacobinism," parliamentary opinion was gradually won round to the view that the trade must be abolished, and an act was eventually passed in 1807. After the Congress of Vienna in 1815, the European powers abolished the trade too.

Although the United States quickly introduced similar legislation, many of the individual states were unwilling to abolish slavery. The cotton trade of the Southern states depended on the huge reservoir of cheap labor that slavery provided. Yet, even in the South, the price of slaves rose rapidly as a result of the increasing

William Wilberforce.

difficulty of their importation from Africa; during the first quarter of the nineteenth century the price of an able-bodied young male slave quadrupled, and by the outbreak of the Civil War it had again trebled in price to over $1,500. The harnessing of steam power was, however, to reduce the need in some industries—though not in the cotton trade—for unskilled labor. It was to bring other benefits too, particularly for the traveler.

1807

The Voyage of "Fulton's Folly"

By taking his North River Steamboat—*called the* Clermont *by the press and by posterity—from New York City to Albany and back, Robert Fulton demonstrated to a skeptical world that steamboat navigation was both feasible and economically viable. Others had built steamboats of sorts before Fulton, but he was the first to put together the requisite elements and design one that was both technologically and commercially successful.*

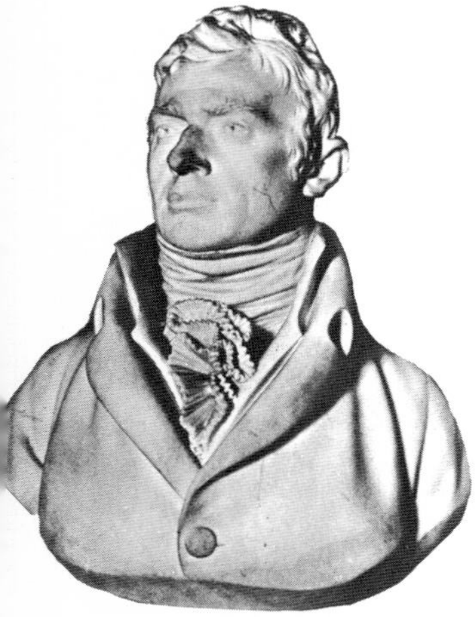

Robert Fulton, American engineer and inventor. By originating the first commercially viable steamship he opened the way for the worldwide development of steam-powered shipping in the nineteenth century.

Opposite A diagram of Fulton's double inclined plane, published in March, 1796.

The *Clermont* was the world's first commercially successful steam-driven ship. Her designer, Robert Fulton, has been variously regarded as an inventive genius whose pioneering strides advanced many fields of engineering, and as a thief who robbed worthier men of the fruits of their labor. Somewhere in between lies the truth.

Fulton was born into a family of Scottish-Irish descent on a four-hundred-acre farm in Little Britain township, Lancaster County, Pennsylvania, on November 14, 1765. Various domestic problems troubled the Fulton household, but his mother nonetheless saw to it that Robert's education did not suffer. Many improbable stories are told of his precocious talents for invention—of his making skyrockets, for example—but we do know that he showed ability as a draftsman and became involved at an early age in designing decorations for guns (Lancaster, during the Revolution, being an important gunmaking center). As he suffered from a protracted illness, Fulton established his widowed mother on a Pennsylvania farm and set out for the spa town of Bath, Virginia (now West Virginia), from where, in 1787, he left for England. On the advice of friends, and under the patronage of a Samuel Scorbitt, he resolved to follow in the footsteps of the Fulton family's friend, Benjamin West, who had earned enormous acclaim as a painter.

Fulton's art, especially in comparison with that of West and his fellow Royal Academicians, can best be described as "primitive." While his style may have appealed to his relatively unsophisticated clients in Philadelphia, it was just competent enough to enable him to exhibit a few works at the Royal Academy and to earn him a modest living. However, it was clear to the ambitious Fulton that he was unlikely to earn great fame or a large fortune from his canvases, and he began to look elsewhere. At this time in England, in response to the demands created by the Industrial Revolution, canal building was booming. Quick, cheap transport was required, and many canal schemes, some highly successful, some total disasters, were launched—frequently under the auspices of a member of the aristocracy. Within a few years of his arrival in England, Fulton had become acquainted with two such noble canal builders, the Duke of Bridgewater and Earl Stanhope, and, becoming enthusiastically involved in their projects, gave up his career as a painter.

Among Fulton's early achievements as an engineer were his invention of an "inclined plane"—a device for raising and lowering canal barges without the need for locks—and a power-driven dredging shovel—the first attempt at mechanical excavation. He also invented a number of machines not connected with canals, including one for sawing marble, and others for spinning flax and twisting hemp rope. In 1796 he published *A Treatise on the Improvements of Canal Navigation*, illustrating it with his own diagrams, and describing himself as "Robert Fulton, Civil Engineer." In this work he advocated with cost-benefit calculations, the introduction of networks of small canals, utilizing such inventions as his inclined plane. He was not successful in his attempts to persuade George Washington and others to build canals.

Since Fulton had received no direct reward for his many patented inventions, and as he now had no paid profession, he was continually in debt and dependent upon the charity of such rich patrons as the social reformer, Robert Owen, who financed his dredging machine developments and other projects. This state was alleviated in 1797, when Fulton was able to sell all his patents for £1,500. Taking advantage of a temporary halt in the Napoleonic Wars, Fulton took the opportunity to visit France. There he met and stayed with the American statesman and poet Joel Barlow. Perhaps under Barlow's influence, Fulton developed a political awareness that prompted the next turn in his career.

R. Fulton inven...

The Double Inclined Plane.

London Published by I & J. Taylor Holborn March 1 17..

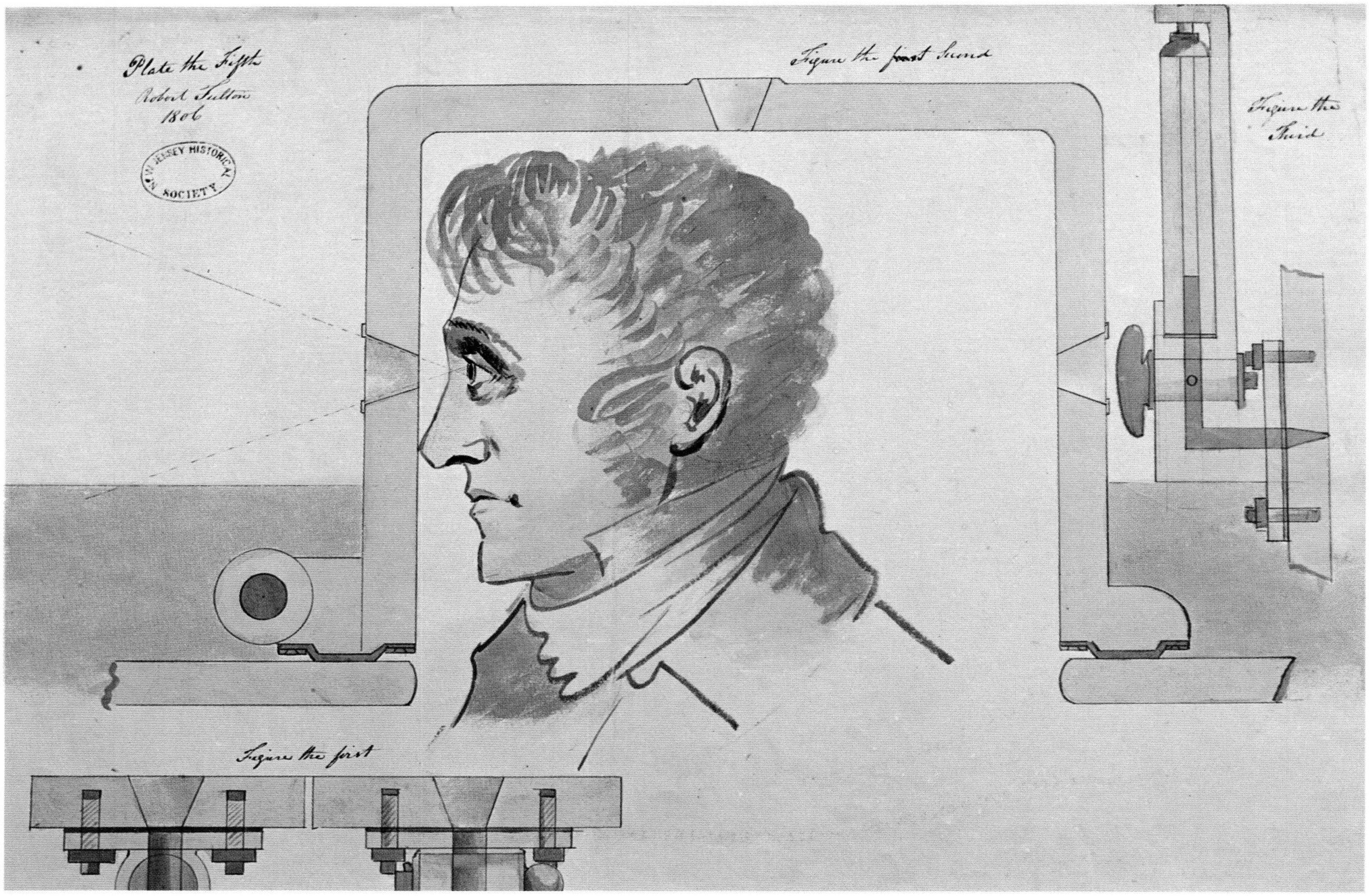

A watercolor self-portrait by Fulton, possibly in the turret of a projected submarine. His first such vessel had been bought by Napoleon. A subsequent model was ordered by the British, but dropped after Trafalgar ensured them naval supremacy.

As an advocate of free trade, and believing that unchecked naval power threatened the liberty of the seas, he began to apply his talents to the invention of a weapon that would make it impossible for any navy to achieve and sustain dominance. It is surprising, considering that we are referring to the 1790s, to realize that the invention Fulton had in mind was a torpedo-carrying submarine. The American inventor David Bushnell probably deserves the credit for the creation of the first practical midget submarine, with his pedal-and-screw-propeller-driven *American Turtle* of 1776, but Fulton's project was more ambitious, and involved the use of a submarine capable of carrying several men, able to remain submerged for several hours and to plant explosive charges on the hulls of ships. He named the vessel the *Nautilus* and on December 13, 1797, proposed its use to the French Directory. By 1800, with the backing of Napoleon, it had been accepted, and the ship was built and successfully tested on the Seine, at Rouen and Le Havre. In 1801, it was launched against the British fleet, but despite its ability to dive and surface efficiently, it was slow and cumbersome, and never managed to get close enough to any ship to destroy it. Although submarine warfare remained Fulton's long-term ambition, he began work on the development of a practical steam-driven surface boat.

The story of the invention of the steam engine is long and complex. Some writers assert that the first steam engine was that named after Hero, the Alexandrian mathematician, who before the birth of Christ described an engine consisting of a globe of water that rotated on an axle when it was heated and emitted steam from two jets. Even if it was ever made, Hero's engine never had any practical application, and it was not until the seventeenth century that the first *useful* steam engines were devised by the Marquis of Worcester and Thomas Savery in England. These early devices, like those of Denis Papin and Thomas Newcomen, which followed in the early eighteenth century, were primarily built to pump water from mines which, as surface workings became exhausted, had to be moved deeper underground. Several early inventors, including Papin and Jonathan Hulls of Gloucester, foresaw the possibilities of applying steam power to ships, by means of propellers, pumps, paddle wheels and other systems, but until the work of James Watt, the steam engine was too heavy and inefficient.

As a result of the experiments of Watt in the 1770s and 1780s, the steam engine became more sophisticated and, theoretically, of a suitable power/weight ratio for use in a boat. The first minor successes in

applying steam to shipping did not therefore come until the last quarter of the eighteenth century. A French government-sponsored vessel designed by Count Joseph d'Auxiron, built in 1773, sank before it could be tested, but in 1775, Jacques Périer's steamboat chugged a short distance on the Seine, and in 1783 Marquis Claude de Jouffroy d'Abbans sailed his paddle steamer, *Pyroschape*, on the Saône River near Lyons. In the U.S.A., James Rumsey devised a system for drawing in water and forcing it out through a jet by means of steam power, and tested a boat working on this principle on the Potomac in 1787. An intense rivalry developed between him and John Fitch of Connecticut, the inventor of a boat using steam-driven oars that sailed more than two thousand miles on the Delaware, in the first attempt to operate a steamboat as a commercial venture. But both Rumsey and Fitch were doomed to failure. Neither of them had attracted sufficient financial support to exploit their inventions properly. Rumsey died before the completion of his promising *Columbia Maid*, and Fitch, a broken and disappointed man, drank himself to death.

In Scotland in 1788, James Taylor and William Symington built and sailed a fairly successful steamboat on the lake on the estate of their patron, Patrick Miller of Dalswinton, Dumfriesshire, and by 1803, Symington's steam tug, *Charlotte Dundas*, was operating on the Forth and Clyde Canal. This project ended when its backer, Lord Dundas of Kerse, was unable to continue his support.

Fulton's first interest in the problems of steam navigation dates from his correspondence with the Earl Stanhope in 1793. Stanhope himself experimented with a vessel, *Kent*, which he described as an "ambi-navigator," but he made no great advances. By the turn of the century the groundwork was complete; steamboats were in theory workable propositions. But to make them more than expensive scientific toys—to make them commercially practical and sufficiently reliable for the public to put their trust in them—was the next hurdle to overcome. As Fulton realized, there was growing demand for a rapid and economical form of transport, independent of the power of wind, animals or men, not only on the booming canals of Europe, but also on the extensive rivers of the United States, and, perhaps, ultimately on the world's oceans. The man who could turn the steamboat from an eccentric dream to a commercial reality could make a major contribution to civilization—and make a fortune.

It was not until Fulton met the new American Ambassador in France, Robert R. Livingston, that

Fulton explaining his steamboat to Robert R. Livingston, American Ambassador to Paris. Livingston threw his wealth and influence into the project, and on its successful completion, Fulton cemented their partnership by marrying Livingston's cousin.

he began to think seriously of the question of the invention of the steamboat. Livingston, well aware of the potential of such vessels, had taken over the lapsed monopoly granted to John Fitch, which gave him the exclusive right to operate steamboats on the rivers of New York State. He had experimental vessels built for him by Nicholas J. Roosevelt and John Stevens, but refused to allow them to use such basic features as paddle wheels. As a result their efforts were not successful, and the venture was temporarily abandoned in 1801.

The partnership of Fulton and Livingston, however, was to be highly profitable. Livingston allowed Fulton a free hand, and the union was an amalgam of Fulton's extensive inventive skills and practical mindedness with Livingston's wealth and political influence. In 1802, Fulton had a clockwork-driven model ship built to experiment with various fundamental design principles, and tested it on an artificial lake. There can be little doubt that he was fully aware of most of the work of earlier experimenters in the United States, England and France, and with no pretence at originality he was prepared to adapt features proposed by others to produce a workable machine. He was convinced that the solution to the problem was a mathematical one—of applying sufficient power by the right means in a suitably constructed boat to produce a result at an acceptable cost. He wrote: "For this invention to be rendered useful does not consist of putting oars, paddles, wheels or resisting chains in motion by a steam engine." What he believed most important were the calculations necessary to determine the optimum size of all these parts.

Fulton's method was curiously similar to that adopted by the Wright brothers in solving the problems of powered flight a century later. They were not content to accept the results of previous inventors, but worked patiently and meticulously devising new experiments to produce their own calculations. Thus they succeeded in building machines that worked in practice as well as theory, and machines that worked efficiently and consistently. Furthermore, the inventors knew *why* they had succeeded and were able to repeat the achievement and rectify any errors. Both Fulton and the Wrights used basic principles devised by other workers in the same field, but they used them in such a combination that the result was bound to work as they anticipated. For this reason, while Fulton was obviously not the inventor of the steamboat, he was the first to combine all the essential elements into a workable whole, and had the financial vision—and backing—that most of his predecessors had lacked. At last the steamboat was not only technically, but commercially possible.

As Fulton stood on the brink of success, he made another bid to win acceptability for his submarine plans by offering them to the British government. It must be remembered that his motives were purely pragmatic—it did not matter to him which country used his weapon, since his goal was to make the world's navies ineffectual in order to guarantee the freedom of the seas. Negotiations dragged on with the British, and Fulton traveled to England under the alias of "Mr Francis." The British applied pressure for better terms by refusing to grant an export license for the steam engine that Fulton had ordered from Boulton and Watt of Birmingham (since at this time there were no steam-engine manufacturers in the United States). After much procrastination, the British victory at the Battle of Trafalgar removed their immediate need for submarines, and the matter went no further. The

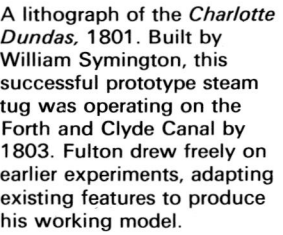

A lithograph of the *Charlotte Dundas,* 1801. Built by William Symington, this successful prototype steam tug was operating on the Forth and Clyde Canal by 1803. Fulton drew freely on earlier experiments, adapting existing features to produce his working model.

export restriction on the engine was lifted, and by 1806, both Fulton and the Boulton and Watt engine were able to leave for the United States.

At the yard of Charles Browne at Corlear's Hook on New York's East River, the keel of his steamboat was laid, and the partly completed vessel then towed to Paulus Hook Ferry where Fulton had set up a workshop. At the outset, Fulton called his ship the *Steamboat*. She was later renamed the *North River* (the Lower Hudson River) *Steamboat*, and later still, the *North River Steamboat of Clermont* (the location of Livingston's estate). This name was shortened on occasions to the *North River*, but by 1810 the press—though not Fulton himself—had latched on to the more romantic *Clermont*, and *Clermont* she remained. After trials on Sunday, August 9, 1807, proved successful, the first epoch-making voyage of this vessel took place on Monday, August 17. Only one newspaper, the *American Citizen*, carried a preview of the event.

The *Clermont* was long and narrow—an almost dangerously unstable 133 foot by 13 foot, weighing 100 tons; she was 7 foot high, with a draft of only 2 foot, and the bow and stern were cut off in sharp 60° triangles. The engine, with a 20-foot boiler, was completely exposed in the center, and two 15-foot diameter paddle wheels were open to view at the sides. An onlooker saw her as ". . . an ungainly craft looking precisely like a backwood sawmill mounted on a scow and set on fire." Until she proved her worth, she was well described as "Fulton's Folly." The forty passengers on her epic maiden voyage were mostly members of society and friends or relatives of the influential Livingston family. The spectators who witnessed the journey up the Hudson, made at about five miles per hour, were astonished, especially during the night, to see this noisy, sparking alien craft—at Poughkeepsie, an argument arose as one group declared that it was a sea monster, while another was convinced it was a sign of the impending Day of Judgment. By day, it was somewhat less awesome, and many spectators traveled out in yachts to view it and to offer their congratulations to Fulton. He, flushed with success, announced his engagement to Livingston's cousin, Harriet, and thereby consolidated his position in the wealthy circles in which he was beginning to move. He was delighted with the performance of the *Clermont*, and wrote to his old friend Joel Barlow:

> My steamboat voyage to Albany and back has turned out rather more favorably than I had calculated. The distance from New York to Albany is one hundred and fifty miles. I ran it up in thirty-two hours and down in thirty. I had a light breeze against me the whole way both going and coming, and the voyage has been performed wholly by the power of the steam engine. I overtook many sloops and schooners beating to windward and parted with them as if they had been at anchor. The power of propelling boats by steam is now fully proved.

Upon her return, some modifications were made to the boat's structure. Berths were added, and the paddle wheels boarded in. Fulton started to advertise the trip from New York to Albany as a regular service, three round trips per fortnight.

> *The North River Steamboat* will leave Paulus Hook Ferry on Friday the 4th September at 6 in the morning and arrive at Albany at 6 in the afternoon. Provisions, good berths and accommodations are provided.

At the beginning of her service as a public conveyance, there were numerous problems to be overcome —many breakdowns occurred, and competitors in traditional boats deliberately rammed her on

A steamboat on the Clyde near Dunbarton, 1817. Henry Bell's three-horsepower steamboat *Comet* marked the beginning of steam navigation in Europe.

Right The *Clermont* on the Hudson River, 1810. Despite much public cynicism, the *Clermont's* maiden voyage from New York to Albany and back in 1807 proved an immediate success.

Below The machinery of the *Clermont*; a contemporary drawing.

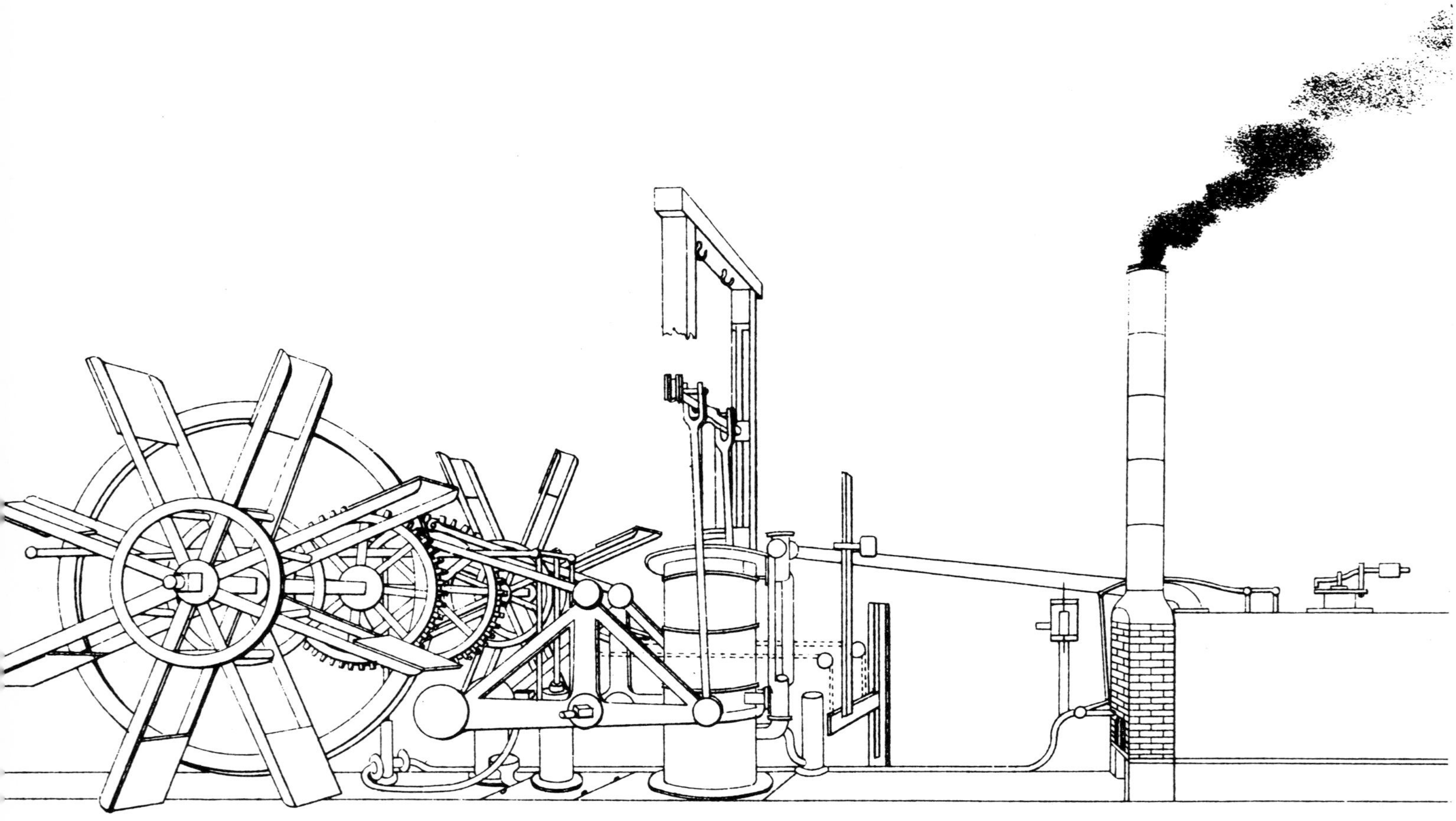

several occasions, causing extensive damage. But despite these setbacks, the *Clermont* began to attract an ever-increasing clientele and was soon showing a profit. At the end of the first season of operation, she was extensively rebuilt. Her dimensions were increased to 149 foot by 17 foot 11 inches, and her weight to 182 tons. She was improved by the addition of decorative woodwork and paintings, and the accommodation was expanded to fifty-four berths in three cabins, with food served from a galley.

Fulton, through his adroit marriage and the success of his steamboat venture, became wealthy and influential, and an important patron of art. By March, 1809, the *Clermont* had produced a profit of over $16,000, and new boats were projected. He became involved in a number of legal wrangles over the patents relating to his steamboat and the scope of the monopoly granted to Livingston, which had been extended from 1803 to 1823.

In 1812, in Scotland, Henry Bell's *Comet* steamboat began operations on the Clyde, marking the beginning of successful steamboat enterprise in Europe. In the same year, Robert Fulton, having published a pamphlet, *Torpedo War*, resumed his interest in submarine warfare, and built an unsuccessful torpedo boat during the War of 1812. He also projected the first steam battleship, *Demologus*, or *Fulton the First*—a double-hulled 156-foot ship with a single paddle wheel shielded in the middle, carrying thirty 32-pound guns. The war ended before she could be put into action. Fulton returned to the painting interests of his youth, but, ever concerned with his steamboat venture, he visited one of his ships on an intensely cold day, caught pneumonia, and on February 23, 1815, died. He was buried, after a magnificent procession through the streets of New York, in Old Trinity Churchyard.

Fulton was not the first man to invent or put a steamboat into use. His unique success and the importance of the voyage of the *Clermont* in 1807 lies in his uniting, for the first time, the various elements of a workable steamship and then putting it into commercial operation with adequate financial backing. In demonstrating that steamboat operation was a feasible commercial enterprise, and not a scientific stunt, Fulton opened the way for worldwide development of steam-powered shipping that became a vital factor in the expansion of international trade in the nineteenth century and in the growth of navigation on inland waterways. The *Clermont* was unstable, inefficient, slow and primitive, but she was the model from which every successful steamboat enterprise derived. RUSSELL ASH

A watercolor of the *Clermont* by Richard V. De Witt, 1861. Modified and refitted, the *Clermont* became the first of a "line" of commercial steamers.

1807-1811 Grinding poverty and social

Industrialization

Trafalgar freed Britain from fears of invasion, but the Napoleonic Wars continued to exert a great influence on the British economy. The need to clothe and equip the home and allied armies artificially stimulated the new factory industries. Between 1806 and 1808, Birmingham manufacturers turned out three million gun barrels. British coal production doubled. A Leeds haberdasher was commissioned to outfit British, Prussian and Russian troops. Speculators and profiteers made and lost fortunes. Blast-furnace magnate Samuel Fereday, for example, on hearing of Wellington's victory at Waterloo, could throw a banquet for 1,500 employees; yet, after the war's end, Fereday went bankrupt. Overall, Britain was launched on a half century of extraordinary growth, growth in the gross national product (the total value of goods and services) at the rate of 2·9 percent per year. In certain industries, this progress was even more rapid. Raw cotton imports into England, for example, went from 13,400 tons per year in 1790 to 55,000 tons in 1810.

Cotton factories in Union Street, Manchester.

As industrialization came into its own, technologists the world over rose to the challenge. The year 1800 saw the American Eli Whitney (1765–1825), inventor of the cotton gin, introduce interchangeable parts for manufacturing muskets—an innovation that pioneered American mass-production techniques. In 1801, France's Joseph Jacquard (1752–1834) invented a loom for figured silk fabrics. In the following year the Englishman Richard Trevithick (1771–1833) built the first high-pressure steam engine and also patented a steam carriage. Two years later, in 1804, he designed and built a locomotive to run on rails. 1806 saw the first gas lighting of British cotton mills; 1807 the maiden voyage of the steamboat *Clermont*; and 1810 and 1811, the power-driven and flatbed presses. In Birmingham, between 1808 and 1813, power was successively applied to wire drawing, iron forges and nail making.

In industrial innovation and growth, Britain was the undisputed leader of the world, yet the pressures of war dealt the British public, especially the laboring classes, several social and political setbacks. Radical British sympathy for the French Revolution had not gone unnoticed. The fears expressed by Prime Minister William Pitt (1759–1806) that home-grown rebels might establish a British republic resulted in the suspension of habeas corpus between 1794 and 1802: subsequently a hundred suspects were jailed without being brought to trial. In 1765, Parliament had passed the Treason Act, prohibiting any expression of contempt toward the king (after George III had been attacked in his carriage), the government or the constitution. Under the Seditious Meetings Act of the same year, any gathering of fifty or more was illegal without a magistrate's permit. Finally, the Combination Acts of 1799–1800 outlawed all trade-union activity.

A constant food shortage fed inflation, as bad harvests from 1795 to 1800, and a concomitant need to import more expensive grain caused prices to rise. In these conditions, farm workers with their own allotments or access to common land might just have scraped by. Instead, the demand for agricultural produce stepped up the process of enclosing previously public land, and more and more of the rural laborers, forced off land where they had previously tethered animals and grown crops, were deprived of an essential part of their sustenance. Thus, as war taxes and prices increased, so did the number of rural poor competing for jobs. For those who had saved anything before disaster descended, so much the worse, for it meant exemption from the means-tested Poor Law benefits. To compound their problems, the Act of Settlement prevented such people from leaving their parish to look for work, unless they wished to brave the industrial north, where labor shortages had relaxed parish vigilance. As Eden's *State of the Poor* indicated in 1795, a typical laboring family's weekly income in the depressed south might break down as follows:

Father (a carter)	12s	od
Mother (part-time roving cotton)		6d
Child aged 12 (baby-sitting)	2s	6d
Child aged 9 (baby-sitting)	2s	od
	17s	od

Yet, on the basis of contemporary prices, the same family needed *18s 6d* simply to live!

Poor Law changes

In 1795, these conditions prompted the Poor Law officials at Speenhamland, in Berkshire, to initiate a system of supplementary allowances. Calculated on the price of three "gallon" loaves per week, the Speenhamland allowances worked out to a maximum of 30 pence weekly per child. At contemporary prices, this could be a crucial contribution to the family budget, but the system had undesired side-effects. Farmers could now pay low wages confidently, knowing that the Poor Rate would keep their workers from starving. Since unmarried men were excluded from benefits, early marriages were encouraged. And finally, a great many people, through no fault of their own, were forced to accept public assistance at a time when that meant far greater social obloquy than it does today. Soon, however, the system spread to other counties. A guaranteed minimum wage would have been a much saner step, and Samuel Whitbread, son of a prosperous brewing magnate, did bring such a measure before the Commons in 1795. Pitt, however, was determined to oppose it. His college reading of the economist Adam Smith (1723–90) had firmly instilled in him noninterventionist sentiments; the "free economy," supposedly working on pure supply-and-demand principles, could not be tampered with. (As commentators have observed, it is unfortunate that Pitt's mentor was no longer living, as he might have pointed out the land monopoly held by the aristocracy.) Instead, the Prime Minister introduced his own Poor Bill, which removed the means test, provided agricultural workers with loans for garden plots and established training schools. But the bill was given a cool—even a derisory—reception, and Pitt withdrew it.

Meanwhile, economic crisis was looming for another section of society—the hand weavers. The labor surplus was also flooding this low-skilled trade. In 1797, their average weekly wage was about 29 shillings a week. By 1815, it would decline by half, and in 1834 (when between 500,000 and 800,000 were employed in the trade) it actually went down to 5s 6d!

In terms of comparative wages, life in the industrial north was undoubtedly better. Where the southern laboring family earned 17s a week in 1795, a Manchester

The inhabitants of Monmouth Street relax in the evening. By Cruikshank.

disorientation attend the new Industrial Age

A Yorkshire collier at the turn of the century.

family of cotton workers earned £1 3s 6d:

Father	16s	0d
Child aged 12	4s	6d
Child aged 9	3s	0d
	£1 3s	6d

Yet it was towns such as Manchester that produced the real horrors of the industrial age. Wages were increasing, but actual living conditions were declining in a variety of ways.

Effects of industrialization

For the first time in history, people were working not at their own rate, or at that of their overseers, but at the rate of unflagging, inhuman machines. Since women and children were better suited to the cramped conditions of machine-crowded factories, women and children were hired. (Besides, they could be paid less than men, and laying off the traditional breadwinner could bring several other members of the family in for the same wage.) Where the machines were, so were the workers taken. In 1795, John Aiken (1747–1822), physician and author, reported:

> Children of very tender age are employed; many of them collected from the workhouses in London and Westminister, and transported in crowds as apprentices to masters resident many hundred miles distant where they serve unknown, unprotected, and forgotten by those to whose care nature or the laws had consigned them.

And the conditions within the factories, and the factory towns, were appropriate only for machines.

In 1784, infectious fever broke out in a factory near Manchester. Thomas Percival, a local doctor noted for his progressive attitude and knowledgeability, was asked to conduct an investigation. He and his colleagues reported that the fever had been

> supported, diffused and aggravated by the communication of contagion to numbers crowded together, by the accession to its virulence from putrid effluvia; and by the injury done to young persons through confinement and too long continued labor; to which several evils the cotton mills have given occasion . . . .

Immediately they had received the report the Manchester magistrates passed resolutions against night work for children, and against a child's work day of more than ten hours. The resolutions were evaded. Ten years later, Percival again reported that factories were breeding grounds for contagion; that factory work and the factory environment were debilitating to all; that night work and long hours impaired strength and reduced life expectancy; that factory children were "generally debarred from all opportunities of education." In consequence of such reports, the First Factory Act was passed in 1802. It provided for a twice-yearly cleaning of the factories, an annual suit of clothes for apprentices, a maximum twelve-hour working day for children, an hour's religious instruction on Sunday, a physician's visit in case of factory epidemics and a five-pound fine for disobeying the Act. Naturally, in a country where industrialists held extensive powers, such feeble measures were of little use. And even had they been, the first generation of industrial workers had problems outside as well as inside the factory.

The new manufacturing cities and towns were not pleasant places to live in. By 1800, back-to-back houses were common in Manchester. Opportunities for personal hygiene were limited when sewage disposal consisted of a ditch running between rows of back-to-backs, and uncontaminated wells and cisterns were rare. And the city's ecology had ambitious—and effective—enemies. A Prussian traveler who came to the city in 1814 noted:

> The cloud of coal vapor may be observed from afar. The houses are blackened by it. The river which flows through Manchester is so filled with waste dye stuffs that it resembles a dyer's vat.

As England's population rocketed from eight million in 1801 to ten million in 1811 to twelve million in 1821, industrial urbanization happened to an unwary public. Suddenly a whole roster of unknown services was essential—waste disposal, garbage collection, street lighting, sidewalks, hospitals, police protection. But a profit-conscious society, whose more comfortable and powerful members dwelled nowhere near these slums, was not likely to provide them.

London going out of Town—or—The March of Bricks and Mortar! by Cruikshank.

1811 "General" Lud's Army

Ned Lud, a Leicestershire laborer whose name became synonymous with industrial sabotage in the first decades of the nineteenth century, was an unlikely candidate for even so dubious an honor. "General" Lud, as he was sometimes called, was a feebleminded "stockinger" whose isolated act of industrial anarchy took place some thirty years before the general outbreaks of 1811. Those outbreaks were perpetrated by roving bands of jobless textile workers who called themselves "Luddites" and who operated under cover of darkness. Their acts of vandalism, although directed at the new labor-saving machines that had robbed many of them of their livelihood, were inspired by discontent over living conditions and inflationary prices as well. Little more than a decade after the first Luddite riot, trade unions were formed to redress workers' grievances.

Cotton workers in 1813.

Opposite John Bull and his burden, a cartoon of 1819 lampooning the social structure of England.

From early 1811 until early 1813, during the turning point of the Napoleonic Wars, three regions of England were disturbed by a series of industrial riots involving the destruction of machinery: the Midland hosiery and lace-making districts of Leicestershire, Derbyshire and Nottinghamshire; the West Riding of Yorkshire; and the cotton areas of Lancashire and Cheshire. It eventually became necessary to employ a force of 12,000 soldiers—a larger army than the one with which Wellington had started his Peninsular Campaign in 1808—to suppress the riots. Some thirty years earlier, Ned Lud, a laborer from Leicestershire, had smashed two lace frames belonging to his employer and in the process gave a name—"Luddism"—to the whole phenomenon.

The anger of the rioters vented itself largely against textile machinery of various kinds. For that reason it was generally assumed that the immediate cause of the riots was the introduction of new labor-saving machinery into the affected industries. This view is a far too simple one of a complex situation. Only to a limited extent did the riots of 1812 have as their main objective the destruction of labor-saving machinery, for such labor-saving machinery was not new. The immediate causes of the disturbances were the high price of foodstuffs, the collapse of the British export trade to the United States after February, 1811, and the effects of Napoleon's Continental System, which aimed at the exclusion of British goods from Europe.

Both at home and on the Continent, 1811 and 1812 were bad harvest years. By August, 1812, the price of wheat in Britain had reached the shockingly high price of 160 shillings a quarter (the average for 1792 had been as low as 43 shillings), and the prices of such coarse foodstuffs as oatmeal and potatoes also rose as the masses began to substitute them for wheat in their diet. In February, 1811, the United States, which had been trying desperately to avoid entanglement in the Napoleonic Wars, announced that the Non-Importation Act of 1809 would henceforth be enforced against Britain only. (That act had originally prohibited all trade between the U.S.A. on one hand and Britain and France on the other.) The measure cut down British exports to the U.S.A. from 11 million pounds sterling in 1810 to less than 2 million in 1811. Textile areas were particularly affected by this cutting off of their largest market.

Luddism is best understood by examining what went on in each of the three districts. In 1811 the counties of Nottingham, Derby and Leicester contained about 90 percent of all stocking and lace frames in the kingdom. Those frames, which were used for knitting cotton, woolen and silk fabrics, were spread widely through the villages as well as the towns, but the preponderance were found in the Nottinghamshire countryside. The industry's entrepreneurs were wealthy merchant hosiers who owned the frames and supplied cotton, woolen and silk yarns to the journeymen stockingers and lace knitters. The merchant hosiers organized the collection of the finished articles through agents, middlemen, or "bagmen," and then sold them to the London wholesale houses. Those merchants also collected frame rents from the stockingers, usually one shilling a week per frame.

Following the collapse of both home and export markets in 1811, warehouse stocks accumulated rapidly and soon one-fifth of the knitting frames in the Midlands stood idle. Many other stockingers were only partially employed, and they often had to accept payment in kind at unfavorable rates. Those stockingers, caught between the double misery of high food prices and unemployment, grew increasingly irate over the use of wider—and therefore more productive—frames in the workshops where they were employed. They also objected to using knitted fabric produced on those wide frames to make cheap and inferior "cut-up" articles. Stocking shapes, for example, could be cut out of a large piece of knitted fabric and those shapes could then be sewn together in pairs to make stockings.

Pension
Sinecure
Budget
TAX
TAX
TAX
TAX
TAX
TAX
GAGGING BILL

Rioting broke out in Nottinghamshire in March, 1811, spread to Leicestershire and Derbyshire by the following November, and finally died down in February, 1812. Gangs of young stockingers, organized and paid by the older men in the trade, roamed the Midlands countryside at night and demanded admittance to cottages and knitting sheds so that they could smash up the wide frames. The stockingers who had the custody of those frames put up very little resistance; the frames, after all, were owned by the merchants, not the weavers. The rioters claimed to be acting in the name of "General" Ned Lud, the apprentice stockinger of Leicester. (According to folklore, when Lud was reprimanded by his master for bad work, he took up a hammer and beat some knitting frames to pieces.) The participants in those nighttime raids took an oath of secrecy when they were initiated—or "twisted-in"—into the organization. Old narrow frames—those that could not be used to produce material for cut-ups—were generally left intact, and the mobs seldom stole anything except firearms. In all, some one thousand frames were destroyed by workers who directed their anger not so much against the new machines as against a new use to which old but recently improved machines were being put. Only after numerous regiments were drafted and sent into the Midlands did the troubles gradually cease; in the aftermath seven men were sentenced to terms of transportation—but no one was hanged.

Rawfold's Mill, where William Cartwright beat off an attack of 150 Luddites in 1812. This incident formed the basis for Charlotte Brontë's *Shirley*.

Bottom Luddites shooting Mr. Horsfall, by Phiz.

In Yorkshire, Luddism broke out only in the region known as the West Riding, and it flourished mainly in the district north of Leeds and in the Huddersfield area. In those areas the trouble was confined to that section of the woolen cloth industry that had to do with the raising of nap on rough cloth and its subsequent close shearing. Two labor-saving machines, the gig-mill and the shearing frame, were gradually coming into use for those purposes. The gig-mill consisted basically of two large rotating cylinders covered with hundreds of teasels, and it raised the nap on cloth much more expeditiously than hand-teaseling. With such a machine, a man and a boy could do the work of seven skilled men, and the gig-mill's use spread in Yorkshire during the 1780s and 1790s. Once the nap had been raised, the shearmen or croppers trimmed it off with a pair of shears weighing between thirty and forty pounds, leaving the surface regular and smooth. A mechanical shearing frame had been invented during the eighteenth century, and it further economized the industry by rendering five skilled men out of six unnecessary. There had been riots against the shearing frame in Wiltshire and Somerset between 1797 and 1802, but by 1807 about fifteen hundred frames were at work in the north of England. Thus the riots in the West Riding were more specifically against the introduction of labor-saving machinery—but hardly against *new* machinery, for gig-mills and shearing frames had been known for years.

Had the times been more propitious, the triumph of the machines would probably have taken place without much public disturbance, but in the West Riding, as in the Midlands, the distress of 1811 and 1812 set off a violent reaction. In January, 1812, small bands of men (similar to those in Nottinghamshire) moved about the affected areas, smashing gig-mills and shearing frames with large sledgehammers. Many of the small manufacturers stopped using the machines temporarily; others—those with greater resources and more guts—defied the Luddites. Two mills near Leeds were successfully attacked in March, 1812, and on April 9 some 300 Luddites sacked and fired Joseph Foster's cloth mill at Horbury. In the same month, however, William Cartwright of Rawfold's resolutely beat off an attack by a mob of 150 Luddites, killing 2 of them. (Charlotte Brontë's *Shirley* is based on that episode.) During the summer of 1812, the Continental System collapsed, trade revived, and the troubles died down. However, seventeen of the rioters were sentenced to death by hanging at York Assizes in January, 1813.

In the third Luddite area, Lancashire and

The Peterloo massacre; the Manchester and Cheshire Yeomanry breaking up a meeting in favor of universal manhood suffrage in 1819. Unrest, both industrial and political, was endemic in early nineteenth-century England.

Cheshire, the movement showed itself to be less an antimachinery movement than a series of food riots that led, almost by accident, to attacks on cotton mills. In those shires, competition between power-loom weaving and the handloom had not yet reached serious proportions. In the Manchester-Stockport area, less than 2,400 power looms were in operation in 1813—at a time when handloom weavers in the district numbered in the tens of thousands. In Manchester itself the worst riots took place in the potato market when mobs of women, having failed to get the farmers to bring down their prices, seized the loaded carts and either sold the potatoes at a low rate or looted them. At Oldham a mob of miners from the Hollinwood coal pits—men who worked in an industry largely untouched by machinery—went around to the food shops enforcing a list of maximum prices. Then, almost as an afterthought, they launched a couple of unsuccessful attacks against Daniel Burton and Sons' power-loom factory at Middleton. These and other riots in Lancashire and Cheshire led to death sentences for twenty-three people.

The next major outburst of machine breaking occurred in April, 1826, when large-scale riots involving the destruction of power looms took place in East Lancashire. Attacks on power-loom factories in Manchester itself proved generally unsuccessful. Once again, a close connection existed between the riots and the state of trade. The great economic boom of 1824–25 had been followed by a severe recession in the winter of 1825–26, causing great distress in the manufacturing districts. As a result of the new series of riots, ten persons received death sentences, but all ten were eventually transported for life instead of being executed.

Surprisingly enough, the final spasm of machine breaking took place in agriculture—where the degree of mechanization was low—rather than in industry. The riots that erupted in the agricultural counties of southern and eastern England in 1830 were sparked by a hard winter. The prices of foodstuffs had risen rapidly throughout 1830, and riots raged from the September to the December of that year, with November as the peak month. The rioting agricultural laborers directed their main efforts against threshing machines, which robbed them of the labor of hand-threshing during the long winter months. The threshing machine, worked at first by horses and later by small steam engines, had proved increasingly popular in Scotland, northern England and North Wales during the Napoleonic Wars.

After the peace of 1815 the prosperous farmers in the wheat-growing counties of eastern and southern England rapidly adopted the threshing machine, despite the fact that labor was now abundant. A newly invented portable threshing machine proved very popular, particularly in Suffolk, and laborers watched the progress of mechanization with increasing alarm. Threatened with the prospect of being thrown onto the public charity of the Poor Law during the winter months, mobs attacked farmhouses, burned hay ricks and destroyed the threshing machines on a large scale. Some farmers deliberately left their machines out in the open—where the laborers could destroy them more easily—in the hope that their action would divert the mob's attention from more vital property. (The

Charlotte Brontë, whose novel *Shirley* describes the Luddite troubles.

A Yorkshire cloth hall; the cloth industry was most affected by the Luddite disturbances.

Complaints about the supposed loss of liberty multiplied during the early nineteenth century.

Home Office roundly condemned this practice as a surrender to the blackmail of illegal force.)

The next large-scale outbreak of rural rioting—which occurred in 1843–44—was much tamer and less violent. The 1830 riots, however, appear to have delayed the progress of farm mechanization only to a limited extent; the intervention of the threshing machine and the mechanical reaper was not permanently halted. Emigration overseas and the drift to the towns over the next forty years solved the problem of the labor surplus on the land more effectively than agrarian violence.

In the eighteenth century (and indeed well into the nineteenth), the major output of British industry—with the exceptions of coalmining, iron-making and shipbuilding—was produced under various forms of what has been labeled the domestic or "putting-out" system. The essence of that

Mr Bull removed by the Tax Gatherers over the Way.
NO GRUMBLING
PRAY Remember the poor DEBTORS
Tampering at Elections – allowed to Ministers only!! Lord Lieutenants of Counties & other Local Authorities must be tools of Government — for Necessary Purposes, employ Clerical Magistrates
Free discussion – a farce
Right of Petitioning, reserved to Families only
LAW of LIBEL
MAGNA CHARTA
Bill of RIGHTS
A FREE BORN ENGLISHMAN!
THE ADMIRATION of the WORLD!!!
AND THE ENVY of SURROUNDING NATIONS!!!!!
15. Dec. 1819

system was that the producer, often assisted by members of the household, worked at home on material that he either bought himself or was entrusted with by a merchant manufacturer or middleman. In the latter case, the material—yarn, iron or leather, for example—remained the property of the merchant. Sometimes, as in wool weaving, there was partial mechanization. (Cloth had to be taken to a water-driven falling mill to be cleaned and thickened, for example.) In the Black Country and the Sheffield area, the nail makers and other workers in metal labored in their own homes or in lean-to sheds at the sides of their houses. In the textile trades, which were spread widely over the countryside, the spinning of woolen, worsted and cotton yarns was carried out in the household until the last two decades of the eighteenth century, when spinning rapidly changed into a factory industry, powered by the water wheel and the steam engine. Weaving of all kinds was carried on under the domestic system until the first decades of the nineteenth century, although loomshops containing as many as a dozen looms and their attendant weavers could frequently be found.

Relatively small but complicated machines presented few problems for the domestic system, despite the fact that the looms themselves were frequently extremely complex affairs to operate and service, depending on the quality and nature of the fabric woven on them. The stocking-knitting frame, originally invented in 1589, was perhaps the most complicated machine in use in British industry in the early eighteenth century, yet many thousands had been installed in the workers' homes. Increasing complexity brought other problems than those of installation and servicing, however. Laboring families could easily afford cheap and simple spinning wheels, and even in the eighteenth century looms were usually owned by the weavers who operated them. The more complex and expensive stocking and lace-knitting frames—which cost between £10 and £30 at a time when a skilled worker might earn only £30 in a whole year—tended to be owned by the merchant hosier, and the journeymen stockingers

A coal works in Coalbrookdale, Staffordshire. The growth of industrialization was at the heart of Luddite and later complaints.

paid weekly or monthly rents for the privilege of using them.

The fact that materials and machines were lent out put hostages into the hands of the workers: embezzlement of raw material was a constant problem and legislation against both theft and the detention of work for long periods went on as long as the domestic system lasted. Refusal to complete webs in the loom and the slashing of unfinished pieces of cloth must have been fairly common as early as the sixteenth century, to judge by the legislation against those offenses. A riot among the woolen workers of Melksham in Wiltshire began in 1738 with the cutting of all the warps in the looms of a merchant clothier named Coulthurst who had lowered the piecework prices for cloth. Luddism was foreshadowed as early as 1675 when a mob of London weavers attacked immigrant French weavers for using ribbon looms, called "Dutch engines," that enabled one weaver to weave sixteen or more ribbons at the same time. Moreover, industrial sabotage and destruction were not confined to the domestic trades. In the northeastern coalfields, rioting miners burned down pit-head machinery in the 1740s and set coal stocks on fire in pursuance of demands for higher wages. The eighteenth-century statute book contains frequent Acts of Parliament directed against arson in coal pits, and as late as 1831 striking miners at Bedlington in Northumberland wrecked pit winding gear.

The great strike movement of 1842—known as the "Plug Plot" riots—marks the beginning of a change in tactics. During those riots in Lancashire, Cheshire and north Staffordshire, the strikers concentrated on stopping, rather than wrecking, the mills by removing the lead safety plugs in the steam engine boilers. Their conduct, although extreme by modern standards, compares favorably with the excesses of Luddism. It presented itself as a method of attempting to force a rise in pay and indicates the extent to which some sections of the workers had come to terms with the new industrial capitalism by 1842.

The economists—among them Dr. Andrew Ure, whose *The Philosophy of Manufactures* was published in 1835—labored to explain the necessity for the rapid introduction of improved machinery to enable mass-produced British goods to remain competitive in the world's markets. Ure also stressed the futility of opposing the adoption of inventions designed "to abridge labor," and he cited Richard Roberts' "self-acting" mule of the 1820s as a prime example. (Roberts' invention had been specially commissioned by the master cotton spinners to put an end to continued demands for higher wages from the aristocracy of the cotton workers, the fine mule-spinners.) Ure's propaganda coincided with the beginnings of improvement in both industrial relations and living standards. Trade unions, which had been wholly illegal from 1799 to 1824, received a grudging recognition from Parliament, the law and society from the latter date. By 1851 the first of the new and increasingly respectable New Model trade unions—the Amalgamated Society of Engineers—had been formed from a coalition of older bodies. Those new amalgamated societies placed their prime emphasis on the thorough seven years' apprenticeship to skilled crafts (which had the effect of raising wages by restricting the number of adequately trained workers). To some extent such apprenticeships were a subtler form of Luddism, but they did assure the artisans employed in such developing industries as engineering, ironfounding, printing and shipbuilding a share in any profits accruing to capital investment in new machinery. Such tactics could hardly be employed by workers in the semiskilled and unskilled trades, however, and they began to organize in unions from the 1870s onward. Here cautious and restrictive working rules of various kinds had to be employed at shop floor level.

Luddism therefore survived as a frame of mind, occasionally expressing itself in acts of sabotage during industrial disputes, but more generally acting as a silent brake not only on the introduction of new and more productive machinery, but also on speedier methods of working and better works organization.

W. H. CHALONER

The War of 1812: Britain and America

Economic warfare

Shortly after five o'clock on the afternoon of Monday, May 11, 1812, the Right Honorable Spencer Perceval, who had been Prime Minister of Great Britain for two and a half years, was assassinated in the lobby of the House of Commons by a recently bankrupted commercial agent named John Bellingham. The eminence of the victim and the location of the crime made Bellingham's act unique in the annals of murder. It also emphasized the despair felt by a large section of the business community over the burdens imposed upon them by a never-ending war—for although Bellingham was mentally deranged, his conviction that the government was responsible for the acute economic recession was held, less violently, by thousands of impoverished manufacturers and laborers.

Spencer Perceval, the only English premier to be assassinated.

English morale was lower in the winter of 1811–12 than at any other point in the Napoleonic Wars. Those were the months in which machine breaking spread northward from the Midlands to reach an angry climax in Lancashire and Cheshire. And factors other than the Luddite hysteria were also contributing to the general malaise. After two bad harvests, food was scarce, and in the spring of 1812, wheat was selling at three times the prewar price. Moreover, the Napoleonic Wars that had once stimulated industry were now strangling it. Napoleon had responded to the British naval blockade by instituting the Continental System (which sought to close all northern and western Europe, except Portugal, to British goods). The British had retaliated by cutting off trade not only with Napoleon's Empire but with any state that broke the blockade. As both combatants sought to regulate Europe's trade, manufacturers in England and France began to feel the strain. The most drastically affected areas were regions in England where the wars had earlier brought quick profits. In the new industrial towns of Lancashire and Yorkshire warehouses were filled with exports for which there were no markets. Factories began to close and unemployment spread. In August, 1810, no less than five large Manchester firms went into liquidation, and shock waves of bankruptcy continued to trouble the northern counties for over a year.

On the afternoon of May 11, 1812, John Bellingham stepped out of the drab uniformity of frustration that had gripped England and entered the margin of history. By that time, the British government had already decided to repeal the trade restrictions known as the Orders in Council. The Orders had imposed a disastrous economic burden on English manufacturers and, by encouraging the Royal Navy to search American ships for contraband, they had so alienated the United States that President James Madison was threatening the British with another war across the Atlantic. Perceval's assassination delayed the announcement of repeal until the new Prime Minister, Robert Jenkinson, Lord Liverpool (1770–1828), had formed his government, but on June 16,

James Madison; his enemies called the War of 1812 "Mr. Madison's War."

The port of Liverpool, hub of Lancashire's industrial boom and the center of British trade with the United States.

1812, it was finally announced in the House of Commons that the Orders in Council would be withdrawn. But it was too late to avert war.

War of 1812

The London newspapers, elated by the future Duke of Wellington's successes in Spain, tended to deride the United States and minimize the significance of Madison's action. But the American Republic in 1812 was a far larger and more developed state than the embryonic Confederation that had won recognition of its independence in 1783. The counsels of President George Washington and his Secretary of the Treasury Alexander Hamilton (1757–1804) had both increased the interdependence of the individual states and fostered their "infant industries." It is true that during the presidency of Thomas Jefferson (1801–09) the states had jealously preserved their rights and their fundamentally agrarian economies, but Jefferson had also been responsible for the Louisiana Purchase of 1803.

The population of the United States had grown from just over five million when Jefferson took office to some seven and a half million in 1812. New roads pushed the line of settlement westward through the Appalachians, and explorers crossed the newly acquired territory to the Pacific. Textile mills spread industry across New England and indirectly gave the "peculiar institution" of slavery a new life as a means for producing more and more cotton. Work had also started on a canal to link the Hudson River with Lake Erie and open up the farmlands of the Great Lakes region.

Under such circumstances, war with England was welcomed by some Americans, for an American victory would secure even more territory for settlement by hardy pioneers. Canada's rich farmlands sorely tempted the War Hawks, who felt that the nation's honor was being insulted by the British navy—particularly because it was believed that the British had incited the Shawnee Indian warriors of Tecumseh (*c.* 1768–1813) to rise against the Americans along the Ohio.

The War Hawks' enthusiasm notwithstanding, the Anglo-American War of 1812 was a mistake, as many of the Federalists in New England perceived it would be from the start. On paper, the United States should have been able to achieve the Hawks' prime objective, the subjection of Upper Canada. Statistically, Americans outnumbered Canadians fourteen to one, and as long as the British were committed in Europe against Napoleon, little military assistance could be ferried across the Atlantic. The Americans had three major problems, however: geographical conditions in the Great Lakes hampered communications; the British fleet in the western Atlantic outnumbered the U.S. Navy; and there was opposition to the war from individual American states (which refused to allow their militia to fight outside state boundaries).

The war was characterized by a series of naval duels—the most important of which was the Battle of Lake Erie in September, 1813, which gave the United States control of the lake—and by inept and poorly coordinated land campaigns. American attempts to invade Canada from Detroit, Niagara and Lake Champlain failed in 1812, but U.S. troops, capitalizing on the victory at Lake

Erie, gained a victory between Lakes Huron and Erie in October, 1813. Most of the fighting in 1813 consisted of punitive raids: the Americans successfully set fire to the capital of Upper Canada which was then called York (and is now known as Toronto), and the British burned Buffalo.

After Napoleon's abdication, British veterans of the Peninsular Campaign were shipped to Canada. Those troops made two attempts to strike southward toward the Hudson; on each occasion they were repulsed. In June, 1814, a British expeditionary force was embarked at Bordeaux and conveyed directly to Chesapeake Bay. Meeting little opposition on landing, it advanced on the city of Washington and set fire to the Capitol, to the President's residence (not yet known as the White House) and to other administrative buildings. The British then attempted a similar raid at Baltimore, where they were finally repulsed by the guns of Fort McHenry. On Christmas Eve, 1814, a peace treaty was signed at Ghent that restored relations between the two countries without reference to the issues that had brought them to war. News of the peace treaty did not reach the United States until seven weeks after its signature, and during the intervening period General (and future President) Andrew Jackson (1767–1845) won a resounding victory for the Americans at New Orleans. Such

Detail from an engraving of the Battle of Lake Erie, which gave the United States control of the lake in 1813.

operations reflected no credit on the strategic thought of either of the combatants, although there were many acts of valor. The only gains for the United States were the making of a popular hero at New Orleans and the inspiring of a national anthem by the American lawyer Francis Scott Key (1779–1843) who was detained behind British lines while they bombarded Fort McHenry.

In a sense, the War of 1812 reversed American foreign policy.

The White House, Washington, which was burned by the redcoats in 1814.

When George Washington retired from the presidency in 1797, his farewell message advocated isolation from Europe's affairs. That policy had been followed by his successor, John Adams—despite the opposition of Hamilton and the Federalists—and with occasional lapses by Thomas Jefferson. Madison, on the other hand, had allowed the war fever of backcountry congressmen to stampede him into a conflict whose resolution depended ultimately on the course of battle on the mainland of Europe. Had the Peace of Ghent represented a real victory for either side, the Americans might have become involved in Europe's affairs for several generations. Instead, the treaty admitted—by its very silence—the folly of the war's causes, and consequently Madison and Monroe (his Secretary of State and successor as President) were able to steer the Republic away from the whirlpool of European affairs.

Napoleon's "ally"

Napoleon, of course, had welcomed the rupture of Britain's relations with the United States in 1812. Eighteen months before the war, a dictated note to the American Minister had declared: "His Majesty loves the Americans"—and throughout the dramatic winter of 1812–13, Napoleon was constantly seeking news of American victories from his Foreign Minister. But although the Anglo-American War and the War of the Fourth Coalition ran parallel to each other in time, they were totally different in character and objectives. (In fact, the Russians' victories over Napoleon were publicly celebrated in the then-separate town of Georgetown, D.C., twelve months before the army of Russia's ally burned Washington). For Napoleon, America remained a sanctuary to which he might one day escape; it could never have been a source of military assistance.

By the early summer of 1812 it had become clear that war was returning to the great plains of eastern Europe. Half a year earlier, on December 19, 1811, the Emperor's librarian had received a request for "good books with the best information about Russian topography" and "the most detailed account in French of the campaign of Charles XII (of Sweden) in Poland and Russia." For four months Napoleon remained in Paris, meticulously studying maps and reports. He dictated lengthy instructions for his garrisons, indicating how the army of Italy was to be moved northward across the Alps to the sandhills of Pomerania, how the Imperial Old Guard was to break off its engagements with Wellington in the Sierra de Gata and march seventeen hundred miles through Spain, France and Germany in order to reach the Vistula River by the last week in May, how six thousand horses were to be transported from the Jutland Peninsula to East Prussia, and how rice supplies were to be speeded eastward from Hamburg. All was planned in detail.

The finest military machine in the world had throbbed into action once again. Marshal Louis Berthier (1753–1815), who had learned his staff work as a young officer assisting the Americans in their struggle for independence, immersed himself in logistic problems. Louis Nicolas Davout (1770–1823), the most methodical of Napoleon's marshals, peered through specially designed spectacles at the muster rolls in his army corps—70,000 men from six nations. General Jean Baptiste Eblé (1758–1812), the incomparable military engineer, worked out details of pontoon bridges to be thrown across the Neman, the sluggish stream separating Prussia from Russia. The paladins of Napoleon's Empire—the red-haired Michel Ney (1769–1815); Joachim Murat (1767–1815), magnificent in exotic uniforms; Nicolas-Charles Oudinot (1767–1847), with saintly face and tyrant's temper; and many others—journeyed eastward to the woods of birch and pine along Europe's eastern border. No one could doubt that Napoleon regarded the forthcoming campaign against Russia as the climax of his military career. He left Paris on May 9, 1812, held court at Dresden for his brother sovereigns and allies from Vienna and Berlin, and reached a Polish village on the banks of the Neman in the late evening of June 21. Moscow lay five hundred miles to the east. "I am embarking on the greatest and most difficult enterprise I have so far attempted," he had told one of his counselors as he set out from Paris.

1812 Retreat from Russia

Death and desertion had thinned the ranks of Napoleon's vast Grand Army by the time it reached Smolensk in August of 1812, but even these difficulties had failed to dampen the Emperor's optimism. "Within a month we shall be in Moscow; within six weeks the war will be over," he declared. Time was to prove him half right. By September the Corsican's troops had indeed conquered Moscow—but the war was far from over. Because the Tsar refused to negotiate a peace treaty, Napoleon was faced with the prospect of retreating or attempting to quarter some 700,000 troops in the gutted capital through the oncoming—and legendarily severe—Russian winter. The Emperor chose to retreat—over the same scorched earth that his army had trod little more than a month earlier. By the time the army reached France, all but 30,000 members of the original force were dead or missing, and Napoleon's Grand Empire was toppling.

Alexander I, Tsar of Russia. He ordered that Moscow should be left deserted for Napoleon's troops to capture.

On June 24, 1812, Napoleon Bonaparte crossed the Neman River in command of the most powerful army that had ever existed in Europe. Every allied and vassal country was represented: Italy, Belgium, the Netherlands, Switzerland, Austria and Prussia. The Army of Twenty Nations, as it came to be known, was a microcosm of Napoleonic Europe.

A few nights earlier, the orderly officers sleeping near Napoleon's room had been astounded to hear him singing some verses of a patriotic song, the *Chant du Départ.* Now the Emperor was playing with his riding whip while humming another tune to himself. This show of gaiety, however, may have concealed a certain anxiety. Napoleon had just declared war against Russia.

The Treaty of Tilsit, which had been concluded between Tsar Alexander I and Napoleon in 1807, was already verging on collapse when the two rulers held a meeting at Erfurt. After the signing of the Treaty, Russia had reluctantly joined in the Continental System, a scheme of economic warfare aimed at closing the European markets to British goods. As a result of these measures, however, the Russian textile industry had suffered from a shortage of cotton, while the cessation of exports of wool and hemp to England had created enormous difficulties for the wealthy landowners. Thus the Franco-Russian alliance was unpopular in Russia, and a pro-English party was plotting to overthrow Alexander I. The Tsar too was exasperated by the meager advantages he had gained from the Tilsit agreement. Although he had obtained Finland, Bessarabia and a section of Galicia, he was still waiting for Napoleon to implement the plan to divide the Ottoman Empire between them. Moreover, some of his conquests were in jeopardy. The presence in Stockholm of Bernadotte, the heir presumptive to the Swedish throne, represented a threat to Finland. Also, Napoleon's creation of the Grand Duchy of Warsaw was a step toward the reconstitution of the ancient Kingdom of Poland, of which Galicia had been a part. Finally, when the Emperor annexed the Duchy of Oldenburg, which belonged to a relation of the Tsar, the alliance broke down.

Napoleon too had decided on a direct confrontation with the Tsar. The extremely ambiguous attitude of Alexander during the Emperor's Austrian campaign in 1809 had persuaded Napoleon that the Franco-Russian alliance would not work. In 1812 he believed the right moment had come to attack his rival. His alliance with the Hapsburgs through his marriage to Marie Louise made him optimistic about German support. Furthermore, he knew he could count on a second front, since war had broken out again between Turkey and Russia in 1809.

Napoleon considered Russia a threat to Europe, and he saw himself in the role of defender of civilized Europe against the Russian invasion. In fact, he aspired to be the successor to the Roman emperors and drive back the northern barbarians as far as the plains of Central Asia. Napoleon is reported to have told his confidant Narbonne, "Marius created Caesar. The extermination of the Cimbri [a German tribe] was the first step toward the foundation of the Roman Empire; and by steeping itself in the same blood, or similar blood, the Empire renewed its strength during the reigns of Trajan, Aurelian and Theodosius." Then, considering the problem within a contemporary context, he added, "Remember Suvorov and his Tartars in Italy—the only solution is to drive them back beyond Moscow, and what better moment than now for Europe to do this—under my leadership?"

Although Napoleon believed that the campaign would be a short one, he made extremely careful and detailed preparations. He ordered the War Office to draw up the most accurate maps possible of the Moscow and St. Petersburg regions, and he collected a vast mass of information about the Tsarist Empire. Nonetheless, he was convinced that the Russians would soon collapse in the face of his

Opposite Napoleon as First Consul.

Napoleon at the Battle of Wagram in 1809.

Right The emperors of Russia (Orthodox) and Austria (Roman Catholic) and the King of Prussia (Lutheran) giving thanks to God after the Battle of Leipzig, 1813, in which the French were decisively defeated.

attack and that the maps and statistical information would not be needed.

Napoleon explained his plan to Narbonne:

> The barbarians are superstitious people with simple ideas. A deadly blow aimed at the great, sacred city of Moscow, the very heart of the Empire, will gain for me in a single stroke this blind, inert mass of people. I know Alexander. . . . Perhaps he will acknowledge defeat at the mere sight of the unparalleled stockpile of armaments that I am building up and at the huge European army which I shall display for inspection at Dresden.

The Emperor was planning even further ahead. He still cherished the old dream that had haunted him ever since the Egyptian campaigns: to strike at India, the very source of British power and wealth in Asia. He confided to Narbonne:

> Supposing Russia is defeated, tell me whether a great army of Frenchmen and auxiliaries, setting off from Tiflis, would not be able to make their way directly overland as far as the Ganges and then whether one touch from a French sword would not suffice to destroy the whole structure of the great British mercantile system throughout India.

A total of 700,000 allied troops were engaged in the Russian campaign, divided into three corps and a reserve force. In the Russian camp, 200,000 men under Prince Mikhail Barclay de Tolly had been divided into three armies. The huge, unwieldy size of Napoleon's army was to be his downfall. Communications and transportation were most inefficient, and military headquarters was soon in a state of chaos.

It is incorrect to claim that the Russians deliberately planned their strategy to draw Napoleon into the heart of Russia, thus allowing the vast spaces of the countryside and the rigorous climate of the Russian winter to destroy him. In fact it was more a lack of coordination among the Russian generals, combined with their fear of being confronted with the Emperor, that drove them into retreat. The idea of making use of space and climate occurred to them only afterward. The Prussian officer Karl von Clausewitz, who later was to write a famous treatise on warfare and who was in the service of the Tsar at that time, was quite categorical on this point:

> The Russian retreat was not the outcome of a carefully thought-out plan; but resulted from the fact that each time they were about to join battle with the enemy, they decided that they were still not strong enough to confront him.

The French army fleeing through Leipzig after its retreat from Moscow.

The retreat from Russia was hindered by the cruelty of the winter weather, which decimated Napoleon's army.

Left Joachim Murat, Marshal of France and King of Naples.

Prince Barclay de Tolly eluded Napoleon at Vilna, abandoning that town on June 28. Here Napoleon received the Tsar's envoy, who had brought him a letter. When Napoleon asked him how to get to Moscow, the envoy replied: "One can choose one's own route to Moscow. Charles XII went there via Poltava."

Napoleon next hoped to catch the main Russian force unawares at Smolensk, but once again Barclay de Tolly eluded him. At Smolensk several of his advisers urged Napoleon to take up winter quarters until the following spring. More than half of the cavalry were already dismounted, and the number of deserters was continually growing. Napoleon, however, was not to be swayed from his purpose. "Within a month we shall be in Moscow; within six weeks the war will be over."

The Russians, however, could not allow Napoleon to enter Moscow, their sacred city, without putting up a fight. On September 7 they joined battle with Napoleon's Grand Army at Borodino. Entrenched behind strong defenses, Field Marshal Mikhail Kutuzov, who had succeeded Barclay de Tolly, repulsed the French attack at first but finally was forced to retire. Napoleon, however, by refusing to engage his Imperial Guard, lost a great opportunity to destroy the Russian army. The French casualties were very heavy: forty-seven generals and one hundred colonels were killed.

As a result of the Russian retreat at Borodino, Napoleon's Army entered Moscow on September 15. "The whole of this empty, uninhabited town was filled with a deep, mournful silence," noted General Armand de Caulaincourt. "Throughout our long march through Moscow, we did not come across a single person." The following day, fire broke out in the capital. The Emperor was visibly upset. One witness has described the scene:

> He walked slowly down the steps of Ivan's Tower, from where he had been watching the fire, followed by the Prince of Neuchâtel and some of his officers; then, leaning on the arm of the Duke of Vicenza, he crossed over a small wooden bridge leading to the quayside of the Moskva River; there, he found some horses.

Despite the conquest of Moscow, the Tsar refused to negotiate peace terms. Napoleon was faced with a dilemma: he thought of launching an attack on St. Petersburg, but this idea was frowned on by his colleagues. A number of staff officers suggested that it would be better to remain in Moscow, where they were well provided with supplies. At the same time, the Grand Army was in danger of being cut off from its bases by Russian reinforcements.

Napoleon's study at Fontainebleau.

After a month of procrastination, Napoleon finally made up his mind to withdraw, and on October 19 the Grand Army evacuated Moscow. It was already getting late in the year, and the first frosts had appeared. Napoleon's plan was to withdraw along the road leading to Kaluga, which lay farther south than the route they had followed on their way to Moscow and thus would afford a milder climate as well as more abundant supplies. Kutuzov, however, barred his way to Maloyaroslavets on October 24. The Emperor was forced to take the road to Smolensk, through the devastated countryside where everything had been destroyed by the Russians or by French pillagers. In addition to famine and the terrible cold (the thermometer fell as low as −30°F.), the retreating army had to contend with guerrilla attacks carried out by the bands of Cossacks pursuing it. The withdrawal turned into a complete rout, and soon Napoleon's Grand Army had deteriorated into a shapeless, undisciplined mass of troops who abandoned vehicles, guns, and frozen corpses in their wake.

When they finally reached the Berezina, Napoleon's forces had been reduced to 30,000 men and an unending procession of stragglers. Moreover, the survivors nearly lost their lives in the Berezina, the ice of which had broken during a sudden thaw. They were saved, however, by the heroism of General Eblé's *pontoniers* who bravely worked away in the frozen water and built two bridges, one for the soldiers and the other for vehicles. Sergeant Bourgogne has described the scene vividly: "The foot soldiers dragged themselves painfully along, nearly all of them with frost-bitten legs swathed in rags and pieces of sheepskin, and dying of hunger." These were the remnants of the Imperial Guard. Then came Napoleon:

> The Emperor was on foot and carried a stick in his hand. He was enveloped in a large cloak lined with fur and wore a purple velvet cap on his head with a band of black fox.

Bourgogne includes this description of a veteran of the Old Guard who was watching the scene: "I saw large tears rolling down his cheeks into his moustache from which icicles were hanging."

Finally, in the middle of December, the remnants of the Army of Twenty Nations recrossed the Neman.

Earlier, however, (on December 5) Napoleon had handed over the command of the survivors to his brother-in-law Murat and had hurriedly returned to Paris on hearing of the conspiracy of General Malet. The General had attempted to take over power in the French capital by spreading the false rumor that the Emperor had been killed outside Moscow. Napoleon left behind him in Russia 400,000 dead and 100,000 prisoners. Never before had an army experienced such a disaster.

The fall of the Grand Empire dates from the time of the Russian defeat. At the beginning of 1812, the Empire included not only France but also Belgium, Holland, the Hanseatic cities of Bremen and Hamburg, the left bank of the Rhine, Catalonia, northern Italy, Rome and the Papal States, and the Illyrian provinces. Napoleon ruled over three political formations: the Kingdom of Italy, the Swiss Confederation, and the Rhine Confederation, which included nearly the whole of Germany apart from Austria and Prussia, as well as the Grand Duchy of Warsaw. This vast area constituted nearly half of Europe and had a population of 71 million inhabitants. War against England lay at the root of the Grand Empire; Napoleon had become involved in a series of conquests in order to close the Continent to English goods and to ruin the pound sterling by an economic blockade. This was, however, never effective.

Under his rule, the Empire became unified. The Civil Code was introduced in every country. New judicial principles of social equality and civil liberty replaced the old feudal system. Napoleon wrote to Joseph Fouché, his Minister of Police: "What I want is a European Code, a European Supreme Court of Appeal, the same currency, the same weights and measures, the same laws for everyone." To the Council of State he declared, "If you unite every country as far as the columns of Hercules, as far as Kamchatka, the laws of France must be introduced there."

There were many additional unification projects. The highway became the chief coordinating factor in Napoleonic Europe, just as it had been in the days of the Roman Empire. The great Simplon and Saint Gothard highways were constructed at this time. Vast works were undertaken that changed the face of the ancient capitals (in Rome, for instance, the Pontine Marshes were drained). Nationalities intermingled in the army. Even the arts were not exempt from this desire for unification. Henceforth it was in the Louvre that the works of Rubens of Antwerp or the masterpieces of Italian or Spanish art could be admired. It was even planned to transfer the archives of the subjugated countries to Paris. And Napoleon created the Order of Reunion to replace the old European decorations, symbolizing the fusion of different countries into the Empire.

Would this Napoleonic Europe have been a workable system? Even at the time of the Russian expedition, cracks were already beginning to appear in its structure. In 1810 Napoleon had modified his concept of the Continental System. Because he was unable to prevent smuggling with England, he decided to become a smuggler himself. He authorized the importation of English goods under a system of licenses. (The high duties he levied on these goods enabled him to finance the Russian expedition.) This limited trade with England was restricted to French ports, which later redistributed the products imported from Great Britain to the rest of Europe. At the same time Napoleon stepped up the campaign against smuggling in the allied and subjugated nations, especially in Germany, where English merchandise worth millions of francs was burned in Frankfurt.

Europe, already reluctant to put up with the shortage of sugar, coffee and cotton imposed by a blockade that also was proving economically disastrous, was even more reluctant to suffer these privations when it saw that France was exempt from them. Indeed, by his system of licenses and by the restrictions imposed on industrial development in certain countries such as Italy, Napoleon planned the creation of a gigantic market in Europe for the benefit of French businessmen and manufacturers. "My ruling principle," he stated, "is that France comes first." The blockade, which started as a means of attacking England, became from 1810 onward the instrument with which to maintain French economic hegemony over the rest of Europe.

But Napoleon lost his reputation of invincibility in the snows of Russia, and Europe took advantage of the French Emperor's failure to rise up against him. The revolt began in Prussia, where poets, academics and politicians inspired the growth of a patriotic movement that spread throughout Germany. Thousands of volunteers joined in the fight for freedom and wore the black, red and gold cockade. Austria allied itself with Prussia and Russia, and in October, 1813, they defeated Napoleon at Leipzig. From then on Germany was lost to the Emperor.

Above Metternich, who led the Austrian peace delegation in 1813 and presided over the Congress of Vienna.

An English printed cotton handkerchief commemorating the Battle of the Berezina, one of the bloodiest episodes in the retreat of the French.

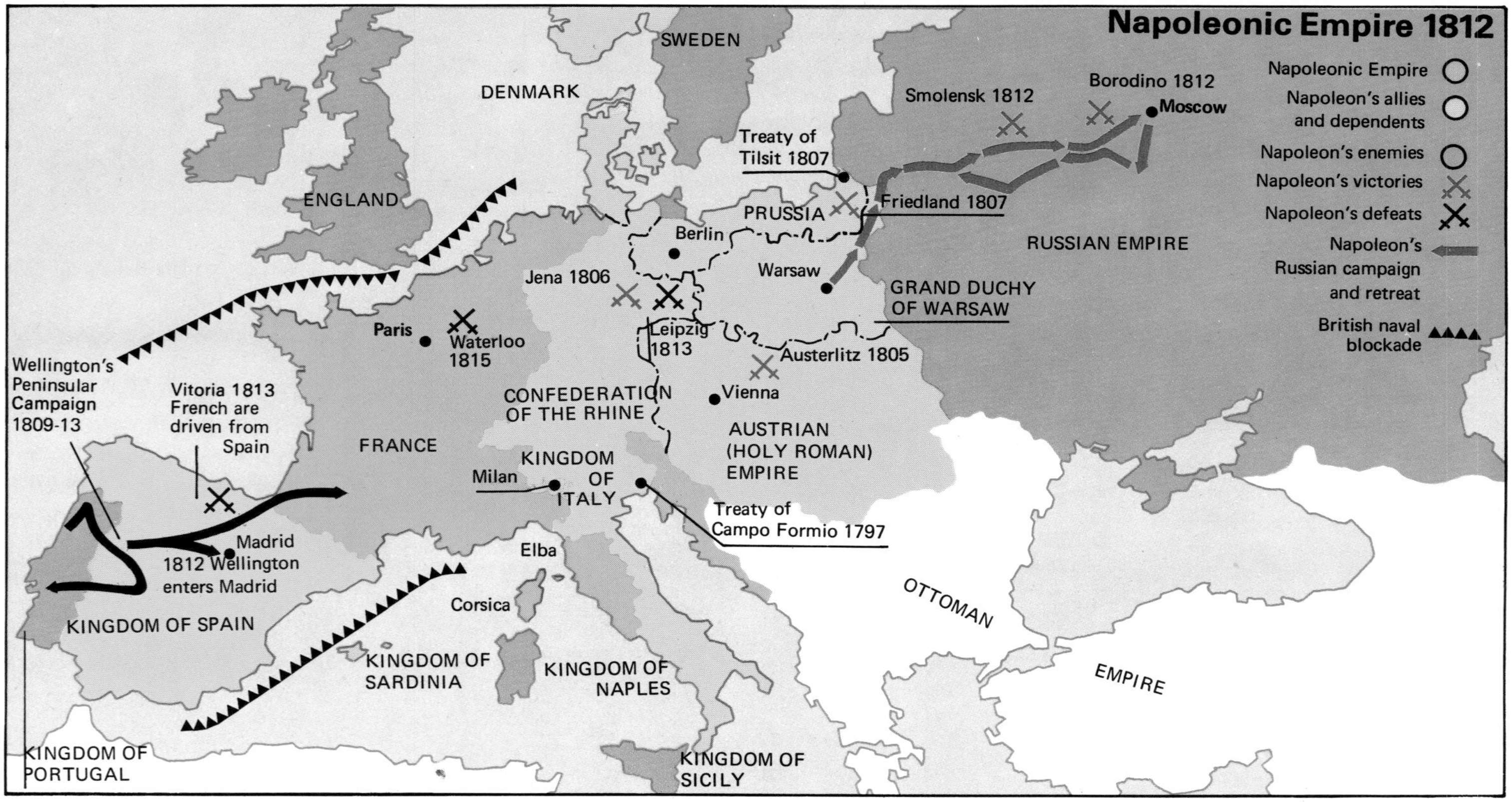

Napoleonic Empire 1812
Napoleonic Empire
Napoleon's allies and dependents
Napoleon's enemies
Napoleon's victories
Napoleon's defeats
Napoleon's Russian campaign and retreat
British naval blockade
SWEDEN
DENMARK
ENGLAND
Smolensk 1812
Borodino 1812
Moscow
Treaty of Tilsit 1807
Friedland 1807
PRUSSIA
Berlin
RUSSIAN EMPIRE
Warsaw
GRAND DUCHY OF WARSAW
Jena 1806
Paris
Waterloo 1815
Leipzig 1813
Austerlitz 1805
Wellington's Peninsular Campaign 1809-13
Vitoria 1813 French are driven from Spain
CONFEDERATION OF THE RHINE
Vienna
FRANCE
AUSTRIAN (HOLY ROMAN) EMPIRE
KINGDOM OF ITALY
Milan
Treaty of Campo Formio 1797
Madrid
1812 Wellington enters Madrid
Elba
Corsica
OTTOMAN EMPIRE
KINGDOM OF SPAIN
KINGDOM OF SARDINIA
KINGDOM OF NAPLES
KINGDOM OF PORTUGAL
KINGDOM OF SICILY

Holland was the next to revolt. On November 15, 1813, the Dutch drove out the French occupation troops and invited the Prince of Orange to rule them. In the meantime, the Swiss Confederation had withdrawn from the French sphere of influence and had proclaimed its neutrality. The raising of troops for the Russian campaign had depleted the French forces stationed in Spain, and in June of 1813 British forces under Wellington defeated them in a bloody battle at Vitoria, driving them out of the Iberian Peninsula with the help of the Spanish.

Thus the disastrous Russian campaign speeded up the disintegration of the Empire by bringing to the surface all the discontent with French domination that had been felt for a long time in Europe. All those countries that had been merged into the Continental System regained their former independence. The Emperor himself was forced into exile, first on Elba and then, after escape and the abortive attempt to regain power that ended at Waterloo, on St. Helena.

The Congress of Vienna, called in 1814 to remake Europe after Napoleon's collapse, was a major effort at European cooperation. Yet the victors, obsessed by their own interests, ignored the nationalist movements that had begun to emerge at the time of the Russian campaign. These violent nationalist movements, especially in Germany and Italy, were to provoke a long series of revolutions and wars. Thus the collapse of Napoleon's Empire marked the beginning of a long period of division in Europe.

The Napoleonic balance sheet was not totally negative, however. The Russian disaster did not jeopardize the radical changes that the Emperor had introduced into Western Europe, particularly the destruction of feudalism. Moreover, although he envisioned a united Europe that would exclude both Russia in the east and England in the west, Napoleon had simplified the map of Europe to a large extent and had broached the idea of European unity—a concept that had lain forgotten since the time of Charlemagne.

JEAN TULARD

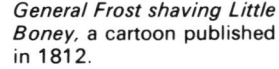

General Frost shaving Little Boney, a cartoon published in 1812.

Napoleon's study at Fontainebleau.

Russia after 1812

Even under the two great rulers of the eighteenth century, Peter (1672–1725) and Catherine (1729–96), Russia had remained isolated from the rest of Europe, and in 1800 could still be regarded largely as an oriental power. Under Alexander I (1801–25), however, largely because of her almost disastrous involvement in the Napoleonic Wars, Russian interest in Europe developed rapidly. Alexander saw Russia's future as a European power. The sign of Russia's new western interest was that on March 31, 1814, the Tsar became the first foreign conqueror to enter Paris since Henry V of England in 1420. For the rest of the century, despite its Asian interests, Russia had all the characteristics of a European state, and saw itself as the rival of Britain, France and (later) Germany. Russia also became an enthusiastic upholder of the Quadruple Alliance formed with Britain, Austria and Prussia originally to overthrow Napoleon.

An immediate result of this new European role was the abandonment of the liberalizing program that Alexander had sought to introduce during the early years of his reign. In the years before 1812, a wide-ranging, although not wholly effective, string of measures had been brought into operation. The invasion of 1812 swept away both the reforms and their architect, Count Michael Speransky (1772–1839), who was accused of being a "Russian Jacobin." Over the next few years the government became increasingly opposed to any change. Rigid censorship and government surveillance of universities and schools was introduced, and a secret police organization was set up. As a result many liberals left Russia to live abroad, while others joined secret revolutionary societies. The death of Alexander in 1825 was the signal for the outbreak of a rising, the Decembrist Revolt, which was, however, easily crushed. Because of this rising, the new Tsar Nicholas I, who ruled from 1825 to 1855, felt justified in continuing his brother's autocratic methods.

Mikhail Speransky, who was the Tsar's adviser on domestic policy until 1812.

Reaction in Britain

While Russian autocracy continued undiminished, there was little enough sympathy in those years between the social classes in Britain. The English country gentlemen profited from the wars as more and more land was enclosed in order to meet the demand for grain (which could not be imported so long as Napoleon kept the Continent closed to English ships). Manufacturers, too, benefited from the continued hostilities: the need to clothe and equip the armies of Britain and her allies artificially stimulated the new factory industries. In fact, only the working population fared badly; prices were high, food was scarce and hours of work in the mines and heavy industries were long. There were waves of anti-Jacobin hysteria among the landowners, who used the emergencies of war to justify action against demonstrations of social and political discontent. In 1799 and 1800 all radical associations were suppressed by acts of parliament, and workmen's "combinations" (which sought improved conditions from employers) were declared illegal. Ironically, a similar prohibition of workers' associations, the *Loi le Chapelier*, had been introduced into the French National Assembly in 1791 and was retained, in a modified form, in the Napoleonic Code. But in Britain, incipient trade unionism was regarded as a symptom of the revolutionary virus from beyond the Channel.

Political liberty was increasingly curtailed in England and Scotland as the war with France dragged on. After the death of Prime Minister William Pitt in 1806, it seemed for a moment that a more liberal program might prevail; the radical Charles James Fox (1749–1806), who had been deprived of office by Pitt, became Foreign Secretary in a "Ministry of All the Talents," but within a few months he, too, was dead. The next three administrations proved unresponsive to demands for reform. Indeed the Tory government met pressure for reform by tighter and more far-reaching treason and antisedition laws. Reformers were silenced or prosecuted for preaching "sedition," and in 1810, William Cobbett (1763–1835), the most patriotic of radical pamphleteers, was imprisoned for two years for protesting the flogging of local militiamen by German mercenaries. "The mass of the people have nothing to do with the laws but to obey them," Bishop Samuel Horsley (1733–1806) had declared stridently in 1795. That uncompromising mood prevailed among the Tory governing class for a quarter of a century, culminating four years after the war had ended in the notorious Six Acts of 1819 (which among other things blocked free speech, free assembly and freedom of the printed word).

It was only when men like Robert Peel (1788–1850) and William Huskisson (1770–1830), the voices of commerce and trade, began to pierce the inner ring of Tory legislators in the 1820s that sanity returned to political life.

Lord Liverpool, English Prime Minister and a leader of reaction.

The fall of Napoleon

When Alexander I of Russia entered Paris in 1814, he was accompanied by the insignificant King of Prussia, Frederick William III, and was followed a fortnight later by the Emperor Francis I of Austria. Thus there were three allied sovereigns in residence in Paris on May 4 when Louis XVIII, brother of the Bourbon King who was executed in 1793, claimed a throne that was his by inheritance rather than by the will of his subjects. Prince Klemens von Metternich and Robert Stewart, Viscount Castlereagh (the foreign ministers of Austria and Britain) and the Duke of Wellington, who had commanded the Allied troops in Portugal and Spain, watched the return of the Bourbons with apprehension, for all three suspected that the French people would never take this fat and forgotten representative of the Old Order to their hearts. "It made a most painful impression upon me," Metternich later wrote in his memoirs.

While Louis XVIII was being crowned in Paris, Napoleon—still an emperor in name—departed to rule the tiny island of Elba off the coast of Italy. It was anyone's guess how long he would play out the parody of power.

The downfall of Napoleon had meant far more than a change in regal personalities, for the Emperor had transformed Europe more rapidly and more comprehensively than any sovereign since Charlemagne, a thousand years before. It became the task of the victors not only to dismantle the imperial apparatus of government, but to control the national aspirations stimulated throughout the Continent by the years of revolution and warfare. At the same time, it was essential for them to build up a lasting settlement that would be safe both against renewed aggression by France and any attempt by one of the Allied powers to establish military domination over its neighbors. The settlement came just in time; the Russians' successful eastward thrust in 1813–14 had already cast a heavy shadow over the deliberations of the Austrians, the Prussians and the British. Their suspicions were fanned by French foreign affairs minister Talleyrand, who, in the

forces of reaction in Europe

The grand entry of the Allied sovereigns into Paris in 1814.

last months of war, had shifted his allegiance from Napoleon to Louis XVIII and now exercised his talent for diplomatic negotiations on behalf of the Bourbons.

By the First Peace of Paris (May 30, 1814), the territory of France was limited to the frontiers of 1792, with minor adjustments. It took far longer to determine the character of the new Europe. The task of so doing fell upon the Congress of Vienna, a gathering of six emperors and kings, two dozen German princelings, and a host of plenipotentiaries and diplomats who met in the Austrian capital from September, 1814, to June, 1815. A spate of formal entertainment and the gossip of an overcrowded city won the Congress a dubious reputation for frivolity and scandal—much of which was unjustified. The statesmen worked hard to achieve their principal objective, the "general repose of the European Continent," and although there was a major rift between Russia and her Western allies, they were successful. Europe was given the opportunity to convalesce for a decade.

An allegorical depiction of Napoleon's departure for the island of Elba off the coast of Italy in 1814.

The Treaty of Vienna

The Congress' final act (which is generally known as the Treaty of Vienna of June, 1815) set up three new political entities and two subject kingdoms. The territorial creations were: a United Kingdom of the Netherlands (Holland, Belgium and Luxembourg); a German Confederation of thirty-nine loosely linked independent states with no central government; and a Free City in the ancient Polish university town of Cracow. The subject kingdoms were Lombardy-Venetia, which was ruled by the Austrian Emperor, and Congress Poland (the area around Warsaw), which was ruled by the Tsar of Russia.

The treaty also called for the Swiss Confederation to be reestablished and given a guarantee of permanent neutrality, the pre-Napoleonic dynasties in Spain, Piedmont, Tuscany, Modena and Naples to be restored, and Norway, which had previously been linked to Denmark, to be handed over to Sweden. Prussia obtained new territories in the Rhineland, an area of great future significance both because of its untapped mineral resources and because of its strategic importance as a launching pad for the invasion of France. The British, more interested in colonies than in Europe, secured Malta, Heligoland, the Cape of Good Hope, Tobago, Mauritius and Ceylon. They were also given a protectorate over Corfu and the Ionian Islands (which remained under British administration until 1863).

The German and Italian peoples were particularly disappointed by the settlement, and so, in time, were the Poles and the Belgians. But as an exercise in the statecraft of reciprocal compensation, the Congress was without a parallel in the history of diplomacy. The principle of a balanced "Concert of Europe" that the Congress established lasted for the remainder of the nineteenth century. No great powers fought each other for almost forty years after the Treaty of Vienna, and there was no war involving all Europe for ninety-nine years.

Not all the credit for the long peace rests with the statesmen in Vienna. For example, it can be argued that the opening up of other continents lessened the likelihood of a long and exhausting war in Europe. But there is no doubt that the delegates to the Congress were conscious of the need for some international order that would curb the anarchy of competing states.

Escape from Elba

The last months of the Congress were disturbed by a dangerous threat to the new settlement. In February, 1815, Napoleon precipitously left Elba. Three weeks later he was back in Paris, Louis XVIII was in exile and French loyalties were swiftly shifting back to the Emperor. Although the Congress of Vienna did not discontinue its sessions, it was necessary for the statesmen of Europe to form a coalition once again against "the international outlaw." Wellington left Vienna to command an Anglo-Dutch force in Belgium; Marshal Blücher concentrated a Prussian army on the Lower Rhine; and the Austrians and Russians slowly mobilized.

1815 The Reshaping of Europe

In an atmosphere of opulence, splendor, and festivity, the European powers that had overthrown Napoleon—Russia, Prussia, Austria and Britain—met in Vienna to work out the shape of the post-Napoleonic world. At first they met with disagreements and mutual distrust and only the dramatic return of Napoleon from Elba and the Hundred Days culminating in the victory of the Allies at Waterloo prompted their accord. The agreements worked out at Vienna, while autocratic and arbitrary, nevertheless helped keep the peace in Europe for half a century.

Arthur Wellesley, Duke of Wellington, victor of Waterloo.

Opposite The Battle of Waterloo, by Denis Dighton. Napoleon's dramatic return from exile galvanized the quarreling statesmen in Vienna into resolving their disputes.

On the last day of March, 1814, Tsar Alexander I, resplendent in gilded stirrups, gold epaulets and a golden collar to his blue uniform, led an allied army of Russians, Austrians and Prussians through the eastern gate of the city of Paris. No foreign conqueror had entered the French capital for nearly four hundred years, and Alexander was deeply conscious of presiding over one of the great turning points in history. Eighteen months previously, Napoleon I's Empire and its dependencies stretched from the Baltic to the Mediterranean, from the banks of the Polish Vistula to the upper waters of the Spanish Tagus. Now the years of French primacy on the Continent were at an end and Napoleon, a loyal remnant of the Old Guard around him, waited forty miles away at Fontainebleau, hoping that his emissaries could obtain reasonable terms from the new master of Europe. It seemed, that spring, as if the fate of the Western world depended upon the word of the thirty-seven-year-old ruler of All the Russias, who had himself so recently reeled before the shock of a French invasion.

For eleven days Tsar Alexander remained the principal spokesman of the Allied cause. He worked closely with a five-man provisional government in Paris that was headed by Talleyrand, for long the ablest of Napoleon's foreign ministers and the first major public figure in France to have foreseen his downfall. Together Alexander and Talleyrand speedily settled the French dynastic question: Louis XVIII, who had spent most of the preceding twenty years in Russia or England, was invited to the throne his brother had occupied before the proclamation of the Republic in 1792. Napoleon was induced to abdicate, though permitted to rule the Mediterranean island principality of Elba and to retain the title and dignity of Emperor. The other Allies, particularly the Austrians, thought it foolish to allow Napoleon sanctuary so close to the Italian mainland, the Austrian Foreign Minister, Prince Metternich, even predicting that if Napoleon settled on Elba, war would be renewed within a couple of years. But the Tsar refused to believe the fallen Emperor would seek to disturb the peace of Europe. Alexander had already given solemn assurances to Napoleon's emissaries and he would not go back on his pledged word. As it was, Napoleon reached Elba on May 4, the day after Louis XVIII returned to his Palace of the Tuileries.

Castlereagh, the British Foreign Secretary, traveled to Paris hoping that it would be possible to conclude a general settlement of all the major European problems before midsummer. He soon saw that this was impossible, for there was too much suspicion among the victorious powers. The Tsar's territorial ambitions in Poland ran directly counter to those of the Austrians, and there were serious differences between the Allies over the future form of the German and Italian lands liberated from French rule. The Tsar argued that the first task was to prepare a treaty of peace with France; only when this was done would it be possible to tackle other problems. The Allies agreed with him, though for differing reasons; the passage of time, they thought, would reduce tension while permitting them to form new combinations against Russia. France was treated generously. By the First Peace of Paris (May 30, 1814), Louis XVIII was allowed to retain the frontiers of 1792, with the addition of the Chambéry and Annecy districts, and the French were spared the humiliation of an Allied army of occupation or the crippling burden of reparations. At the same time, the treaty invited all the states which had taken part in the recent wars to send representatives to a congress that would meet in Vienna and determine the formal character of the new map of Europe.

The Congress was Metternich's brainchild. He believed the four great powers—Austria, Britain, Prussia and Russia—would take all important

The Congress of Vienna, from a contemporary cartoon. The bickering and intrigue that surrounded the proceedings were the source of much cynicism, especially on the part of European liberals.

decisions. The smaller states, and France, would then be consulted over minor details and left to approve the work of their masters. He thought—and so, for that matter, did Castlereagh and Alexander I—that the whole business would be over in six weeks; if the Congress opened on October 1, as planned, everyone would be home by Christmas.

Metternich was wrong. He had not allowed for the masterly diplomatic skill of the French representative, Talleyrand, who exploited differences between the Russians and their allies while, at the same time, appearing as champion of the lesser European states. As soon as Talleyrand arrived in Vienna he began to encourage the smaller powers, claiming that France, Spain, Portugal and Sweden had as much right to be heard as the big four. "The intervention of Talleyrand . . . hopelessly ruined all our plans," wrote Gentz, Metternich's right-hand man, in his diary. The opening of the Congress was postponed for a month, and during that period the rift between the Tsar and Metternich became so great that it seemed they might even fight a duel. They differed, first and foremost, over policy. Alexander wanted to be king of a vassal state embodying all the Polish lands, while Metternich favored a return to the partitioned Polish boundaries of 1795. Over most questions the Prussians supported the Tsar and the British supported Metternich. With so many divisions and such a varied clash of interest it is hardly surprising that the Congress lasted, not for six weeks, but for nine months—and then completed its work only under the pressure of external emergency.

The statesmen of Vienna were remarkably haphazard in the day-to-day business of making peace. "A kingdom might wax or wane in the course of a ball, an indemnity be settled during a dinner, a constitution be drafted at a hunt," declares the Count de la Garde-Chambonas in his memoirs of the Congress. His impression would not have been shared by the minor civil servants who met week after week in the stifling constriction of overheated conference rooms to work out the details of the new European order; but there was enough truth behind the Count's generalization for this picture of the "dancing Congress" to have survived in the public imagination for more than a century and a half. Never before had the cosmopolitan aristocracy of central Europe mounted so flamboyant a gala occasion—balls, banquets, concerts, ballets, military reviews, a medieval carousel, a balloon ascent, hunting expeditions by horse or sleigh followed each other with protracted carnival zest from the beginning of October until the coming of Lent, in the

An official version of the Congress; by Isabey. The main points of difference lay between the Russian and the Austrian interests, supported by Prussia and Britain respectively.

second week of February. The Emperor Francis of Austria established a Festivals Committee with responsibility for planning diversions for the thousands of visitors to Vienna that winter, and before long it was being said in the city that the Festivals Committee was the most hard-working body in the whole Congress.

There was an air of unreality about all this frenetic festivity. The social calendar for January, 1815, invited delegates to the Congress to share the delights of no less than sixteen grand fetes during the month, to say nothing of numerous other distractions in the snow-covered countryside. And yet there was a really deep division between the Allies that month. In the first week of the new year, for example, the great-power relationship was so bad that Metternich and Castlereagh signed a secret military convention with Talleyrand, providing for joint action should Tsar Alexander insist on imposing his solution of the Polish Question by force of arms. It is unlikely that Alexander, or anyone else, would have risked war over Poland, for the long struggle against Napoleon had left every country materially exhausted and the prospect of another winter campaign in central Europe had little attraction. Nevertheless, the political stalemate in Vienna was significant. It strengthened the hands of liberals on the Continent and in England, many of whom were resolutely opposed to a general settlement dictated by the Eastern autocrats. Feeling at Westminster ran so high that Castlereagh was summoned back to London in February, 1815, in order to control an increasingly factious House of Commons. He was succeeded as the chief British representative at the Congress by the Duke of Wellington, who already enjoyed great prestige among the Allied leaders for his victories in Portugal and Spain.

It was not only the Opposition members of Parliament at Westminster who were excited by the crisis in Vienna. Rumors of discord reached Napoleon on Elba before the end of January. He knew already that Louis XVIII and the restored *émigrés* were unpopular—indeed, he had a personal grievance against the new French government for witholding pensions to which he was entitled by treaty—but it was the reports from Vienna that interested him most, and visitors to the island found him shrewdly seeking to assess their significance. His greatest fear was that, with the increasing influence of Metternich and the Austrians, his own position on Elba would be in danger; for he knew there was talk of removing him to a remote outpost in the West Indies or the southern Atlantic. If his former enemies were quarreling among themselves, it was

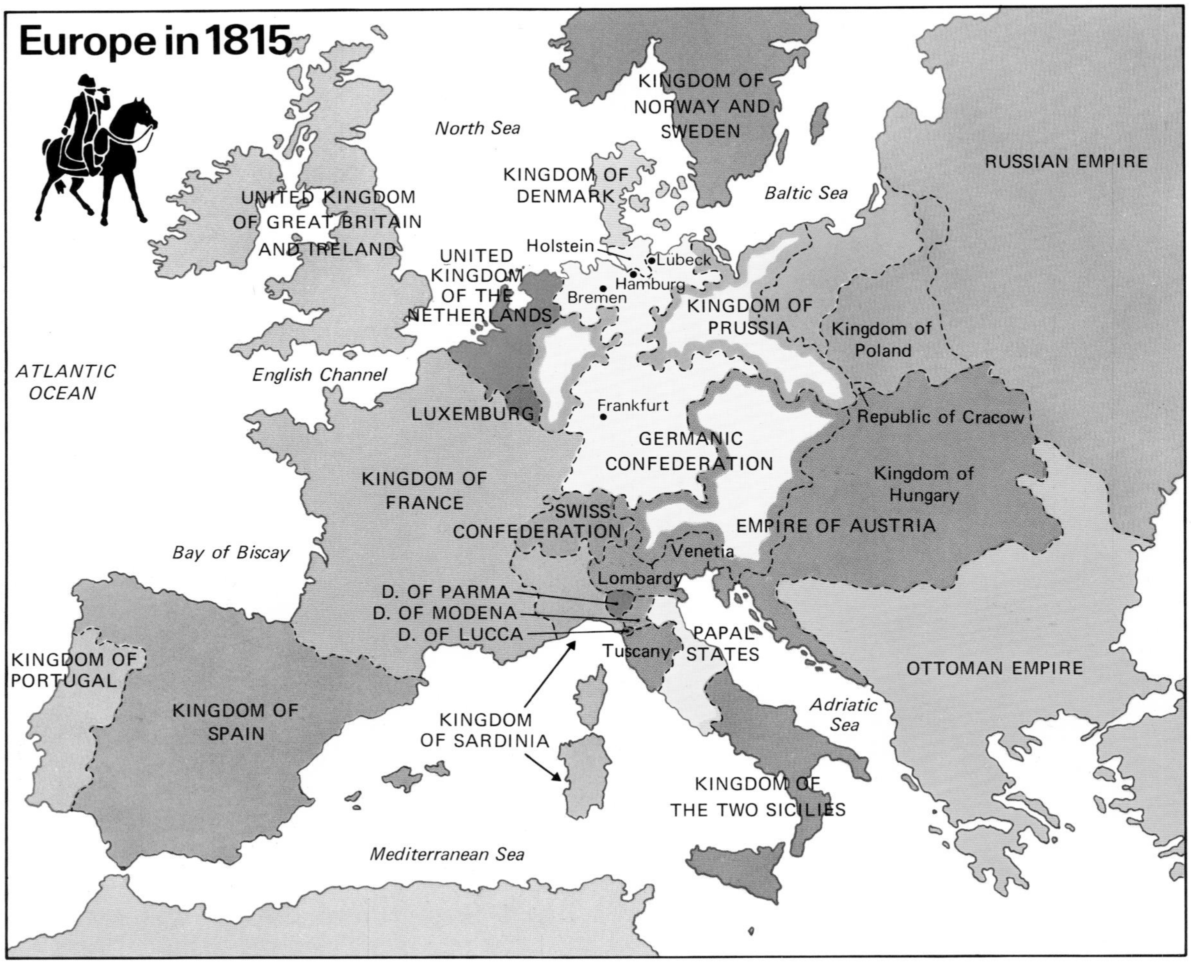

tempting to intervene and seek to improve his status. What if he marched on Paris and recovered his throne? Rather than face another long war it seemed probable that the Allies would accept a negotiated settlement in which he would demand for France her natural frontiers. In the third week of February he accordingly decided on a gambler's throw, and gave secret orders to fit out an expedition to sail from Elba for France. On the night of February 26, the brig *Inconstant* slipped away from Elba with the Emperor and four hundred veterans aboard. Six smaller vessels, each tightly packed with soldiers, made an inconspicuous escort. Three days later the tiny force reached the French coast between Cannes and Antibes. "I shall enter without a shot being fired," Napoleon declared confidently. He was right.

News that he had disappeared from Elba only reached Vienna on the morning of March 7, and by then he had been in France for a week, gaining support daily as he moved steadily northward through Grenoble and Lyons. The Allies did not know Paris was his objective until four days later, although they had already taken steps to brand him as an international outlaw and a "disturber of world repose." On March 20, King Louis XVIII fled to Belgium and that evening Napoleon arrived back at the Tuileries, borne shoulder-high across the courtyard of the palace by ecstatic veterans of his campaigns. It was, however, the limit of his success. His return reconciled the Tsar and Metternich and induced the wavering diplomats in Vienna to introduce some order into the proceedings of the Congress. A new treaty of grand alliance was made public on March 25: the Austrians, British, Prussians and Russians undertook to raise an army of 600,000 men to defend the Peace of Paris from the outlaw "Buonaparte." There was little sign of a rift between the great powers: the problems of Poland, Germany and Italy were speedily resolved. On March 29, the Duke of Wellington left Vienna to take command of the Allied vanguard in the Low Countries, knowing that the rulers of Russia, Austria and Prussia were already beginning to concentrate supporting armies on the Rhine. If Napoleon was counting on spreading mischief between his old enemies, he was soon disappointed.

Throughout the early summer of 1815 there were thus two centers of intense activity in Europe. Rival armies massed in the traditional cockpit of the Continent, the triangle formed by Lille, Brussels and Sedan, for no one doubted that Napoleon intended to enter Belgium and challenge the will of his adversaries in battle. But, seven hundred miles away in Vienna, the statesmen were still preparing a comprehensive treaty that would embody all the decisions of the peacemakers. At last on June 9 the Vienna Treaty was ready for signature. Its territorial provisions were more extensive than any earlier

Above Victory banquet of the City of London in the Guildhall, June, 1814, with the Prince Regent, Tsar Alexander, Frederick William of Prussia and Metternich seated at the high table.

Left A French Hussar or light cavalryman.

Far left An officer of the Hussars. Napoleon's more experienced troops and his superiority in guns convinced him the prospects at Waterloo were favorable.

PORTRAIT OF A NOBLE DUKE.
Salamanca
Waterloo
"I should think this head possest some talent for Military affairs."
Wellington
Phrenological Lecture

Above A caricature of Wellington, the "Iron Duke." The totality of his victory at Waterloo diminished Russia's influence and ensured for Britain a say in European affairs greater than she had known for a century.

Right Field-Marshal Blücher, commander of the Prussian forces that outflanked the French, enabling Wellington to move into attack at Waterloo.

settlement. Three new political entities and two subject kingdoms were set up: Holland, Belgium and Luxembourg became a United Kingdom of the Netherlands; thirty-nine states were loosely knit together in a German Confederation; a Free City was established in the ancient Polish university town of Cracow; the Emperor of Austria was given the crown of Lombardy-Venetia; and the Tsar of Russia became King of "Congress Poland," the central Polish lands around Warsaw and the Vistula. At the same time the Treaty reestablished the Swiss Confederation, with a guarantee of permanent neutrality, and restored the pre-Napoleonic dynasties in Spain and most of the Italian peninsula. Norway, which had previously belonged to Napoleon's Danish allies, was transferred to Sweden, and there were major changes within Germany, the most important being the extension of Prussian power in the Rhineland. The British (who were mostly interested in consolidating colonial acquisitions in southern Africa, the West Indies and the Indian Ocean) were content in Europe with the possession of Malta and Heligoland and a protectorate over Corfu and its dependencies.

None of these territorial changes paid any regard to national rights, for Europe's rulers still tended to think in dynastic terms and distrusted "national feeling" as a subversive and Jacobin doctrine. The settlement was therefore denounced by liberals throughout the Continent as an example of cynical bargaining in statecraft. Yet it is clear in retrospect that, despite its frivolity, the Congress of Vienna possessed in the end a certain moral dignity. The statesmen made pronouncements of general significance for international well-being. They accepted, for the first time, the principle of free navigation of the great European waterways, applying it in this instance to the Rhine and Moselle Rivers, and they established a regular system of diplomatic precedence. The slave trade was condemned and a recommendation made by the great powers that the liberties of the Jewish peoples should be broadened, especially in Germany. However much men of liberal sentiment might despise the Vienna Congress, its spokesmen were not unaware of fundamental human rights.

At the time, however, these virtues remained unappreciated in Europe. Nor indeed did the final stage of the Congress excite wide interest. Everything depended on what happened in Belgium, and the drama of this latest Napoleonic campaign held public attention throughout the Continent. At dawn on June 15, Napoleon led an army of 125,000 men across the Franco-Belgian border and occupied Charleroi. Facing him were 117,000 Prussians under Marshal Blücher and a cosmopolitan force of 95,000 men (one-third British and the remainder Dutch, Belgian and German) under Wellington personally. The next day, Napoleon defeated the Prussians at Ligny but failed to follow up his success, partly through confusion in the subordinate command. Wellington, withdrawing an exposed corps from the town of Quatre Bras, established a defensive line along a ridge south of Waterloo, a village twelve miles from Brussels.

The weather turned on June 17, and the two armies prepared for a decisive engagement under driving rain, which gave way to a damp mist before nightfall. At breakfast on Sunday, June 18, Napoleon studied the maps and the latest reports from his outposts. He had the more experienced troops and superiority in guns. After the events of the previous two days he discounted the possibility of intervention by Blücher. Wellington, he thought, was at his mercy. "We have ninety chances out of a hundred in our favor," he declared.

So, indeed, thought many of the citizens of Brussels, though Wellington was optimistic. He had chosen a strong defensive position, a plateau with a steep southern slope and ground made swampy by the heavy rain at its foot. Moreover there were several small copses, good for cover, and sound solid farmhouses, with stone gateways and brick walls. Napoleon hoped for a quick victory, with cavalry breaking through along the Brussels road and separating Wellington from the badly mauled Prussians. The weather, however, was against him. He had originally ordered the initial assault for nine in the morning, but the ground was too waterlogged and it was not until four hours later that his batteries opened fire. At that very moment someone drew Napoleon's attention to a strange darkening on a ridge four miles to the east. Was it the shadow of a cloud, or the massing of an army? Soon captured prisoners left him in no doubt. What he had seen were Blücher's columns, bearing down on the French flank. There was no time to lose.

Through the afternoon the Allied line held fast against repeated French attacks until Napoleon had to divert men to meet the challenge from Blücher and the Prussians on his right. There followed an uneasy pause, when the battle remained in the balance as the evening shadows lengthened. Forty squadrons of cavalry harassed the Allied squares, as Napoleon and his deputy Marshal Ney threw in all their resources. At half-past seven the Old Guard moved forward, the finest troops under Napoleon's command. They were repulsed and, as they reeled under the shock of counterattack, Wellington ordered the whole Allied line to advance. For perhaps a quarter of an hour there was utter confusion at the foot of the plateau but, at last, with the light failing fast under gathering clouds, Napoleon realized he had lost the day and rode off toward Charleroi, the broken commander of a broken army. He had hoped for a victory that would prove he had lost none of his military genius. Instead he suffered the most decisive of defeats. Within four days he had abdicated for a second time and within a month he was on his way to the remote south Atlantic island of St. Helena, a prisoner of the British.

Snuffing Out Boney! by Cruikshank. The wild, if cheerful, Russian giant menacing a miniscule Bonaparte reflects the preeminence of Alexander I as leader of the Allied cause in 1814.

The totality of Wellington's victory surprised the Allies. Tsar Alexander, with the rulers of Austria and Prussia and their main armies, was at Heidelberg, ready to march against France if Napoleon became heavily committed in Belgium. But as soon as news of Wellington's victory arrived at Heidelberg, it was clear that Europe and the Vienna frontiers were secure from the menace of another Bonapartist upheaval. Hurriedly Alexander set out once more for Paris, eager to reestablish the primacy he had enjoyed fifteen months previously. But this time he was too late to shape policy. The victor of Waterloo, not the Tsar of All the Russias, was the new master of France. A valiant advance in the fading light of a June day ensured for Britain an influence over Europe's affairs greater than she had known for more than a century.

ALAN PALMER

The Quadruple Alliance

The immediate consequence of Napoleon's Hundred Days was the Second Peace of Paris (November 20, 1815), which redrew French frontiers as they had been in 1790 and imposed a war indemnity of seven hundred million francs on the French people. The terms of the treaty further stipulated that Allied troops were to occupy France for a period of from three to five years.

An indirect consequence of the Second Peace of Paris was a new endorsement of the need for international cooperation to safeguard the whole Vienna settlement. The foreign ministers of both England and Austria, Castlereagh and Metternich, believed such cooperation could best be achieved through a system of "diplomacy by congress," and a legal basis for such conferences was provided by a clause in the Quadruple Alliance that was signed in November, 1815, by Austria, Britain, Prussia and Russia.

Tsar Alexander favored an even more elevated concept—a "Holy Alliance of Justice, Christian Charity and Peace"—to which he induced most of his brother sovereigns to subscribe (although both Metternich and Castlereagh regarded it with considerable cynicism). Unfortunately, the Tsar chose to inform the world of his Holy Alliance at a review of the Russian army of occupation in Paris, and his alliance became the particular butt of Europe's liberals. Within a few years the term Holy Alliance was being applied to the entire policy of repression followed by the three Eastern autocracies, Russia, Prussia and Austria. The Tsar's original idea, a muddled and mystical call for something more exalted than mere reactionary government, had been lost.

At first, the Congress System favored by Metternich and Castlereagh functioned effectively. Although, unlike the League of Nations or the United Nations, the Congress System had no permanent secretariat, it was nonetheless a genuine experiment to test the possibility of international administration. The first meeting, held at Aix-la-Chapelle (Aachen) in 1818, was highly successful. But a fundamental difference separated Britain from her old allies at the remaining congresses. The Austrians and Russians believed that the great powers had a right and a duty to intervene if other states were threatened by internal unrest. The British, however, refused to associate themselves with repressive measures against liberal revolutionaries in Spain and southern Italy. The congresses at Troppau in 1820 and at Laibach in 1821 were inconclusive, and when the British withdrew from the Congress of Verona in 1822 the whole system fell apart.

The "Holy Alliance" of Tsar Alexander I of Russia, Emperor Francis I of Austria and Frederick William III of Prussia, by which they pledged to maintain the status quo.

The Sick Man of Europe

Long before Britain's insistence on nonintervention killed the Congress System, there were signs of a deep rift between the two main champions of repression, Russia and Austria. Ever since the first sessions of the Congress of Vienna, Metternich had tried to avoid discussions about southeastern Europe. The weak and incompetent government of the Turkish Empire had been challenged by a major revolt in Serbia in 1804, and there were powerful movements for national independence in the other Balkan states as well. Metternich knew that the Russians were eager to benefit from the increasing feebleness of the Sultan's Empire, and he feared that if Turkey-in-Europe broke up into small national states, the process of disintegration would also affect the Austrian Empire (for many of the submerged historic nationalities in southeastern Europe were subject to both Austrian and Turkish rule). Friedrich von Gentz (1764–1832), who was Metternich's chief adviser in foreign affairs, wrote in 1815: "The end of the Turkish monarchy could be survived by the Austrian for only a short time." This prophetic warning was to prove accurate at the end of World War I.

So long as the principal challenge to Turkish rule came from Serbia, Metternich had some hopes of maintaining "a state of repose" in the Balkans, for there was bitter feuding between the leading Serbian families (one faction of whom favored cooperation with the Sultan). But a new spirit of national and cultural regeneration was at work among the Greek communities, not only in the Aegean but in the Turkish ports on the Black Sea and even in Constantinople. The prospect of a revolt in Greece appealed to the Tsar because of the close links between the Russian and Greek branches of the Orthodox Church. And there were others besides the Russians who felt kinship with the Greeks. The Romantic spirit, harnessed to a Classical education, ensured that if Greece sought her independence, the echoes of her struggle would resound throughout Western Europe and even beyond the Atlantic.

On April 6, 1821, Archbishop Germanos (1771–1826) of Patras called on his compatriots to free themselves from Turkish rule. The Greek War of Independence had begun. Metternich, who deemed the move a catastrophe, complained that the headquarters of the European revolution could never have shown more cunning than in selecting Greece as the center from which the whole Continent would be set aflame. The Greek revolt rallied Europe's liberals—and from among the philhellenes, democracy was soon to find its martyr-hero, Lord Byron.

Skulls on a tower at Nis in Yugoslavia, commemorating the first Serbian uprising.

Revolution in Latin America

Between 1810 and 1822, new republics sprang up from the Rio Grande to Tierra del Fuego with a rapidity unmatched until the ending of colonial rule in Africa in the 1960s. The desire for independence was originally stimulated by the example of the North American colonists in their struggle with Britain, but the timing of the individual revolts was determined by events in Europe and, in particular, by Napoleon's dominance of the Iberian Peninsula. The bonds linking Spain and her colonies had always been tenuous in time of war, and with Spanish administration breaking down, it appeared an easy task to cast them aside entirely.

The struggle was to prove a difficult one, however. The wars that ended Spain and Portugal's three-hundred-year domination of Latin America passed through two principal phases. During the first phase, from 1809 to 1816, the colonists were repressed everywhere except in the area around the Plate River. But during the second phase, between 1816 and 1825, the independence movement gained striking successes, and the colonists cast aside colonial exploitation in four million square miles of South America.

Basically, the Latin American revolt was a struggle for liberation from Spain rather than for individual liberty, and some of the new governments were as reactionary as any in Europe. Agustín de Iturbide (1783–1824), who proclaimed Mexico's independence from Spain in 1821, relied on support from the Church and the landowners to suppress a genuine republican movement and to ensure the survival of the constitutional monarchy over which he presided as Emperor. Brazil, declaring itself independent of Portugal in 1822, kept a monarchical structure of administration and accepted the rule of the Portuguese royal family.

Despite these fundamentally conservative elements, the wars for independence produced three outstanding leaders who may be regarded as the founding fathers of Latin America: Francisco de Miranda (*c.* 1750–1816), Simón Bolívar (1783–1830) and José de San Martín (1778–1850). Miranda, a Creole from Caracas, Venezuela, was a failure in his own lifetime but blazed the revolutionary trail that Bolívar followed to free Colombia and Venezuela, and San Martín followed to liberate Chile and Peru. Miranda had witnessed the triumph of the American colonists in 1781, had enlisted in the army of the First French Republic and had risen to the rank of general. In 1811 he commanded the Venezuelan rebels, but the Spanish loyalists outclassed Miranda's forces militarily and he was captured and sent to Spain. He died in a dungeon in Cadiz in 1816, and his death marked the nadir of the rebels' cause. It was now that Bolívar took up the leadership of the rebels. Also a Carqueño Creole, he came from a well-to-do family, and the young Simón was well-read, widely traveled, and had many interests. He was especially interested in new agrarian techniques—estate irrigation and the planting of indigo. He married in 1802, but ten months later his wife died of yellow fever and Bolívar distracted himself with a trip to Europe, where he enjoyed an agreeable mixture of casual intellectual bonhomie and elegant dissipation. Bolívar first met Miranda in London and he soon became his principal lieutenant. After Miranda's death he was forced to flee from Venezuela and seek refuge in Jamaica, and it seemed as if the whole future of Latin America rested with San Martín.

San Martín was a veteran officer who had fought for Spain in the homeland and in Africa. His Peninsular experiences served him well in 1817. Few battle feats in the nineteenth century surpass the achievement of San Martín's "Army of the Andes," an intrepid force of five thousand men who dragged wagons and guns over the hump of Mount Aconcagua and through the Uspallata Pass into Chile. It was a grim but effective march. The Spaniards, taken by surprise, were overwhelmed in the Battle of Chacabuco on February 12, 1817, and Santiago, the principal Spanish stronghold, was occupied. A revolutionary government was established under Bernardo O'Higgins (1778–1842), the son of an Irish soldier who had enlisted in the Spanish army, and on the first anniversary of the Battle of Chacabuco, Chilean independence was formally proclaimed. In the north, Bolívar returned from his sanctuary in Jamaica, organized a base at Angostura, and proceeded westward across the Andes to destroy Spanish power in the northwest.

Bernado O'Higgins.
The son of an Irish soldier, he established a revolutionary government in Chile.

A great pincer movement then began to threaten the heart of Spanish authority in Peru, and in Quito—as Ecuador was then called—San Martín made use of a fleet improvised by Admiral Lord Cochrane (1775–1860), an independently minded British naval officer and former Member of Parliament. Cochrane's squadron had mastery of the Pacific coast and was able to transport San Martín's troops northward so that they could land where they chose and shape the military campaign by command of the sea. The Spanish Viceroy was forced to evacuate Lima, and the independence of Peru was proclaimed on July 28, 1821. Two years earlier Bolívar had defeated the Spanish armies in Venezuela and established Great Colombia, a region comprising the whole of the northwestern quarter of the subcontinent. The Latin American peoples seemed at last to be masters of their own fate.

José de San Martín.

The Monroe Doctrine

Toward the end of 1823, the British Foreign Secretary, George Canning (1770–1827), proposed joint Anglo-American action to ensure the integrity and independence of the newly emancipated colonies. It was clearly to the interest of both governments to safeguard the right of trading freely with Spanish America and to exclude, so far as was possible, intervention by other European states. But President James Monroe and his Secretary of State, John Quincy Adams (1767–1848), distrusted Canning's proposal. They had no wish, as Adams told his cabinet colleagues, "to be a cockboat in the wake of the British man-of-war." Adams proposed a definition of American policy that he left to President Monroe to enunciate. Thus it was that in December, 1823, the President dispatched to Congress the famous Monroe Doctrine: no part of the Americas should be used for future colonization; any attempt by European powers to extend their influence across the Atlantic would be interpreted by the United States as a danger to its own peace and security; the United States would not interfere in Europe's quarrels but expected Europe to accept that the political system of the Americas was essentially different and distinct. For more than a hundred years this doctrine was the lodestar of American foreign policy, though at the time Canning maintained that the young Republic could effect such proud isolation only by the grace of the Royal Navy. It marked the final interment of the Spanish Empire on the mainland of South America (although Cuba was to remain a Spanish possession until the end of the century).

The real importance of the Monroe Doctrine lay in the future—at the time when the United States fleet was sufficiently powerful to cast a shield of defense around the whole continent. But even in 1823, Monroe's bold words were significant. They reflected a new national self-confidence and an assumption that the armies of Europe would never be permitted to traverse the American lands. The fledgling Republic, ignored or at best disdainfully patronized by the European states, had come of age. This development would soon be reflected in her domestic politics as well as in her world standing.

San Martín's resignation

Meanwhile in South America at the end of July, 1822, one of the most surprising abnegations in history took place in Guayaquil, a small port almost equidistant from Lima and the Isthmus of Panama. In this steaming equitorial harbor, San Martín met Bolívar and acknowledged the primacy of the man who had liberated the north. Believing that Bolívar's plans for a broad confederation were politically more ambitious than anything that he could offer, San Martín retired from political life. (He died a quarter of a century later in voluntary exile in France.) Bolívar assumed responsibility for the armed forces of Peru and in the following year landed in Peru and was proclaimed dictator.

End of an Empire

1824

Determined to cast aside the tradition of colonial exploitation that had characterized Spanish rule in South America, Simón Bolívar led the rebel colonists of Peru to victory at Ayacucho in 1824. His triumph—which was the climax of a sixteen-year-long struggle—marked the end of the most stable empire in European experience and the beginning of a new era in Latin American history. Spanish power and European influence on the South American mainland collapsed, but Bolívar's wider ambition—to create a united Spanish American republic—never materialized.

At Ayacucho, Peru, high up in the Andes Simón Bolívar's deputy, Antonio José de Sucre, led the insurgent South Americans to final victory over their Peninsular Spanish masters on December 9, 1824. The battle was itself unspectacular, but after sixteen years of intermittent warfare it heralded the end of what had been the most stable empire in European experience. For the first time a colonial power was conclusively defeated by an army recruited largely from Indians, Negroes and *Mestizos* (colonists of mixed European and Indian descent). Moreover, the South Americans had demonstrated their skill not only in conventional warfare but also in guerrilla tactics, on a scale then unknown in colonial conflicts. After Ayacucho, Bolívar had only to round off a campaign that caused hardship and deprivation far greater than Napoleon's Russian adventure. In South American history, however, Ayacucho represented but a moment of triumphant euphoria, for the alliance that coalesced to oust the European soon fell into disarray.

As early as the 1790s the privileged groups of Venezuela had been alarmed by a series of disturbances. A slave revolt had swept the French Caribbean island of Santo Domingo in 1791; "liberty" and "equality" were proclaimed by malcontents in Coro, Venezuela, in 1796. The possibility of a great insurrection fanned by imported revolutionary rhetoric was apparent to all, and Creoles and *Peninsulares* joined together to stave off class and ethnic warfare. But the alliance was shortlived.

In 1808, Napoleon invaded Spain and deposed the ineffectual Charles IV. The invasion left a power vacuum in the colonies and consequently a clash of loyalties. Since it was the nearest colonial capital to Spain, Caracas received news of the invasion first. The majority of Caraqueño Creoles insisted on the urgency of a preemptive coup, arguing that public order could be preserved and local interests defended only by dislodging the colonial government. The *Peninsulares* and a Creole minority were equally adamant that public order depended upon the monarchy, and answered that any concession to separatists would only encourage the Negroes and *Mestizos* to press their demands violently. Essentially, each elite group considered itself conservative and depicted the other as about to unleash smoldering discontent. Events in Caracas followed closely upon those in Spain: a royalist clampdown in Venezuela in 1809 gave way during 1810 to a revolt purporting to defend the deposed Ferdinand VII against the constitutionalist Spanish regency in Cadiz.

The Creoles were unprepared. Though debate in the municipal councils and trading associations grew heated and patriotic associations multiplied, it took time for a convincing Creole leadership to emerge. Miranda—the independent monarchist—and Bolívar—the republican—sailed for Venezuela in different boats. Because he admired his foresight and persistence in championing a cause that had been unpopular for a generation, Bolívar deferred to Miranda and together they established Venezuelan independence on June 5, 1811. But the trend in favor of republicanism was reversed as royalists exploited the accumulated grievances of slaves and *llaneros* (plainsmen) against Creole landlords and tax-collectors. The First Republic tottered as ammunition ran short, coffee and cocoa prices fell, revenues diminished and an enfeebled government had to resort to paper currency and even then could not pay its soldiers. The royalists exploited popular anxieties over the effects of paper currency, and took advantage of an earthquake in Caracas to direct religious hysteria against the Republic. But Miranda did not grasp the gravity of the situation, and failed to unite a Caraqueño elite that was too immersed in ideological debate to be effective in suppressing revolt. He posted Bolívar

Simón Bolívar, *El Libertador*. Widely traveled and deeply influenced by French republican ideas, Bolívar dedicated himself to the liberation of Spain's American colonies and became one of the great figures of the independence movement.

Opposite Bolívar leading the insurgent Venezuelans to independence in 1811. This victory was shortlived, and Bolívar fled to New Granada where he organized continued resistance to the Spanish royalist forces.

to a secondary theater of war to keep him on the sidelines. Bolívar, however, was too alarmed to remain a mere spectator. Miranda's pre-Napoleonic style of warfare had been responsible for a "generation gap" in the military command, which his arrogance and insensitivity to local feelings after so many years in Europe only served to deepen. Moreover, Bolívar regarded as treacherous Miranda's capitulation to loyalist forces in 1811, without consulting his subordinates. Thus, when the occasion arose, he handed Miranda over to the loyalist leader, General Juan Domingo Monteverde, and secured for himself a free passage to the chief port of New Granada, Cartagena, which in 1812 had an independent government.

From Cartagena Bolívar organized to recapture Caracas. In his celebrated *Manifesto of Cartagena* he exhorted republicans to go onto the offensive and to regain the initiative in Venezuela. After taking part in an onslaught upon royalists controlling the Magdalena River, the main artery of New Granada, Bolívar launched a new attack on Venezuela. Modeling his strategy and tactics upon Napoleon's, Bolívar swooped on Caracas from the Andes. The despotic behavior of Monteverde now played into his hands: Caracas fell, and the Second Republic was formed.

Bolívar had first to restore a severely dislocated economy and reinstate the Venezuelan government. He encouraged exports and trade with the British. He was careful neither to offend the propertied classes with confiscations (as Monteverde had done) nor to arouse their anxiety with rhetoric that might be considered Jacobin-inspired. He insisted on the superior durability of republican government and the urgent need for a centralized political system. But the republican attempts at recovery were thwarted by a royalist blockade. Having lost the initiative, Bolívar had nothing to fall back on except his rhetorical talents: he resorted to the theatrical gestures that he had seen in Europe and which were novel in a Venezuela accustomed only to the stylized performances of colonial administrators.

The departure of Napoleon from Spain allowed Ferdinand VII to reassert his rule in the colonies in 1815, with an expeditionary force led by General Pablo Morillo and by means of undercover agents sent to reinflame *llanero* resentments. The *llaneros,* hunters and cattle-herders for the most part, were accustomed to the rigors of subsistence living and fought with a ferocity unknown in Europe. The atrocities committed by the *llanero* "Legion of Hell"—rape, mutilation, torture, brandings, sacrilege—horrified the Caraqueño elite, and Bolívar felt obliged to retaliate with similar guerrilla tactics: bloody reprisals, scorched-earth policies, relentless harassment and swift, unexpected forays. The niceties of European warfare were forgotten. To keep the war going, each side had to take emergency measures, including the melting down of gold and silver belonging to the Church and the promise of freedom to slaves after the fighting ended, in exchange for their services in battle.

Defeated, with his army crumbling behind him, Bolívar withdrew up the Andes. He hoped to stage a comeback from New Granada, but his command was precarious. His guerrilla activities had earned him an unsavory reputation that had not been salvaged by success. Believed to harbor dictatorial ambitions, he was known among the lawyer-class of Bogotá as the Man of Terror; the Archbishop had excommunicated him, and he was distrusted as a Venezuelan. At a hastily convened congress in Tunja, therefore, Bolívar set out to win the sympathy of the New Granadines before entering Bogotá.

Morillo, in the meanwhile, was pursuing his strategy of successively capturing Venezuela, New Granada, Peru and the Plate River. After consolidating his position in Venezuela, he marched toward New Granada. The Congress of New Granada, hesitant to recognize Bolívar's military talents, was less reluctant about posting him to the periphery, and furnished him with men and supplies to relieve the Caribbean port of Santa Marta. Bolívar failed to accomplish this, took refuge in Jamaica, and sailed from there to Haiti, where he convinced the President, Alexandre Petión, of his need for resources. Petión, President of the only Negro Republic in the world, was sympathetic to Bolívar's vision of an independent, republican Spanish America. He fitted Bolívar out with a small force of two hundred and fifty men, arms for six thousand and a printing press, and exacted from him the one promise that all slaves be freed in the states he liberated.

In 1816, Bolívar landed successfully in Venezuela and set up headquarters in the lower Orinoco basin at Angostura. Entering into alliance with a newly emergent *llanero* leader, the illiterate General Antonio José Páez, a man who was particularly sensitive to the needs of warfare in the jungle and plains. he recaptured the Orinoco basin within three months. Ill-equipped, he had no choice but to recruit primitively armed Indians who, though a match for the royalists in exceptional conditions, were no match for them in normal ones. Bolívar, therefore, looked for men in Europe: in Spain he found republican sympathizers; in Britain demobilized troops, unemployed during an economic depression, readily composed a British legion. But although European troops were good for propaganda in Europe they were not always an asset in the field, since they were resentful of receiving orders from South Americans.

In 1819, a congress convened at Angostura and established the independent state of Venezuela with Bolívar as President. With Venezuela semi-pacified, Bolívar now set out to recapture Bogotá, supported by the New Granadine General Francisco de Paula Santander. The 1819 campaign was the most spectacular yet. Bolívar hoped to surprise the royalists by letting it be known that he would take the normal mountain route for Bogotá, when, in fact, he intended to cross plains and jungle to

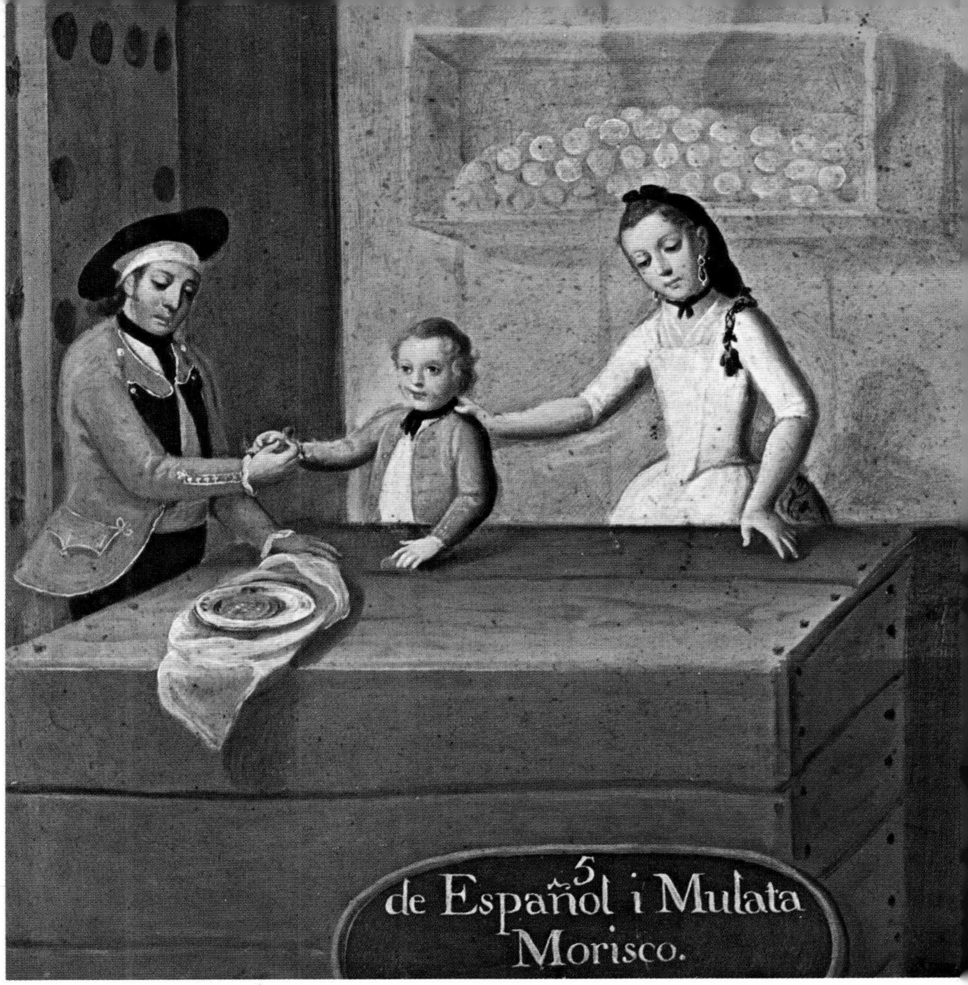

reach it. He set up his base in the Casanare region, convenient because the Spaniards had not recaptured it in 1816, and because it was too extensive to flush out. From the Casanare, Bolívar marched on Bogotá. His officer corps was young—no one was over forty. Their progress overland was arduous; the troops endured tropical rainfall and mosquitoes without uniforms or boots—they even had to improvize loincloths as substitutes for trousers, and to extemporize coracles out of cowhides. The loss of animals was heavy. Then, on climbing the Andes, the men, accustomed to tropical climates, had to adapt to Arctic conditions. But despite these hardships, Bolívar's ruse was successful. Because their intelligence was poor and their troops scattered over the three hundred miles between Bogotá and Cartagena, the Spaniards were caught unprepared. A tired royalist army, demoralized by his mastery of guerrilla tactics, was defeated at the Battle of Boyacá, and Bolívar entered Bogotá, this time hailed as a hero and deliverer. Republican morale was reestablished with the defeat of the Spanish crack troops and, in 1821, Venezuela and New Granada were formally united as one republic, Colombia, with its capital on the frontier between the two, at Cucutá.

Bolívar now set about giving Colombia institutional stability. Santander, aged only twenty-nine, was elected Vice President and was to exercise presidential powers in Bolívar's absence. In the event, tensions soon crystalized: civilian New Granadines feared dictatorship by the Venezuelan military; Venezuelan soldiers felt that armchair

Above The union of a Spaniard and a Mooress. The victory at Ayacucho was remarkable in that for the first time a multiracial army conclusively defeated a colonial power.

Opposite The cloister where Bolívar lived for a while behind the village church of Cayma on the outskirts of Arequipa.

Below The equestrian statue of Bolivar in Tunja, Colombia.

Above Bolívar by the side of a wounded soldier. He attributed the failures among his campaigns to the oppression of the native-born for whom he sought independence.

Right A pass in the Cordillera Occobamba in Peru. The ranges of the Andes served the revolutionaries both as routes and place of refuge. However, altitude sickness and Arctic temperatures took a toll on troops who were mostly from the tropical lowlands.

lawyers in Bogotá were not entitled to the same influence over policy as those who had taken the risks of fighting. Bolívar, meanwhile, had returned to Venezuela to expel the remaining Spaniards, and a victory at Carabobo in June, 1824, effectively ended the war there.

The new Republic could not feel secure. The Spaniards still had a strong base in the mining zones of southern New Granada and Upper Peru. Further south the movement for independence had been more successful. From the Plate River General José de San Martín, an outstanding professional soldier of monarchist sympathies, had undertaken a dramatic march over the mountains of Upper Peru and was aiming for Lima. More willing to negotiate with loyalists than the republican Bolívar, San Martín, after being recognized as "Protector of Peru," discussed with the Viceroy the possibility of an independent monarchy in Peru with a Spanish prince as ruler and an interim regency. This solution was unacceptable to Bolívar, who would not contemplate any form of monarchy bordering Colombia. He therefore chose a trusted lieutenant, Marshal Antonio José de Sucre, to take Ecuador. Sucre was defeated by the Spaniards, and Bolívar marched on Ecuador himself. At the port of Guayaquil Bolívar met San Martín. Although the content of their conversation remains a matter of speculation, San Martín appears to have requested Bolívar's help in consolidating his position in Peru and Upper Peru, and was prepared to put himself under Bolívar's command. Bolívar was hesitant, for three reasons: he feared overstretching his slender resources; he anticipated the unpopularity of an alien Colombian army in Peru; and he knew how unreliable the Lima aristocracy was—it always shifted its allegiance to whoever was on top at the time. However, as San Martín was prepared to sacrifice his monarchist sentiments, the risk of a personality clash was averted.

In 1823 Bolívar entered Lima. The liberation, as he predicted, caused little jubilation. Peru was in a state of endemic civil war—war not only between royalists and republicans but between different shades of republican. A difficult situation was complicated by the unpredictable behavior of the navy. Bolívar and Sucre were disheartened to find they could not avoid involvement in local in-fighting. The return of Ferdinand VII to power in Spain had given a fillip to royalists in Peru. But the royalists were divided too—between royal absolutists and liberal constitutionalists.

The royalists, however, assembled to meet Bolívar. In response, he led his army southward along precipitous mule-tracks. Supply networks were uncertain, and once more men from the tropical lowlands were subject to altitude sickness and Arctic temperatures. Faced by a very real risk of mutiny, Bolívar had ensured that all his soldiers were paid adequately and regularly. And in a short encounter with the royalists at Junín, he emerged victorious. Bolívar then returned to Lima where political problems were as pressing as military ones. The Colombian Congress, concerned as always that power should not be concentrated in one person, ordered that Bolívar should not rule another state and run the army at the same time. Thus it was that Bolívar remained in Lima, and, ironically, left it to Sucre to win the victory on December 9, 1824, that put a seal upon Spanish-American independence. The Battle of Ayacucho was itself curiously anticlimatic. The Spanish Viceroy was captured, and the royalists left without hope of further reinforcements from Europe. It only remained for Bolívar and Sucre to undertake mopping-up operations in Peru and assert their authority in Upper Peru, which had already unilaterally declared independence, naming itself Bolivia after the liberator.

The sense of exhilaration that followed this triumph was brief. Still envisaging a united nation that could compete with the European powers on equal terms, Bolívar expressed his hope first for a Confederation of Hispanic Nations and then for a Federation of the Andes. The romance of his exploits captured European imaginations—Byron mentioned emigrating. And the independence struggle hypnotized the more hard-headed Britons: businessmen who had once been dismayed at the prospect of a republican solution were now impressed by Bolívar's emphasis on stability and invested heavily in Peruvian mining.

Disillusionment soon set in, however, as the mining industry crashed and hopes of republican stability began to sour. In New Granada factionalism was rife. For Bolívar's victories in Peru and his popularity in Bolivia soon aroused New Granadine suspicions of personal and military aggrandizement. In Venezuela relations between Caracas and the *llanero* outback were fraught. In Peru Bolívar had assumed dictatorial powers to deal with turbulent dissidents; it proved easier to assume these than to shed them. Slowly losing his idealism, he looked increasingly to workable government and less to ideal solutions. Finally disillusioned, and convinced that the Americas were ungovernable, Bolívar died near Santa Marta in 1830.

The Spanish American revolutions were not "revolutionary" in the modern sense of the word. There was no major redistribution of wealth. Indeed, widespread destruction had meant a serious loss of wealth and Spanish America did not recover its trading position of the 1790s till the 1840s. Nor were there major adjustments in status: Indians and Negroes remained suppressed and neither slavery nor the slave-trade was abolished. Yet the potential for violence of the submerged ethnic groups was recognized and calculated upon by the politicians of the nineteenth century. Uprisings based on the plains of Venezuela and Argentina became commonplace; the memory of Indian revolt was imprinted upon the political consciousness of Mexico, Peru and Bolivia; and race war was never out of the question in Colombia or Venezuela. But by the criteria of the early nineteenth century, the Spanish American revolutions were remarkable. Absolute monarchy had been thrown off, and republican institutions, however imperfect, and republican modes of debate, however glibly imitated, had been substituted. The absolute power of the Church throughout Spanish America had been curtailed by the crisis in ordination that accompanied the war and precedents for later anticlericalism had been set. Conflict, too, between civilian and military sectors became a common phenomenon.

The optimism of the younger Bolívar was not entirely unwarranted. Despite the fact that the successor states sank into a mood of unmitigated pessimism, and that they were disrupted by constant frictions, Bolívar did provide a guideline for the action of subsequent generations. Throughout the nineteenth century he remained the symbol of unfulfilled hopes qualified by a realistic appraisal of local possibilities. Even in the twentieth century the Andean countries have lacked heroes of the same stature although Bolívar's vision has remained something of a yardstick. This vision may have proved less than luminous, but it has at least outshone that of his successors.

CHRISTOPHER ABEL

Below French troops defeating the forces of Toussaint L'Ouverture, the Haitian Negro ruler who resisted Napoleon's attempts to reestablish slavery. His eventual successor, Alexandre Petión, gave Bolívar asylum, aid and support for the South American struggle.

1824 Death of a Poet

Insurrection engulfed the Ionian Peninsula in the early spring of 1821 as a determined band of Greek patriots attempted to free their homeland from Ottoman oppression. Their cause found widespread international support—particularly in England, where John Hobhouse, a close friend and traveling companion of Lord Byron, founded a committee to assist the insurgents. Byron, England's foremost Romantic poet, found the rebels' cause a particularly compelling one, and on July 13, 1823, he sailed for the strife-ridden peninsula. In his youth Byron had toured Greece with Hobhouse, and he remembered the country as a place of unending beauty. Instead, he encountered inclement weather, earthquakes, riots and mutiny. Discouraged and embittered, Byron lingered at his headquarters in Missolonghi until April of 1824. On the ninth of that month, the poet-soldier caught cold while riding; ten days later Lord Byron, the personification of Romanticism, was dead.

Byron's signature carved on a column at the east end of the Temple of Poseidon at Cape Sounion in Greece.

Opposite Byron in Albanian national dress. Byron's sympathy for the Greeks was largely based on romantic ideas.

In mid-May of 1824, dispatches from the Gulf of Corinth reached London announcing that a month earlier, on April 19, George Gordon, Lord Byron, had died at Missolonghi. The first to open the dispatches was Byron's friend Douglas Kinnaird, who immediately forwarded their contents to another old friend, John Cam Hobhouse. "I can scarcely write to tell you," Kinnaird said, "yet delay is absurd and I know not how to soften what your own fortitude alone can make you bear like a man—Byron is no more. . . ." The news, Hobhouse noted in his diary, threw him into "an agony of grief." No less agonizing were the emotions of Augusta Leigh, the ill-fated sister who had loved Byron far too well. A cousin reported that even Lady Byron, his former wife, was "in a distressing state," and that "she said she had no right to be considered by Lord Byron's friends, but she had her feelings." Of Byron's one-time Italian circle, the widowed Mary Shelley remembered him with especially deep affection. "Albé," she recorded in her journal, "the dear, capricious, fascinating Albé—has left this desert world! God grant I may die young!"

Meanwhile the story of Byron's death had "come upon London like an earthquake" and had reverberated throughout the length and breadth of England. To the generation that was then emerging from childhood, it seemed as if some tremendous natural calamity had shaken the framework of the universe. In Lincolnshire, fifteen-year-old Alfred Tennyson hurried down to the cold little stream that ran below his father's garden, and scratched the momentous phrase "Byron Is Dead" upon the surface of a sandstone rock. Jane Welsh wrote to her stern young suitor, Thomas Carlyle, that she had heard the report while she was surrounded by a crowd of people. "My God, if they had said that the sun or the moon had gone out of the heavens, it could not have struck me with the idea of a more awful and dreary blank in the creation. . . ."

Nor were Byron's only mourners his friends, or those who had eagerly studied his works and passionately admired his genius. At Belvoir, the Duke of Rutland was entertaining a large party of jovial country neighbors. When the news was brought to him as he sat at the dinner table, he stood up and commanded silence. "Gentlemen," he exclaimed, "Lord Byron is dead." And without discussion, the company rose from their chairs, called for their servants and carriages, and quietly made their way home.

Few great men, in any country or period, have left behind them so acute a sense of loss. Yet only eight years earlier, on April 26, 1816, Byron had said good-bye to England, an exile and a social outcast who appeared to have realized in life the tragic predicament that he had frequently portrayed in literature. He was as solitary as his own *Childe Harold,* the subject of as many alarming legends as *The Corsair* or *The Giaour.* Over his head hung a heavy cloud of scandal, and on his journeyings he was to be pursued and harried by a crowd of hostile English tourists. They scrutinized him impudently if they encountered him face to face, or followed his daily round, however pedestrian it might be, with the help of opera glasses. Once, in Switzerland, some tablecloths happened to have been hung out from the windows of the Villa Diodati; his fellow English travelers naturally imagined that what they saw was an array of petticoats belonging to the women of his harem.

Byron, it is true, did not always discourage such legends. The course of debauchery into which he had plunged after settling in Venice in 1817 was just as outrageous as any of the exploits with which the most spiteful gossips credited him. The easy-going Venetians themselves had sometimes looked a little grave, murmuring that milord was a *giovane stravagante,* indeed a very wild young man. True, he had tired of his random sexual adventures, but the

Byron and Marianne. Byron's reputation as a philanderer scandalized London high society.

damage was already done. And his association at Pisa and elsewhere with the notorious atheist, Percy Bysshe Shelley, and other English expatriates of the same kind did not do much to improve his reputation.

Yet he remained the Romantic poet par excellence, the artist who had caught and fixed the vague imaginings and the restless, unsettled desires of his literary and social age. Keats and Shelley were still seldom read; the powerful influence of Wordsworth and Coleridge was confined to a relatively small group. In Byron alone did English writers and critics find a full-blooded personification of the new Romantic mode of feeling that, having begun to take shape as a self-conscious literary movement during the second half of the eighteenth century, had reached its climax with the appearance of *Childe Harold* and the series of highly dramatic and brightly colored verse tales—*The Giaour, The Bridge of Abydos, The Corsair, Lara, The Siege of Corinth, Parisina* that Byron had written, usually at breakneck speed, during the last three years before he left England.

Nothing could dim the renown of *Childe Harold*. But once Byron had settled down in Italy he embarked upon a very different type of epic, and some of his admirers, Hobhouse included, began to grow a trifle restive. Byron himself considered that *Don Juan,* written in Italy, was a much more important production than any of his earlier poems—it gave a far less distorted view of his own protean personality. But readers who had enjoyed his romantic panache were shocked by the "quietly facetious" tone (an astringent mixture of wit and lyricism) that he now applied to solemn subjects.

Above right The east front of the Parthenon, as it was in Byron's day.

Further, they were often bored by the elaborate blank-verse dramas that Byron always persisted in regarding as his finest and least perishable works. The reception of his dramas was somewhat lukewarm; and after his foolish Italian mistress, the Countess Teresa Guiccioli, had voiced her disapproval of *Don Juan,* which hurt her idealistic conception of love, Byron decided he must cut the poem short.

In 1823, Byron was living in Genoa, a lonely, bored and disappointed man. At thirty-five, he felt old; he believed that his popularity was waning; moreover, he had long since fallen out of love with

Fireplace in the house of John Murray, Byron's publisher.

Byron at Missolonghi with his huge Newfoundland dog, Lyon.

Above left Missolonghi, with its shallow stagnant lagoon. Here Byron spent three purgatorial months.

Teresa Guiccioli, though she remained an inseparable companion. He sometimes considered deserting Italy and seeking a new refuge beyond the Atlantic Ocean, perhaps in the United States (though he distrusted Americans, whom he regarded as members of a coarse-minded race), or possibly in Venezuela. The South Americans, he thought, might suit him excellently. "Those fellows," he told Hobhouse, "are as fresh as their World, and fierce as their earthquakes. . . ."

Then, in the early days of 1823, he received a heartening piece of information, which gave his thoughts a much more cheerful turn. Hobhouse and other English liberals had recently set up a committee to assist the cause of the insurgent Greek patriots. For nearly two years those Greeks had been conducting a desperate struggle against the armed forces of the brutal Ottoman Empire. What Byron heard of the committee and its aims immediately aroused his interest; and when delegates, on the way to Greece, arrived at Genoa in April, he not only welcomed them and was delighted to discuss their plans, but "even offered to go up to the Levant in July, if the Greek provisional Government think that I could be of any use."

His motives were mixed. For Byron, "dearly beloved Greece" had a profound emotional significance. In no other country, he declared, had he ever been completely happy. Greece symbolized youth and love, sensuous gaiety and the carefree life of action. In his gloomiest moments, Byron's imagination constantly turned back to its rocky, sunlit islands and its dangerous, white-capped seas. He would sometimes talk of the "grey Greek stone" under which, once he had finished his wanderings, he hoped he might be laid to rest.

Thus Byron's attitude toward the Greek cause was both emotional and altruistic. On one hand, he saw the opportunity of reliving an old dream and throwing off his lassitude. On the other, all his most generous instincts were excited by the idea of human freedom. In *Childe Harold* he had delivered a poetic message to the Greek people, bidding them remember their splendid past and reassert their ancient dignity. Now he considered the practical side of the problem: what the insurgents were most likely to need (money, ammunition, medical stores) and what he himself could supply. At the end of April he learned that he had been elected to the Hobhouse Committee, and early in June he decided that he would definitely undertake the expedition. On July 13, 1823, he boarded the *Hercules,* accompanied by Teresa Guiccioli's brother, Pietro Gamba; that strange ruffian, Edward John Trelawny; his personal physician, Dr. Francesco Bruno; two servants; his English valet, William Fletcher; and Tita, his Venetian gondolier. On the fifteenth, after some exasperating delays, the *Hercules* set sail for Greece.

When Byron reached the Ionian Islands at the beginning of August, 1823, Greece was hopelessly divided among a half-dozen warring leaders, of whom the most conspicuous were Alexander Mavrokordatos, a wily Phanariot politician; Colokotronis, head of the provisional government; the gallant brigand Odysseus; and Marco Botzaris, a chieftain of the savage Souliot tribe. Each was eager to secure the Englishman's support—and each was equally determined to lay hands upon the committee's well-stocked war chest. Byron was obliged to remain on the island of Cephalonia until the year

Lady Caroline Lamb, one of Byron's mistresses.

had almost ended before he was able to sort out their conflicting claims and make plans for his future movements. Finally, he decided to join Mavrokordatos and his allies on the north shore of the Gulf of Corinth. After escaping many dangers (once his light vessel was nearly shipwrecked; once it narrowly avoided capture by a watchful Turkish frigate), he landed at the dismal little town of Missolonghi early in January, 1824.

During the three months that he spent at Missolonghi, Byron's life was purgatorial. He had remembered Greece as a place of unending beauty. But his new headquarters, located in a ramshackle house, looked out over a shallow and stagnant lagoon that was divided from the sea by a ridge of sand and mud. Beyond the dilapidated town itself stretched gloomy and unhealthy marshes. Byron, however, had come to Missolonghi as a soldier, not as a tourist. He immediately made himself at home in his uncomfortable lodgings where he received his guests seated, like a Turk, upon a mattress and a cushion, a heavy cloak wrapped around his shoulders. In his bedroom—the only room where this fastidious and oversensitive being could enjoy a few hours' solitude—he kept his books, his uniforms, and one or two treasured possessions.

Far worse than the petty discomforts of his life was the atmosphere of dissension against which Byron had to contend almost as soon as he reached the mainland. Alexander Mavrokordatos was an earnest and high-minded patriot; but this subtle Levantine gentleman, with his commonplace European clothes, his gold-rimmed spectacles, his drooping moustaches and long untidy locks, was not the perfect fellow warrior, and Byron presently discovered that Mavrokordatos had little real control over the forces he was supposed to lead. Much more picturesque were the kilted Souliot tribesmen, hung round with weapons and silver ornaments, from whom the poet had recruited his private bodyguard. These "rude soldiers" had been quartered at Byron's house, where they stacked their guns and

The cremation of the poet Shelley, showing Byron in attendance.

played noisy games of cards in a spacious outer room. Unfortunately, they were a greedy, disloyal crew. As early as January 18, they raised a murderous riot; and on February 19, they once again mutinied and shot down a foreign officer. Byron met the crisis with "calm courage."

Meanwhile, every military scheme miscarried. Byron and Mavrokordatos had planned to assault Lepanto, the Turkish fortress farther up the gulf. Byron himself meant to march at the head of the Souliots, and he eagerly awaited his first taste of action. But unfavorable weather—rain had been falling almost incessantly since his arrival at Missolonghi—the defection of the Souliot contingent, and the hurried departure of most of the English mechanics whom he had relied on to produce the artillery he needed brought his hopeful plans to nothing. By February 15 he was almost at breaking point. That evening, when he had withdrawn to his room in an anxious and dispirited mood, he suddenly collapsed with what his attendants believed must be an epileptic seizure.

Nothing is so remarkable about Byron's behavior at Missolonghi as the proud stoicism with which he faced and surmounted the incessant troubles of his daily life. These included the Souliot mutinies, a violent earthquake, the escape of a stranded Turkish brig that had seemed to offer such an easy prize, and the pitiless torrents of rain that lashed down into the muddy streets. On January 22, Byron had celebrated his thirty-sixth birthday; the occasion inspired him to produce some verses that he described as "better than what I usually write":

'Tis time this heart should be unmoved,
Since others it hath ceased to move:
Yet, though I cannot be beloved,
Still let me love! . . .
The Sword, the Banner, and the Field,
Glory and Greece, around me see!
The Spartan, borne upon his shield,
Was not more free . . . .
Tread those reviving passions down,
Unworthy manhood!—unto thee
Indifferent should the smile or frown
Of Beauty be.
If thou regret'st thy youth, *why live?*
The land of honourable death
Is here:—up to the Field, and give
Away thy breath! . . .

Critics have sometimes been puzzled by the poet's reference to his "reviving passions" and to the "smile or frown of Beauty." Yet even at Missolonghi he could not shake off love; the habit of loving was too deeply rooted. There seems no doubt that the object of Byron's last passion was his sixteen-year-old Levantine page, Loukas Chalandritsanos, a

The Massacre of Scios, Delacroix' picture of Greek sufferings.

Left Greece Expiring by Delacroix, symbolizing the struggles of Greece during the rising against the Turks.

A Greek priest fighting with guerrillas during the War of Independence.

youth of "a most prepossessing appearance," as an observant member of his suite noted. Byron's solicitude for his page had long been obvious; and on the voyage to Missolonghi, when they seemed likely to fall into Turkish hands, he declared that he "would sooner cut him in pieces and myself too, than have him taken out by those barbarians ... for you know what his fate would be."

Further significant evidence of his affection for Loukas is provided by a second poem, which was found among his papers after his death but was allowed to remain in manuscript until 1887. The poet begins with a recital of the dangers through which he has stood beside his friend, but adds:

Thus much and more; and yet thou lov'st me not,
And never wilt! Love dwells not in our will.
Nor can I blame thee, though it be my lot
To strongly, wrongly, vainly love thee still.

At Missolonghi, Byron, who in the past had so often succeeded in love, evidently discovered what it was to fail.

Byron's seizure on February 15 had left him weak and shaken. He began to abandon hope, and by the end of February he decided that his situation was "intolerable." All that he could do was to retain his post; and throughout the month of March he hung on grimly, doling out supplies, arguing and advising, and, as often as the weather allowed him, making a brave attempt to raise the Greek morale by riding forth with his attendants and bodyguard into the open country that lay beyond the lagoon. During one of these expeditions, on April 9, Byron appeared to catch cold. Although he was feverish, he rode out again on the next day. Afterward he retired to his sofa, where he suffered from "shuddering fits" and "wandering pains." He then summoned Dr. Bruno, who was joined by Dr. Millingen. Both were inexperienced physicians who hopelessly mismanaged the case. Although their patient at first refused to be bled, he gave way as his strength declined and submitted to a disastrous regime of bleeding and purging, which further weakened his resistance. By April 15 his life was clearly in danger,

and his mind was beginning to grow clouded.

During his lucid moments, he once spoke of consulting a witch—he could not forget a gypsy soothsayer's prediction that his thirty-sixth year was bound to be perilous, and imagined that he might be a victim of the evil eye. However, Dr. Millingen records that he "did not hear him make any, even the smallest, mention of religion." Indeed, he seemed to reject such thoughts, muttering that he would not "sue for mercy." But memories of his past life haunted him; and on Easter Sunday, April 18, he called William Fletcher to his bedside and struggled to impart some crucial message which Fletcher, he insisted, must carry back to Lady Byron. The message, alas, was unintelligible. Later those who gathered around him could distinguish only a few broken phrases: "Why was I not aware of this sooner? Why did I not go home before I left for here? ... Poor Greece—poor town—my poor servants, *Io lascio qualche cosa di caro nel mondo.*" On April 19, as darkness approached, a peal of thunder rolled across the gulf. Soon afterward, at a quarter past six, Byron opened his eyes, then closed them for the last time.

As he had prepared to leave Italy for Greece, Byron had remarked, both to his friend Thomas Medwin and to his last female admirer, Lady Blessington, that he did not expect that he would return from Greece. A fatalist whose character had always included a strongly self-destructive strain, he had hoped to find in death the justification of a life that had ceased to afford him either pride or pleasure. Though he was unprepared for the physical accident of death, it completed the moral pattern that he had already laid down. Not only did it redeem his personal credit and ensure him a lasting place in the hearts of his contemporaries; but it advanced, as nothing else could have done, the cause of Greek and European freedom. Like the far-famed pursuit of happiness, nationalism—the right of every country to determine its own destiny—is an essentially Romantic concept; and Byron was among the first, and certainly not the least effective, of the great Romantic liberators. PETER QUENNELL

The Siege of Neskastron. Europe strongly supported the Greeks, whom they saw as the inheritors of Classical Greece struggling against the barbarians.

In art the Romantic movement reflects

Glory and Greece

In December, 1822, a renowned public figure declared: "The mention of Greece fills the mind with the most exalted sentiments and arouses in our bosoms the best feelings of which our nature is susceptible." The speaker was James Monroe, the fifth President of the United States, and his declaration formed part of his State of the Union address. Monroe's words fell on sympathetic ears; enthusiasm for liberty and the democratic ideal was boundless among the citizens of the proud young Republic, and they were well aware of the struggle being fought in Greece, nine thousand miles from their eastern seaboard. Pro-Greek philhellenic societies had been founded in all the larger cities, and a new settlement along the Michigan frontier had been named Ypsilanti to commemorate one of the earliest heroes of the Greek War of Independence. In Tennessee the principal town in territory that had been recently ceded by the Cherokee Indians was honored with no less a name than that of Athens.

Romanticism and Revolution

Byron, noted for his theatrical good looks, his moody charm, and his rebelliousness, may have been the Romantic Hero incarnate, but he was neither the Romantic movement's most talented nor its most artistically influential figure. Indeed, the witty couplets of his long poem *Don Juan* resemble more the verse of the earlier Classicist Alexander Pope (1688–1744) than anything of the nineteenth century. Other artists—painters and musicians as well as poets and novelists—are somewhat more representative of the European movement known as "Romanticism." That term, more evocative than descriptive, can be applied to an artistic change that coincided with the revolutionary spirit (social and industrial as well as political) of the eighteenth and early nineteenth centuries.

The latter half of the eighteenth century had seen intellectual reaction against the rationalism of the Enlightenment. A new emphasis on feeling and emotion countered the earlier stress on reason

William Wordsworth, Romantic poet.

and intellect. By 1770, the year the Romantic poet William Wordsworth, who died in 1850, was born, England was already confronting the economic and social changes of the industrial and agrarian revolutions. As large-scale farming drove the peasantry off the land, the old intimacy and dignity of rural village life became the subject of epitaphs. Thus Oliver Goldsmith, poet and playwright (1728–74), mourns one deserted village:

> A bold peasantry, their country's pride,
> When once destroy'd, can never be supplied.
> A time there was, ere England's griefs began,
> When every rood of ground maintained its man;
> For him light labour spread her wholesome store,
> Just gave what life required, but gave no more:
> His best companions, innocence and health,
> And his best riches, ignorance of wealth.

But as today's mass society came into being, so did a number of artists and philosophers determined to resist it at every opportunity.

The English architecture of the eighteenth century had been greatly influenced by the revived Classicism of Italy's Andrea Palladio (1518–80). But around 1770, the influential English writer Horace Walpole (1717–97) decided that he would indulge his taste for the romantic past and ignore the rules of "correct" building. Instead, he had his country house on Strawberry Hill near London built in the Gothic style, like a castle. Meanwhile, the British architect William Chambers (1726–96) was studying Chinese architecture and landscaping for the pagoda he would build in London's Kew Gardens. This defiance of a classical aesthetic in favor of individual—and often exotic—tastes was not an isolated phenomenon. In art, as in society, a radical individualism arose to challenge the idealized order of the Enlightenment. Romanticism emphasized individuals, especially artistic individuals, rather than society at large. Byron's pose of the nonconforming genius, so extensively realized in his own life, was central to Romantic thought. "Every individual human soul that develops its powers," observed German poet Friedrich von Schiller (1759–1805), "is more than the greatest of human societies." And in his *Marriage of Heaven and Hell*, the English mystic poet William Blake (1757–1827) thundered: "One Law for the Lion and Ox is Oppression."

This stress on the individual produced radically new theories of human psychology and communication. Blake, on reading the observation of the Swedish philosopher Emanuel Swedenborg (1688–1772) that scientific study, intellectual endeavor and human affection were linked stages in the same continuum, scribbled in the margin: "Study Sciences till you are blind. Study intellectuals till you are cold. Yet Science cannot touch intellect. Much less can intellect touch Affection." And the British statesman Edmund Burke (1729–97) achieved his first intellectual celebrity, not by political writing, but in his *Philosophical Inquiry into the Origins of Our Ideas of the Sublime and the Beautiful.* There he argued for the primacy of the passions over the intellect: "The great power of the sublime . . . far from being produced by them . . . anticipates our reasonings and hurries on by an irresistable force." With the individual and his feelings replacing society and reason as the matter of art, the late eighteenth century saw a vogue of subjectivism. In *Tristram Shandy* and *A Sentimental Journey*, novelist Lawrence Sterne (1713–68) pioneered the stream-of-consciousness narrative nearly two hundred years before it was reintroduced by James Joyce (1882–1941) in his pivotal works *Ulysses* and *Finnegans Wake*. Shakespeare's tragic heroes, individually defying society and its restrictions, enjoyed a new popularity. In Germany, Johann Wolfgang von Goethe (1749–1832) created a hero, Faust, and a tragedy, *Göts von Berlichingen*, in the Shakespearean mold.

Politically, the Romantics seemed more alienated than involved before the French Revolution. But by 1774, the German philosopher Johann Gottfried von Herder (1744–1803) was applying the individualist themes of his *Sturm und Drang* (Storm and Stress) literary theory to politics. Nations, he argued, could be seen as collective individuals, with personalities, cultural identities and disparate claims incompatible with Enlightenment cosmopolitanism. A similar argument was developed in England by Burke on behalf of political parties. Forming parties, he suggested, should not be seen as seditious factionalism, but as the rightful action of collective individualism.

But with the French Revolution political theorizing yielded to real involvement. Blake wrote a long

Horace Walpole's house on Strawberry Hill.

the revolutionary spirit of the times

poem about it, and Wordsworth actually traveled to observe it in 1791. "I . . . believed," he later wrote:

> That a benignant spirit was abroad
> Which might not be withstood, that poverty
> Abject as this would in a little time
> Be found no more, that we should see the earth
> Unthwarted in her wish to recompense
> The meek, the lowly, patient child of toil,
> All institutes for ever blotted out
> That legalised exclusion, empty pomp
> Abolished, sensual state and cruel power
> Whether by edict of the one or few;
> And finally, as sum and crown of all,
> Should see the people having a strong hand
> In framing their own laws; whence better lay
> To all mankind. . . . (*The Prelude*)

Slightly less eloquent lines were penned by another English Romantic, Samuel Taylor Coleridge (1772–1844), on the turnabout by Edmund Burke who after first supporting the French Revolution later denounced it energetically in *Reflections on the French Revolution* (1790).

> I saw the sainted form of Freedom rise;
> She spake! not sadder moans the autumnal gale—
> 'Great Son of Genius! sweet to me thy name
> Ere in an evil hour with altered voice
> Thou bad'st Oppression's hireling crew rejoice
> Blasting with wizard spell my laurell'd fame.'

But perhaps the most vivid expressions of political sentiment came from the Romantic painters. Jacques Louis David (1748–1825) painted in a Neoclassical style, but his subjects were the outstanding individuals and dramatic scenes of revolutionary France. A Deputy during the Revolution, David voted for the death of Louis XVI. Later, as dictator of the arts, he was the Revolution's propagandist, painting heroic portraits of revolutionary martyrs Jean Paul Marat (1743–93) and Louis Michel Lepelletier de Saint Fargeau (1760–93). David also designed the costumes and sets for revolutionary pageants, like the *Festival of Supreme Being* in which Robespierre (1758–94) acted as High Priest. When Robespierre fell from power, David was imprisoned. After his release he met Napoleon and became his ardent supporter. The result was a Napoleonic saga of paintings, including *Napoleon crossing the Alps*, the *Coronation*, and the *Emperor distributing the Eagles*.

Liberty leading the People by Delacroix.

A generation later, another French painter combined political conviction and a Romantic style to great effect. In his *Journal*, Eugène Delacroix (1798–1863) wrote: "If by my Romanticism people mean the free display of my personal impressions, my remoteness from the servile copies repeated *ad nauseam* in academies of art and my extreme distaste for academic formulae, then I am indeed a Romantic." Like David, Delacroix painted tableaux of dramatic moments in revolutionary France. His famous *Liberty leading the People*, with a bare-breasted woman spurring the citizens over the bloody barricades, commemorates the Revolution of 1830, when the reactionary Charles X was replaced by Louis Philippe. And like Byron, Delacroix supported the Greek rebels. His *Massacre at Scios* and *Greece Expiring* lament their sufferings at the hands of the Turks.

Many other Romantic figures urged the cause of individual and national liberty, including Byron's contemporary Percy Bysshe Shelley (1792–1822)—who was expelled from Oxford for his pamphlet on the "necessity of atheism"—and the German Romantic Heinrich Heine (1797–1856).

Less obviously political, but perhaps even more subversive, was Wordsworth's criticism of conventional poetic diction. In place of the abstruse subjects and flowery idiom of the Classicists, he sought to substitute "situations from common life . . . in . . . language really used by men. . . ." His class bias in this theory was stated candidly. "Low and rustic" persons were likely to use poetic language, "because such men hourly communicate with the best objects from which the best of language is originally derived; and because, from their rank in society and the sameness and narrow circle of their intercourse, being less under the influence of social unity, they convey their feeling and notions in simple unelaborated expressions."

But Romanticism also had its conservative aspects. The widespread dismay at the rise of mass industrial society produced reaction as well as reform. Where Enlightenment figures scoffed at the pietism and repressive government of the Middle Ages, Romantic writers, François René de Chateaubriand (1768–1848), in France, Novalis (Friedrich von Hardenberg) (1772–1804), in Germany and Sir Walter Scott (1771–1832), in England, compared the period favorably with their own. The rising materialism, ugliness and disorder of their times produced a nostalgic fascination with nobility, chivalry and piety. This was the era of the Gothic revival in architecture, when monumental public buildings were styled like medieval cathedrals and castles. In 1836, British architect A.W.N. Pugin (1812–52), whose book, *Contrasts*, had praised medieval building, was commissioned to decorate the new British Houses of Parliament. The resulting style is a fitting tribute to the medieval origins of British democracy. Enlightenment skepticism was countered by a return to religion that revived the unifying force of both faith and ritual. The German artist Kaspar David Friedrich (1774–1840) painted scenes that communicate this conviction in a combination of hazy, almost surreal landscapes and Christian imagery.

Cemetery in the Snow by Kaspar David Friedrich.

No simple equation is possible between Romanticism in the literary and visual arts and Romantic music. The traditional assignment of Classicism to the eighteenth century and Romanticism to the nineteenth is obviously undermined by the persistence of Classical forms—the sonata, the string quartet, and the symphony—from one century to the next. The medievalism that suffused the other arts was rare in musical contexts—with the exception of the "Romantic" Symphony of the Austrian composer Anton Bruckner (1824–96), so named because of the composer's description of its opening in terms of medieval chivalry. The Classical system was also largely retained in the nineteenth century. What did unite the outstanding Romantic composers—such as Franz Schubert (1797–1828), Robert Schumann (1810–56), Felix Mendelssohn (1809–41), and Hector Berlioz (1803–69)—was their music's direct aim at the listener's senses and emotions. Like the other Romantics, their emphasis was the communication of feeling rather than the creation of pleasing aesthetic structures—a revolutionary ambition in a revolutionary age.

The People's President 1829

The American electorate overwhelmingly rejected John Quincy Adams and his National Republican Party in the presidential election of 1828 and endorsed Andrew Jackson—the first populist candidate—for the nation's highest office. Adams called the defeat of his aristocratic, Eastern party "the ruin of our cause," but the populace did not agree. Like many of them, Jackson was a tenant farmer's son, a brawler and a self-made man. Soldiers and civilians alike referred to the Democratic candidate as "Old Hickory," and while few of them could remember his enlisting in Washington's Continental Army at the age of thirteen, fewer could forget his stunning victory over Major-General Pakenham at New Orleans in the War of 1812. They swept Jackson into the White House, and he returned the favor by making the Democratic Party the champion of unlimited franchise, free education and equal opportunity.

For weeks before the raw inauguration morning of March 4, 1829, the roads to Washington were clogged with hard-featured homespun figures—farmers and mechanics, rivermen, artisans and backwoodsmen. All of them were converging on the still-unfinished capital to see "the man of the people," General Andrew Jackson, sworn in as the seventh President of the United States. The General's election in 1828 had been bitterly personal: President John Quincy Adams, the incarnation of Eastern aristocratic pretensions, had opposed Jackson, who emerged as hero-general of the West, the very symbol of what Adams had disdainfully called "the common man."

Scurrilities overshadowed issues in the 1828 campaign, a contest that witnessed the emergence of two fledgling parties—Adams' National Republicans and the Jacksonian Democrats—from the single chrysalis of Jefferson's Democratic Republicans. The ascetic Adams found himself labeled a Sybarite, a spendthrift, a monarchist—even a procurer. National Republicans in turn denounced Jackson as a gambler, a drunkard, a duelist, a slave dealer and a cockfighter. They even intimated that he was insane.

The Republicans' most successful propaganda effort was the Coffin Handbill, a lurid broadside edged with coffin silhouettes that accused Jackson of having had six militiamen arbitrarily shot as deserters in the War of 1812. Such accusations fell within the accepted limits of political abuse, but Adams' supporters went beyond those loose limits when they attacked the General's wife—the plump, good-hearted, pipe-smoking Rachel, whom Jackson had married after her first marriage had presumedly ended in divorce. Now, thirty-seven years later, Jackson found himself charged with having cohabited with Rachel before their marriage. "Ought a convicted adulteress and her paramour husband be placed in the highest office of this free and Christian land?" one Adams pamphlet asked. Only Jackson's position as presidential candidate kept him from challenging the pamphlet's author. "How hard it is to keep the cowhide from these villains!" he lamented to a close friend.

For the friends of Jackson, the election's outcome had never been in doubt, but even they were astonished at its sweep. The General triumphed over his rival with 178 votes in the Electoral College to Adams' 83. In the popular voting, Adams trailed by 508,064 votes to Jackson's 647,276. "The ruin of our cause," the defeated President called the final tally—"the overwhelming ruin of our administration."

Jackson's triumph turned to ashes the following month when his beloved Rachel died. He was convinced that she had been hounded to her grave by the vituperative malevolence of Adams' pamphleteers. "In the presence of this dear saint I can and do forgive my enemies," he said as he stood at her graveside. "But those vile wretches who have slandered her must look to God for mercy."

Although it was sensed rather than seen at the time, Jackson's election marked the third American revolution. The first, which gave birth to the Declaration of Independence, was political rather than social, establishing an aristocratic republic. Washington was elected its first President by a propertied Federalist minority. In his aloof dignity—with his state receptions, his canary-yellow coach emblazoned with his family arms, and his wife's assumption of the honorific title of Lady Washington—Washington saw himself as above politics, a Republican regent for the whole people. Jefferson's hairbreadth election in 1800 marked the second American revolution, "as real a revolution in the principles of our government," Jefferson himself concluded, "as that of 1776 was in form." The persistent sweeping away of property qualifications for voting and the continued extension of the franchise to the mass of white American males made the triumph of Jefferson's Democratic Republicans over the Federalists inevitable.

Andrew Jackson, the first President to come from the New West and the first self-made man to live in the White House.

Opposite above The group of rustic log cabins which was Andrew Jackson's home from 1804–19, near Nashville, Tennessee; and (*below*) his home after 1819, again near Nashville, but now a luxurious mansion typical of the antebellum South.

A caricature of Jackson used against him in the 1832 election when he sought and secured reelection. His enemies accused him of monarchical ambitions.

For Washington's courtliness Jefferson had substituted republican simplicity—even going so far as to walk to his own inauguration. Yet Jefferson was a doctrinaire democrat by nature and a patrician by inheritance. Except for the single-term interlude of John Adams, the Virginia-based political dynasty of which Jefferson was a member guided the destinies of the new nation for its first thirty-six years. As the master of the elegant Monticello, he remained a diffident theorist of democracy. Americans of limited means and learning—the bulk of the population—who were no longer content to be ruled by their self-appointed betters, rallied to him.

If Jefferson was the spokesman of common men, Jackson was their embodiment, and his election marked the end not only of Adams but of the Virginia dynasty as well. Though himself a wealthy frontier planter, Jackson personified the radical plebeian element in American politics. "Andy," as his supporters called him, was the first President to be called by his first name and the first self-made man to occupy the White House. The third American revolution, which was brought about by Jackson's election, was in essence a populist revolution. Before Jackson's inauguration, Daniel Webster remarked of the violent, self-willed President-elect that "when he comes he will bring a breeze with him. Which way it will blow I cannot tell."

Rachel Jackson, "Old Hickory's" wife. The fact that Jackson had married her before she was legally divorced was used as propaganda against him in the 1828 election campaign.

The first six Presidents were men set apart by manners, breeding and education, but any ambitious man might measure himself against Andy Jackson, the tenant farmer's son. Jackson's father had come from the north of Ireland to settle in the Waxhaws, an upland frontier region of the Carolinas where he died in 1767, a month before his son Andrew was born. Andy grew up a thin, freckled boy with reddish hair and the proverbial short temper said to accompany such coloring. Considered the bright boy of the local church school (as quick with his fists as with his mind), he soon found his interests turning from books to horse racing, cockfighting and fisticuffs. Yet when the Philadelphia papers (which were brought to the Waxhaws each week by overland mail) began to carry news of the Revolution, young Jackson was often picked as the public reader, since he "could read a paper clean through without getting hoarse ... or stopping to spell out the words."

At the age of thirteen, Andy and his sixteen-year-old brother Robert joined Washington's Continental Army. Andy was promptly taken prisoner by the English. An arrogant British officer ordered the boy-soldier to clean his boots, and when he refused, the officer struck at him with his sword. As Andy raised his hand to ward off the blow, the blade cut to the bone and then glanced aside and laid open his scalp. Jackson would bear the white jagged scar—and a hatred of England—the rest of his life.

After the war, Andy stayed for a time with a family friend in Charleston, South Carolina, where for six months he was apprenticed to a saddler. Relieved from his semiservitude by an inheritance of several hundred pounds (left him by an Irish grandfather), Jackson lived the more expansive life of a gambler and horseman until his legacy ran out. From Charleston he moved on to Salisbury, North Carolina, where he was long remembered as a "most roaring, rollicking, game-cocking, horse-racing, card-playing mischievous fellow . . . the head of rowdies hereabouts." His ambitions kept pace with his amusements as he studied law with his friend, John McNairy. Before he was old enough to vote, he had passed his bar examination and was admitted to practice.

North Carolina's Western District then extended to the Mississippi, and when McNairy was elected judge of that district's superior court, he appointed his friend and fellow student public prosecutor. With Bacon's *Abridgement of the Law* in his saddlebag and a black wench whom he had bought for two hundred dollars his only company, Andy set out across the Blue Ridge Mountains in 1788. He met McNairy along the way and joined the first caravan over the new Nashville Road. By October the two had reached the Cumberland River settlement of Nashville, which consisted of a pair of taverns, a distillery, two stores, a ramshackle courthouse and a fringe of cabins—all surrounded by a rail fence to keep out stray buffalo.

Jackson found Nashville a debtors' haven but within a month the young prosecutor had changed all that as he enforced writs of execution that had been neglected for years. Creditors and property owners soon acclaimed him, and clients flocked to his makeshift office. Money was scarce, but land was cheap, and most of his legal fees were paid in acres or slaves. Almost before he knew it, the zealous young prosecutor found himself a landowner.

Andy first boarded at the widow Donelson's blockhouse, ten miles down the Kentucky Road from Nashville, and there he met his landlady's sloe-eyed married daughter, Rachel Donelson Robards. Rachel was then living apart from her husband, and when she returned to him in 1790 it was for a brief, unsuccessful attempt at reconciliation. Jackson was sent by the Donelson family to bring her home. The aggrieved Robards threatened to follow—until Jackson threatened to cut off his ears.

After Robards sued for divorce, Rachel fled to Natchez, the Spanish city on the Mississippi. Only thirty miles north of Natchez, at Bayou Pierre, Jackson had earlier set up a log house and trading post to sell slaves and supplies to the wealthier settlers flocking west. When he learned of the divorce action, he followed Rachel to Natchez. Unaware that the divorce would not be made final for another two years, he married her in August, 1791, in the mansion of one of his customers.

Jackson brought his bride back to Nashville, to a plantation he had bought from her brother. There, once settled, he not only traded in cotton, slaves, horses and land but also continued to practice law. When the Western District became a state, he is said to have proposed its name of Tennessee. The new governor, John Sevier, once the ruler of the outlaw state of Franklin, appointed Jackson Tennessee's first congressman. Albert Gallatin, Jefferson's urbane former Secretary of the Treasury, remembered the Tennessee congressman as a "tall, lanky, uncouth-looking personage . . . queue down his back tied with an eel-skin . . . dress singular . . . manners those of a rough backwoodsman." After Tennessee's first senator was expelled for "a high misdemeanor," Jackson was appointed to the United States Senate, but he soon resigned because of financial difficulties. In 1798 he became a justice of the state superior court.

On the bench Justice Jackson was fair and decisive, if impatient of legal subtleties. Nor did his judicial robes tame his violent spirit. When, after a falling-out, Sevier taunted him with "taking a trip with another man's wife," Jackson clubbed him down with his walking stick and then challenged him to a duel. (That duel never took place, but several years later Jackson did kill a man on the dueling field because he had maligned Rachel. In return he received a bullet near the heart that would cause him pain for the rest of his life.) While he was still a justice Jackson was involved in his most famous brawl, which took place in Nashville during the War of 1812. He spotted his enemies, Jesse and Thomas Hart Benton, on the street and went for them with a horsewhip. The Bentons replied with pistols, and in the free-for-all that followed, Jackson's shoulder was shattered by a bullet. He was carried, presumably dying, to the Nashville Inn where, in the course of the next few hours, two mattresses were soaked through with his blood. The wound was not a fatal one, however, and a few months later, with his arm in a sling, the indomitable Jackson was able to conduct a militia expedition against the Creek Indians. And when the theater of war shifted to the South, Jackson rallied the defenses of New Orleans against an assault led by Wellington's brother-in-law, Major-General Sir Edward Pakenham.

The Battle of New Orleans—fought a fortnight after the British and American commissioners had met at Ghent and signed a peace treaty—made "Old Hickory," as the soldiers called Jackson, the most popular military figure since Washington. Legend would celebrate the American victory as the triumph of Jackson's iron will and the skill of his freeborn Kentucky riflemen who coolly picked off the advancing redcoats until the British fled the field. The facts were more prosaic. In an example of military folly not to be equaled until Balaklava, Major-General Pakenham sent his men in close formation across a long rice field to assault an earthwork at the opposite end. The sheltered Americans could direct almost pointblank cannon fire from their vantage, and the British were literally blown to pieces. Pakenham was shot dead, and over two thousand of his men fell with him. Jackson lost a mere eight militiamen, with thirteen more wounded. At the battle's end some five hundred redcoats—

John Quincy Adams, defeated by Jackson in the 1828 election. Adams was the incarnation of Eastern aristocratic pretensions.

An anti-Jackson election cartoon of 1832. The election was fought over the future of the Bank of the United States which Jackson was intent on destroying.

who had prudently played dead—rose from the field like ghosts to surrender.

"I cannot believe," Henry Clay later testily observed of his rival for the presidency, "that the killing of 2,500 Englishmen at New Orleans qualifies a person for the various, difficult and complicated duties of the chief magistracy." Nevertheless the battle legend fixed Old Hickory as the nation's hero and the people's friend, and this single engagement almost elected him to the presidency in 1824 and carried him in triumph to the White House four years later. As he rode from his inauguration to his reception, frail-looking and still in mourning for Rachel, crowds followed him on foot and, heedless of invitation, surged through the White House rooms, overturning the refreshment tables, smashing glasses and clambering on damask chairs and sofas with their muddy boots. Women fainted, men fought, liquor was rushed out in buckets. Finally Jackson's friends had to link arms to protect him and lead him away from his exuberant supporters. "The reign of King Mob seemed triumphant," the patrician Supreme Court Justice Joseph Story observed.

Jackson had no definite plans on taking office. Sensing the bond between himself and ordinary people, he felt that he belonged to them and they to him, that where he led they would follow. His fundamental beliefs were few and simple. He believed that the American Union of states was indissoluble; he distrusted banks and paper money; he accepted unreflectingly the premise that the interests of the majority were the measure of national interests. At his inauguration many of his supporters had carried hickory brooms as a token of the "clean sweep" of federal officeholders that they awaited from their leader—and they were not disappointed. Jackson is commonly believed to have introduced the spoils system into American political life.

Actually the spoils system was a practice older than the Republic and one which Jackson never applied as ruthlessly as he has been accused of doing. In his first year in office, he removed approximately a tenth of the 11,000 federal officeholders, many of whom could justly be accused of indifference, inefficiency, corruption and superannuation. Public office, he felt, was not a private right, and he believed that appointments should be for four years only. His attack was directed at the entrenched and encrusted bureaucracy, but his political purge turned out to be worse than the bureaucratic disease itself: he dismissed many able men for partisan motives, and he established a national precedent of favoritism to the detriment of honest and efficient government.

Two issues dominated Jackson's two terms in office: the power of the Bank of the United States, and the threat of disunion, centered chiefly in South Carolina. The Bank of the United States was established after the financial chaos following the War of 1812. Its numerous branches served the country well, aiding commercial operations and providing the country with the soundest paper currency that it had ever known. In the opinion of a present-day economist, "the Bank often served the public and on a few occasions this was done at the expense of the stockholders." Issuing only a fifth of the nation's bank notes, and holding only a third of the total bank deposits, the Bank was never the monopoly claimed by its enemies. Nevertheless it was a private vested interest, not subject to regulation; it did control state bank currencies and dominated the domestic and foreign exchange markets; and it was not above making loans to

Political Billiards, a cartoon showing the Tsar and the Turkish Sultan playing billiards for possession of Turkey, as Europe's sovereigns look on. Jackson, third from the left, watches in civilian clothes.

deserving politicians. For Jackson, the Bank was a "hydra of corruption," a truckler to "the rich and powerful" that stood for "the advancement of the few at the expense of the many." When Nicholas Biddle, the Bank's president, attempted to renew its charter in the 1832 presidential election year, the recharter bill sponsored by Henry Clay easily passed both houses of Congress. "The Bank is trying to kill me," Jackson told his Vice-President, Martin Van Buren, when the measure passed, "*but I will kill it!*"

The 1832 election was fought on the issue of the Bank, with "Harry of the West" Clay, the candidate of the National Republicans, opposing Old Hickory. It resulted in an overwhelming victory for Jackson, who this time swept the Electoral College and carried the country by a two-to-one popular majority. Because the Bank's original charter did not expire until 1836, Jackson effectively undermined its power after his reelection by withdrawing government deposits and placing them in state banks. Jackson, who was intent on destroying the Bank as if it were an opponent on the field of honor, was too economically illiterate to grasp the implications of his actions. As a result, the United States, which had become one of the leaders in bank techniques, soon became one of the most backward. Inflation and depression followed.

Slave-holding Southern planter though he was, Jackson was first of all a Unionist. When, in resentment over the so-called Tariff of Abominations, South Carolina's John C. Calhoun claimed the rights of individual states to nullify "unconstitutional" acts of the national government, Jackson met the challenge at a Jefferson's birthday dinner. Staring grim-faced at Calhoun, the President proposed a standing toast: "Our Union: It must be preserved." Calhoun's fingers trembled so much when he lifted his glass to drink that the wine ran down the side of his glass.

Faced with a takeover of South Carolina's state government and gravely disturbed by the Nullifiers' threat to withdraw from the Union and set up a separate government, Jackson announced that if, in their defiance, they shed one drop of blood, he would hang the first Nullifier he could get his hands on from the first tree he could find. Neither office, age nor sorrow could dim his combative nature. The day after he left the presidency he remarked that he had only two regrets: he had not been able to shoot Clay and to hang Calhoun!

Jackson's predecessors had all been Neoclassicists who shared an enlightenment faith in reason and natural law. Jackson brought the Romantic movement to political life, replacing reason and proportion with energy and feeling. More by instinct than intent, he changed the face of American politics and brought about the emergence of the mass man. He made the Democratic Party the party of those who believed in unlimited franchise, free education and equal opportunity. Through his violent and impulsive person he projected the age's leading ideas: that the unchecked development of the

An anti-Jackson cartoon of 1831 entitled *Rats Leaving a Falling House.* Jackson was hated by the Eastern commercial classes.

individual was paramount; that formal training and traditional learning were unnecessary; that thought should be subordinate to action. Yet Jackson, the people's friend, never saw fit to challenge the institution of slavery, and it was he who was largely responsible for the vindictive anti-intellectualism, the distrust of the educated man, that would subsequently run through American political life.

In his last months, Jackson's thoughts centered on Texas, where he feared that the independent settlers would become "hewers of wood and drawers of water for the ... [British] aristocracy." He lived just long enough to see the Lone Star State become part of the Union. Justice John Catron, whom Jackson had appointed to the Supreme Court, wrote of the fierce, dying old man:

> If he had fallen from the clouds into a city on fire, he would have been at the head of the extinguishing hosts in an hour. He would have blown up a palace to stop the fire with as little misgiving as another would have torn down a board shed. In a moment he would have willed it proper and in ten minutes the thing would have been done. . . . He cared not a rush for anything behind: he looked ahead.

FRANCIS RUSSELL

The July Revolution—Paris sneezes

The House of Rothschild

As the nineteenth century entered its fourth decade, life was changing in Europe no less than in the United States. Revolution, war and its aftermath had imposed a heavy financial burden on the continental aristocracy, many of whom were already in debt to bankers or to less reputable financial adventurers. Extravagance and speculative attempts to improve old properties only further aggravated matters, and even the Austrian Chancellor Metternich (who received annual grants from the Tsar, the King of Naples and his own sovereign) needed personal financial backing from the House of Rothschild and other great Austrian and Swiss bankers.

Nathan Mayer Rothschild, founder of the London branch of the banking dynasty.

In some parts of Europe an almost morbid cupidity was elevated into a cult of money for its own sake, a philosophy that frequently went side by side with harebrained schemes of rash investment. The extremes that such cupidity reached in France were satirized in the novels of Honoré de Balzac (1799–1850)—who was himself a victim of that very vice in his private life.

These developments had effects far beyond the world of finance. In the late 1820s, a bourgeois class of successful bankers, industrialists and traders began to set a tone of cultural taste distinct from the old values of aristocratic society. Indeed, between 1830 and 1848 the emergent bourgeoisie in France, Austria, Germany and Britain imposed their smug complacency and cozy respectability on the classes above them. That mood,

Tsar Nicholas I, who ruled as though government were an endless military parade.

which ultimately pervaded the courts of Europe, was in marked contrast to the Romanticism that still fired the passions of most students. There was a sense in which both views were equally escapist.

Outwardly, however, the old European aristocracy was fighting an obstinate rearguard action to retain its political rights. In Vienna, Metternich continued to believe that the affairs of the whole Continent passed through his elegant hands. He sat at the great window in the Ballhausplatz each day studying reports from secret agents and ambassadors, ever alert against a revival of the Jacobin peril. Tsar Nicholas I—who, as a lad of eighteen, had ridden triumphantly into Paris in 1814 alongside his brother Alexander—ruled in St. Petersburg as though all government were an endless military parade. He was able to cow a mob into submission by the strength of his personality; and in the summer of 1831 he was to have great need of that talent.

By 1830, alarming dispatches were already reaching Nicholas from Warsaw, where the Poles were restive under Russian discipline. Nor were they the only source of disaffection in the Europe of 1829–30. There was trouble among students in Italy and Germany, where nationalist sentiment activated latent unrest, and there was trouble in Brussels, where the citizens had already wearied of the union with Holland that had been imposed on Belgium in 1815. But it was toward France that Metternich and Nicholas looked most anxiously, for as Metternich himself declared, "When Paris sneezes, Europe catches cold."

Revolution in Paris

The political health of France seemed no worse in the summer of 1830 than it had in the preceding six years. A punitive expedition was dispatched to Algiers to discipline its ruler, an Arab dignitary of piratical inclination who had slapped the face of the French Consul with his fan. The city was taken with ease, and Algeria remained a French possession until 1962. It was, however, the last foreign prize to be captured by the restored Bourbon monarchy. Louis XVIII had died in 1824 and had been succeeded by his brother, Charles X. Charles, who had fled precipitately from the kingdom upon the outbreak of the great French Revolution in 1789, was a religious bigot who relied for political advice on the reactionary Prince Jules Armand de Polignac (1780–1847).

As long as France was materially prosperous—a condition that lasted until the very end of Charles X's reign—his subjects treated Charles' stringent laws against sacrilege with tolerant disdain and even accepted measures that safeguarded aristocratic estates. There was much in the capital, however, to remind Parisians of the halcyon days of both the Revolution and the Empire. Lafayette, who had fought beside the Americans at Brandywine and Yorktown and who had commanded the French National Guard in 1789, was still a parliamentary deputy. Talleyrand, the old cynic who was consecrated Bishop of Autun four months before the Bastille fell and who had served the Directory, Napoleon and Louis XVIII as Foreign Minister, waited hopefully in the wings to make a farewell bow on the diplomatic stage. A fading galaxy of Napoleonic marshals—Jourdan, Macdonald, Marmont, Mortier, Oudinot, Soult, Victor—passed tactfully in their memories over days of humiliation and betrayal. Romanticism was turning the Bonapartist odyssey into legend, and it was becoming daringly fashionable to have served the Emperor. Lesser known veterans, gaunt figures with game legs or missing fingers, clustered around the cafés of the Palais-Royal in Paris seeking to rekindle the comradeship of the Grand Army. Frustrated by the tedium of the present, France was shadow-acting the recent past.

Marshal Soult, one of the greatest of Napoleon's generals.

Louis-Philippe I

In July, 1830, the *dramatis personae* of the Revolution re-emerged briefly to startle a Europe that had almost forgotten them. On July 26, Charles X and Polignac attempted a minor coup by issuing ordinances aimed at ending representative government and abolishing liberty of the press. Their move enraged the people of Paris, and for three days barricades choked the narrow streets. The King fled, to settle ultimately in Edinburgh. A courier, bearing an Act of Abdication, sped to Lafayette who had taken over the Hotel de Ville. The revolutionary patriarch was once more master of Paris.

Although republicans had directed the new revolution, France remained a monarchy, for the radical party was not yet organized and the Bonapartists had no candidate at hand. Lafayette, always happier as a constitutional royalist than as a conservative republican, and Talleyrand, who sensed that Europe would not tolerate a French republic, urged the Duke of Orleans to accept the vacant throne. They were supported by such younger liberal intellectuals as Louis Thiers (1797–1877) and François Guizot (1787–1874) and by the banker Jacques Laffitte (1767–1844). The Duke of Orleans, a distant cousin of Charles X and a descendant of Louis XIII, had fought in the armies of the First Republic as a young man. Less than two decades later he was proclaimed "Louis Philippe I, King of the French by the Grace of God and the Will of the People."

and Europe catches cold

The July Revolution reaches Italy and Belgium

As Metternich had feared, the fall of the Bourbon dynasty produced a liberal effervescence throughout the Continent. The rulers of the German states of Brunswick, Hesse-Cassel and Saxony were forced to abdicate, and their successors pledged themselves to introduce liberal constitutions. Early in 1831, trouble spread to Italy as revolts broke out in Modena and Parma and in the Papal States. Those risings were all aimed primarily against Austrian domination of the peninsula, and they were all suppressed by Austrian troops. Tsar Nicholas I,

Charles X, who succeeded Louis XVIII as King of France in 1824.

who was to breathe fire and fury against "that infamous July Revolution" for the next eighteen years, urged his fellow autocrats in Berlin and Vienna to stand together in defense of the monarchical principle and to form a "rampart against revolutionary doctrines." It was an idea that Metternich found wholly acceptable, and it worked for more than a decade (largely because all of east-central Europe was disturbed by an armed rebellion against Russian rule in Poland).

In Western Europe the July Revolution had its greatest effect in Belgium. Four weeks after the flight of Charles X, moderate liberals in Brussels began to demand an autonomous administration. The rebels insisted that

Louis Thiers, a French intellectual who supported Louis Philippe's claim to the throne.

"Belgium is no Dutch colony," but the Dutch ignored them. Social unrest fueled the situation. Tempers mounted, and in the last week of September, 1830, violent fighting broke out in the streets of Brussels. That series of clashes culminated in a withdrawal of troops and a proclamation of independence on October 4.

The breach between the Dutch and the Belgians was broadened three weeks later when Dutch artillery bombarded Antwerp. During this period the Belgians were fortunate in two respects: the Polish revolt neutralized any repressive measures contemplated by the Eastern autocracies, and the British and French both supported the Belgian cause (despite their distrust of one another's motives). Before the end of the year an international conference in London had formally declared the union of Belgium with the Netherlands to be dissolved, but it was not until April of 1839 that the Treaty of London recognized Belgium as "an independent and perpetually neutral state."

Tory rule ends

Belgian independence was the first diplomatic success for Lord Palmerston (1784–1865), who became Foreign Secretary as a member of the cabinet of Earl Grey (1764–1845) in November, 1830. His appointment was a sign that political life was changing in Britain as well as on the Continent under the impact of the news from Paris that the Bourbons had fallen. For over twenty-three years the Tories had held a majority in the House of Commons, that gentlemanly and unrepresentative institution against whose composition the reformers had long railed in vain. A general election held within a few weeks of the July Revolution cost the Tories some thirty seats (although party distinctions were so blurred in those days that nobody could agree on the precise shift of allegiance). The Duke of Wellington, who had been Prime Minister since the first weeks of 1828, struggled to keep the Whigs out of office, but his government was defeated on a minor issue and the King invited Earl Grey to form an administration pledged to parliamentary reform. There had been no Whig government since the days of Charles James Fox (1749–1806); a new era had dawned in British politics.

The birthplace of the radical William Cobbett at Farnham in Surrey.

More than Tory rule was passing out of English life that summer, for 1828 was the year in which William Cobbett (1763–1835), the radical champion of an idealized free peasantry, completed his *Rural Rides*. Cobbett was deeply conscious both of the insidious spread of the towns and of the disappearance of the old interdependence between a yeoman farmer and his laborers. He found it ominous that starving field workers from the southern counties should have rioted to demand two shillings and sixpence a day and should have suffered savage punishment for their protestations. Classes were becoming more sharply segregated, even in the countryside. Farmers who sought "to ape their betters" were stock characters of gentle ridicule for the novelist—but they were unsympathetic employers of labor as well.

The year 1830 also brought a change of monarch. George IV, King since 1820, and Regent for his deranged father for nine years before that, died in June. He was succeeded by his brother, William IV (1765–1837), who shared with Louis Philippe of France an unregal quality of genial approachability. Few people mourned the passing of George IV; he had been a liar, a fop and a selfish hedonist whose monumental rudeness stuck in the mind more easily than his moments of charm. Yet he had shown taste in fashion and architecture and had recognized the genius of the urban architect John Nash (1752–1835), who realized the interdependence of building and space, and whose balanced crescents and terraces were a model for town planning. Under Nash's supervision Regency London and Regency Edinburgh became pioneering achievements in urban vistas, despite the fact that George's grandiose plans remained unfulfilled. Indeed, during the King's last years, the delicate combination of gaiety and Classicism that was Regency at its best had disappeared, and vulgar adornment was becoming an end in itself.

The transition to bourgeois habits was as marked in London as in Paris or Vienna. In 1829, George Shillibeer introduced a horsedrawn omnibus—already a feature of French urban life—to the streets of the capital. For sixpence a Londoner could travel the four miles from the Bank of England to Regents Park in a coach the side panels of which showed the eventual destination in elaborately ornamental Classical seals. And up in Lancashire, the greatest social revolution in many decades had begun to change the face of the English countryside.

BOOKING OFFICE

1st CLASS

L & N.W.R-No 9
LUGGAGE VAN

The Age of Steam

1830

England in 1830 was rent by domestic unrest: persistent demands for parliamentary reform and frequent calls for repeal of the Corn Laws threatened to split the Duke of Wellington's cabinet and topple the Tory regime. In an effort to distract the disgruntled populace, the Duke's unpopular government pumped £100,000 in public funds into the construction of a rail link between Liverpool and Manchester. On September 15, 1830, the Duke and a galaxy of political and social luminaries boarded the eight special trains that were making their maiden run to Manchester. Nearly a million spectators—some jeering, most cheering—lined the roadbed to watch the lead locomotive, Northumbrian, *sweep by at twenty-four miles per hour. The Age of Steam had begun.*

The official opening of the Liverpool and Manchester Railway on Wednesday, September 15, 1830—the climax of eight years of persistent scheming and hazardous construction—marked an achievement that was to have a profound effect on the development of national economies. The Duke of Wellington, Tory Prime Minister, had consented to preside over the ceremonies inaugurating what was appropriately referred to in the press as a "great national undertaking." For not only was the line the first British railway to link two populous towns; the railway company that built it had received a loan of £100,000 from public funds in 1828 to hasten its completion.

The weather on the morning of the fifteenth was fine. Thanks to skillful publicity—including the timely issue of an excellent illustrated history of the project by Henry Booth, treasurer of the Liverpool and Manchester Railway Company, and preliminary trips for directors, their families and friends on three previous Saturdays—large crowds (estimated at from 500,000 to about 1 million people) assembled at both terminals and along the track. The directors and their engineer, George Stephenson, had chosen eight locomotives for the occasion. The leading one, *Northumbrian,* was to be followed at intervals by seven other trains hauled by the locomotives *Phoenix, North Star, Rocket, Dart, Comet, Arrow* and *Meteor.*

At the Crown Street station in Liverpool, the air was festive as passengers boarded the carriages. The lead cars carried not only dignitaries, including the Duke, but musicians as well. At about 10:40 A.M. the carriages began rolling down by force of gravity through the tunnel that took the railway from Liverpool to Edgehill, where the locomotives were attached and the trains dispatched. The passengers were awed by the tunnels and excavations through rock and treacherous shale. The railway viaduct built over the Sankey Brook and the parallel Sankey Canal (where a grandstand had been built to accommodate a thousand spectators) "particularly obtained the Duke's attention, and 'magnificent!' and 'stupendous!' were heard frequently to issue from his lips." The trains reached a speed of twenty-four miles an hour and the three leading locomotives soon arrived at Parkside, seventeen miles from Liverpool.

At this point a tragic accident occurred. The trains stopped, as arranged, to take on more water, and in spite of printed official placards requesting passengers not to dismount from their carriages, many did so. Among them was one of the two M.P.s for Liverpool, William Huskisson, a liberal Tory who had resigned from Wellington's cabinet soon after it had been formed in 1828 and had since been estranged from the Duke. Huskisson had recently undergone an operation, and he also suffered from the aftereffects of paralysis in one leg. The Duke, who wisely did not get down from the state carriage, shook hands with Huskisson in a gesture of reconciliation. Suddenly the *Rocket,* the fourth locomotive in the procession, was heard approaching Parkside on the parallel line of rails. The Duke ordered: "Huskisson, do get to your place! For God's sake get to your place!" But Huskisson held the handle of the wide door open for others hurrying to climb into the car, thus putting himself in the path of the oncoming *Rocket.* He failed to get inside in time. As far as can be ascertained, either the locomotive or the first car hit him. He stumbled and fell screaming onto the line, directly in the path of the second car.

The Earl of Wilton hurriedly improvised a tourniquet from a handkerchief, but Huskisson apparently knew that his wounds would prove fatal and cried out: "Where is Mrs. Huskisson? I have met my death. God forgive me." George Stephenson, who had designed the *Rocket,* now took charge. Two carriages were uncoupled from the *Northumbrian* and the remaining one became an improvised ambulance. The dying politician, together with two surgeons who happened to be in the party, sped forward to Eccles Bridge with George Stephenson at

George Stephenson, designer of the *Rocket* and initiator of many early British railways.

Opposite Uniforms showing the contrast between the coaching era and the age of steam; (*above*) drivers and (*below*) guards of 1832 and 1852.

The Liverpool and Manchester Railway where it crosses the Bridgewater Canal. Railways soon took over the canal's role in transportation.

the controls of the locomotive. Huskisson was taken into the vicarage of his friend the Reverend Thomas Blackburne of Eccles, while George Stephenson set off toward Manchester "at a most terrific rate [after] travelling from the place where the accident happened to Eccles Bridge at the rate of thirty-five miles per hour." Stephenson collected four Manchester surgeons and returned to Eccles. Despite their efforts, Huskisson died the same evening at 9 o'clock.

The terrible accident had dissipated the good spirits of the morning, and the Duke wished to abandon the rest of the trip to Manchester. But the boroughreeves of Manchester and Salford pressed him to allow the full ceremonies to proceed. They gave as their reason the fear that the disappointment of the immense crowds gathered at the Manchester terminus in Ordsall Lane might break out into widespread rioting, particularly as the Duke's government was not outstandingly popular. The Duke agreed to continue, but the fears of the boroughreeves proved unjustified. Although there were occasional shouts in favor of parliamentary reform and against the Corn Laws, together with frequent hissing and hooting at the Liverpool Row Boats as the Duke's train steamed nearer to Manchester, the dissenters "appeared to be gathered from the lowest grades of the community." Another factor dampened any excessive ebullience: the fine morning weather at Liverpool had been replaced by cold winds, driving rain and thunder by the time the locomotives arrived at Manchester.

The Duke acknowledged both the cheers and the jeers in his usual restrained manner. On arrival at Manchester he and "the principal party" remained in their car while the rest of the expedition—almost eight hundred strong—partook of the customary "cold collation" in the upper floor of a railway warehouse. The Duke, however, did not isolate himself from the masses: "... he went through a most fatiguing office for more than an hour and a half, in shaking hands with thousands of people to whom he stooped over the handrail of the carriage .... Many women brought their children to him, lifting them up that he might bless them, which he did, and during the whole time he had scarcely a minute's respite." About 4:30 P.M., after a warning by Joseph Lavender, deputy constable of Manchester, that the Manchester crowds were getting out of hand, the Duke's train began the journey back to Liverpool. The last locomotive reached Liverpool around 11 P.M., and its passengers soon discovered that the splendid entertainments planned for the evening and the following day had been either canceled or much reduced. Politically and socially it had been an unsatisfactory day; from a technological aspect, however, the day had been extremely successful.

Railways had appeared in Britain as early as the 1590s when short lines were laid in Nottinghamshire and in Shropshire. Primitive four-wheeled, horse-drawn trucks carried coal from the mines to rivers and main roads over these early lines. By the end of the seventeenth century the construction of these wagonways had become a task requiring considerable capital and engineering skill, particu-

Below, from left to right
James Watt, inventor of the separate condenser; I. K. Brunel, who pioneered the building of suspension bridges; William Huskisson, one of the first railway accident victims; George Bradshaw, famous for compiling the first railway timetable.

An 1831 engraving of a railway tunnel.

larly on the coalfields of Northumberland and Durham. The early rails were of hardwood, but by the eighteenth century cast iron was being used for the points and crossing rails, the areas of greatest wear and tear. In 1767–68, during a period of low prices in the iron trade, the Coalbrookdale Iron Company of Shropshire laid down a wagonway using only cast-iron rails, and after that time wooden rails gradually went out of use.

In the 1780s the steam engine became sufficiently advanced in design to permit the construction of steam locomotives. Thomas Newcomen of Dartmouth had devised the first commercially profitable stationary steam engine between 1705 and 1712, and by the 1760s hundreds of Newcomen-type engines were at work pumping water out of coal mines. In 1769 James Watt secured his famous patent for the separate condenser, a device that cut fuel consumption in the Newcomen engine by two-thirds. With Watt's second patent (granted in 1781 for the "sun and planet" motion) it became possible to apply the improved steam pumping engine to give rotary motion to machinery. The Frenchman Nicolas J. Cugnot, independently of Watt, built a small steam carriage in Paris in 1769, but found that the carriage lacked sufficient power and was unstable.

As early as 1784 William Murdock, the gifted foreman of Matthew Boulton and James Watt's Soho Engineering Works, had constructed a small working model of a road locomotive, but Watt did not encourage Murdock to experiment further. It was left to Richard Trevithick to build both the first high-pressure road locomotive (1801) and the first locomotive to be used successfully on a railway (1804). The times were propitious for such an innovation. Two of the chief items in the expense of working a colliery were horses and their forage. During the Napoleonic Wars, and particularly after 1808, the demands of the British armies in the Iberian Peninsula forced up the price of horses considerably. It is not surprising therefore that colliery agents and engineers spent considerable time and energy during those years in trying to devise steam-driven "horses."

George Stephenson entered the contest later, and he did not produce his first engine until 1814. But his locomotive was noteworthy because it was the first to run on an edge rail rather than on a flanged plateway. (In the former the wheel has a projecting

Above Rain, Steam and Speed—The Great Western Railway, by J. M. W. Turner.

Below The Railway Station, a painting of Paddington Station, London, by William Frith.

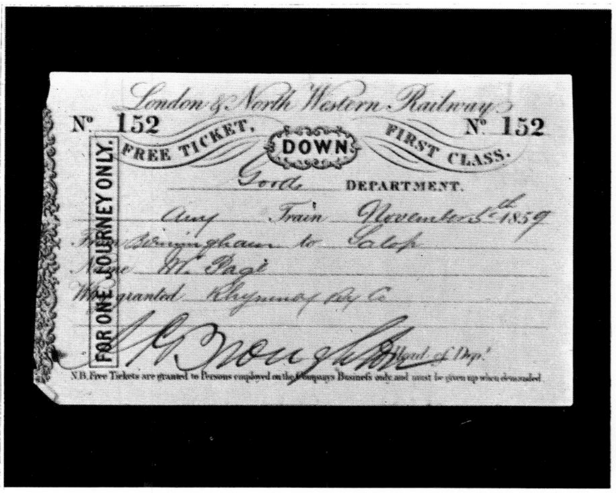

edge, or flange, to keep it on the track; in the latter the rail is flanged.) The old wagonways needed technical improvement once the "point of effort" on the railway had moved from the ground underneath the horses' hooves to the rails underneath the wheels of the new locomotives. Between 1815 and 1819 Stephenson concentrated on improving the fixing and jointing of the rails and the structure of the engine wheels. Birkinshaw's patent of 1820s, which enabled wrought-iron rails to be rolled cheaply enough to be a substitute for the brittler cast-iron rail, also proved to be an important factor in the early success of the locomotive railway.

Stephenson's first great success came with the construction of the famous Stockton and Darlington line. Opened in 1825, it was the first railway used for the public carriage of goods by locomotive (fare-paying passengers were not carried on the line until 1833). Although Stephenson also worked on the Bolton and Leigh line, which opened in 1829, and the Canterbury and Whitstable line, opened in 1830, he is chiefly remembered for his work on the Liverpool and Manchester Railway. That railway project had been discussed as early as 1822. The discussions demonstrated the great power of Britain's newest and fastest growing industry: cotton.

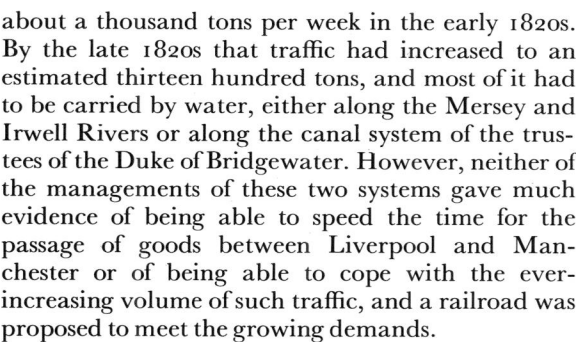

The Industrial Revolution was in full swing, the national production of goods and services of nearly all kinds was expanding rapidly, and the existing network of rivers, canals and turnpike roads needed supplementing by some speedier and more economical method of transport. The traffic of goods between Liverpool and Manchester—largely raw cotton and cotton goods—was estimated to be about a thousand tons per week in the early 1820s. By the late 1820s that traffic had increased to an estimated thirteen hundred tons, and most of it had to be carried by water, either along the Mersey and Irwell Rivers or along the canal system of the trustees of the Duke of Bridgewater. However, neither of the managements of these two systems gave much evidence of being able to speed the time for the passage of goods between Liverpool and Manchester or of being able to cope with the ever-increasing volume of such traffic, and a railroad was proposed to meet the growing demands.

Proponents of the railroad also argued that merchants and industrialists would be able to make the journey between the two cities, transact their business without undue haste, and return home in

Early train tickets. Railway tickets at first were varied in appearance.

Victorian travel was crowded and uncomfortable, as this painting by William Maw Egley shows.

The *Rocket*, one of the eight locomotives chosen for the opening run of the Liverpool and Manchester Railway.

The opening of the Liverpool and Manchester Railway; this picture shows the scene at Edgehill, on the outskirts of Liverpool, where the locomotives were attached to carriages and dispatched to Manchester.

the early evening to their families—something that was not possible using the stagecoach. Passenger traffic was not stressed as much, however, as freight traffic in the debates on the proposed line.

Liverpool merchants, bankers and professional men promoted the measure in Parliament, and after four years of scheming, struggle and disappointment, the Liverpool and Manchester Railway Company finally was incorporated in 1826. By then the promoting group, popularly known as the Liverpool Party, contained a sizable minority from Manchester. The group had substantial links with the Quaker businessmen who had financed the Stockton and Darlington Railway, the Peases and the Richardsons. There were still, however, great difficulties to be overcome. The line had to be run over the treacherous Chat Moss at the Manchester end at a cost of an extra £30,000; at the Liverpool end costly excavations and tunnels had to be made. George Stephenson made serious mistakes in some of his surveys, and as late as 1828–29 no final decision had been taken as to whether the line should be operated by locomotives or by a series of stationary steam engines hauling the trains and wagons over short distances by means of ropes. Stephenson held out strongly in favor of locomotives. To decide the issue, the directors of the company decided to hold the famous Rainhill Trials in October, 1829. The demonstration of the power and reliability of Stephenson's *Rocket* at these trials decided the question unequivocally. As Stephenson had predicted, the locomotive held out the greatest promise for increased power and speed. Railways could now be thought of not merely as feeder lines to rivers, canals and highways, but as potential vanquishers of the fastest form of transport then known—the stagecoach.

Official French, Prussian, Austrian and Russian observers, busy taking note for their governments on the tremendous upsurge of industrial and technological change taking place in post-Napoleonic Britain, watched the growth of British railways with interest. The progress of railway construction in Britain also aroused lively interest in the United States, which was faced with the problems presented by vast distances. At least two British pamphlets on the Liverpool and Manchester Railway had been issued in pirated editions in America by the end of 1830, and by 1840 the United States was not only constructing railways but was building some of its own locomotives. In Britain itself Birmingham was linked to the Liverpool and Manchester Railway by 1837, and one year later the opening of the line from London to Birmingham created the first trunk system.

The 1840s saw a vast extension of the network as

the result of the Railway Mania of 1844–47, and in the 1850s the drive to build national railways spread across Europe from Belgium, which had inaugurated a state-owned system in 1834. At the side of the railways ran the new electric telegraph, which linked capital cities with the provinces and further extended the power of governments that had already started to transport their armies by rail. During the Crimean War (1853–56) the first military railway made its appearance at Balaklava, and the construction of a strategic rail network was pressed forward in India after the mutiny of 1857. Railways proved decisive in the unification of Italy, for in 1859 Napoleon III's troops traveled by troop train from France into northern Italy to defeat the Austrians at Magenta and Solferino.

The Civil War in the United States provided the second example in history of the large-scale use of railways in military operations, and General Sherman's march through Georgia in 1864 effectively cut the Confederacy in two largely because of his systematic destruction of railway track and rolling stock. During the Civil War, construction began on the first through railway from the Atlantic to the Pacific. The Union Pacific Railroad Company extended its New York–Omaha line westward, while at the same time the Central Pacific Railroad Company pushed its track eastward from Sacramento. They met on May 10, 1869, at Promontory, Utah, and the first through train from Sacramento to New York reached its destination on July 29, 1869, after a journey of six and a half days. In the early 1870s railways were being laid down in the United States at the rate of ten thousand miles a year.

The opening up of Argentina and Uruguay by railways financed largely by British capital brought the wheat and meat of the pampas and prairies down to the ports for shipment to Britain. Similarly, in Australia, New Zealand and South Africa railway construction proved to be an indispensable preliminary to the first stages of economic development. Meanwhile the locomotive grew mightily in size and tractive power, and the substitution of steel rails for iron rails from the 1860s on made for smoother and safer running.

By the 1890s Europe was crisscrossed by a complex and efficient railway network. Over these lines, toward Hamburg, Bremen, Gothenburg, Rotterdam, Liverpool and Le Havre, came the surplus peasant population of Europe on its way to the New World, and Russian Jews fleeing before anti-Semitic pogroms. Even backward Russia, with its broad-gauge tracks, was reasonably well provided with railways by 1900, with nearly 48,000 miles open. The construction of the Trans-Siberian Railroad from Vladivostok to Chelyabinsk, where it would join with the Russian European system, was begun in 1891 and completed in 1904, during the Russo-Japanese War.

The Edwardian era marked the apogee of the railway age in Britain, when railways reigned supreme as a means of land transport. Although the gasoline-driven internal-combustion engine came rapidly into use after 1906, no long-distance transport worth mentioning, either of passengers or goods, was done by road before 1914. But World War I ultimately was responsible for the ascendancy of the car and truck; for the widespread use of gasoline-driven vehicles in military operations paved the way for a rapid expansion of road transport at the expense of railway transport in the 1920s and 1930s. The railway age, which had lasted for less than a century, was clearly coming to an end. By then, however, patterns of trade, the development of markets for goods and services, and the movements of populations had been permanently altered.

W. H. CHALONER

Liverpool railway station in the 1830s. The Liverpool and Manchester Railway was the first British railway to link two populous towns.

Trains on the Liverpool and Manchester Railway show the great difference between first-class (*top*) and second-class (*bottom*) travel.

In England an era of reform coincides

The burning of the Bishop's palace at Bristol. Popular dissatisfaction caused riots in many towns.

"Dark Satanic Mills"

The opening of the Liverpool–Manchester Railway more than symbolized a revolution in transport and communication—it also coincided with the start of a reform era in government that was long overdue in Britain. In fact, passengers traveling on Stephenson's new railway were inevitably exposed to one of the political anachronisms of the age. Midway between Liverpool and Manchester, the line passed the village of Newton. Though few in number, Newton's residents were doubly fortunate; they lived in an enclave of rural Lancashire as yet unsullied by the "dark Satanic mills," and in each parliamentary election they enjoyed the privilege of returning two members to the House of Commons. The quarter of a million inhabitants of Manchester, on the other hand, remained politically unrepresented at Westminster. And so did the three great manufacturing centers of Sheffield, Leeds and Birmingham. The removal of such anomalies was essential if the British people were to escape the violence that accompanied every major change on the Continent.

Earl Grey, who put through the First Reform Bill in 1832.

In 1831 and 1832 there seemed to be a real prospect of popular insurrection in the English cities. The Whig government of Charles Earl Grey (1764–1845) had indicated its desire to overhaul the electoral system, redistributing seats to ensure representation for the new industrial towns and abolish "rotten boroughs" (electoral districts with a disproportionately small electorate) and "pocket boroughs" (districts controlled by a single family). But the radical "political unions" that had sprung up in Birmingham and other cities in the Midlands wanted more; they demanded a broad extension of the franchise. The Tory-dominated House of Lords blocked all Grey's attempts at reform, however, and there were serious riots in Derby, Nottingham and Bristol.

In June, 1832, Grey and his colleagues finally managed to steer a parliamentary reform bill through the House of Lords and onto the statute book, but the measure itself fell far short of radical aspirations. The franchise was still limited to comparatively wealthy taxpayers, most of whom were property owners. (Thus the "reformed" House of Commons that met in 1833 had actually been elected by only one-sixth of the adult males in the country.) The radicals complained that the Reform Bill had merely transferred political power from the old landed aristocracy to the new oligarchs of industry and commerce, and working-class agitation continued. For the most part the dissent was conducted through the movements that had developed outside Parliament (and often in opposition to it); the rapidly expanding middle classes seemed content to seek redress of their grievances from the House of Commons.

The ministries that managed British affairs for most of the 1830s were the last collective manifestation of the Whig ideal in politics, although the robustly amateur prejudices that formed the essence of Whig government survived until the mid-1880s. The Whig belief in ordered liberty prompted many reforms whose attainment was rooted deeply in the past. It made possible, for example, the triumph of the great antislavery campaign that the crusading William Wilberforce (1759–1833) had resolutely championed since the 1780s. An act providing for the emancipation of all slaves in British possessions was passed in 1833, the year of Wilberforce's death.

The Utilitarians and the Chartists

Other influences at work at this time were gradually transforming the Whigs into the Liberals of Victorian England. The Utilitarian philosopher Jeremy Bentham (who died in 1832 in his eighty-fifth year) was patriarch of the Philosophic Radicals, a group of political intellectuals who had been seeking to sweep away the centuries-old inefficiency of local and national administration for two generations. It was these Utilitarians who reformed the bumbling government in towns and cities through the Municipal Corporations Act of 1835, and it was they who launched sustained attacks on the entrenched privileges of the Church of England.

There was a less sympathetic side to the Utilitarians, however,

Jeremy Bentham, patriarch of the Philosophic Radicals.

for although they were prepared to give state protection to children employed in the factories, their coldly unemotional belief in the virtues of hard work made them unable to appreciate the rigors imposed on adults by an industrial society. Anthony Ashley Cooper, Lord Shaftesbury (1801–85)—who was, at this time, beginning his twenty-year campaign for improved factory conditions—won far more support from the Whig leaders (and even from that highly individualistic Tory, Benjamin Disraeli (1804–81), than from the archpriest of the Benthamites, Sir Edwin Chadwick (1800–90). The most characteristic piece of Benthamite legislation was the Poor Law Amendment Act of 1834 that made public relief of the destitute more systematic and uniform by establishing workhouses. Unhappily for both the Benthamites and the poor, these "uninviting places of wholesome restraint"—the phrase is Chadwick's—rapidly became a disgrace as was shown so powerfully in *Oliver Twist* by the novelist Charles Dickens (1812–70) before the end of the decade.

The Whigs, distrusting democrats no less than despots, frowned upon movements of popular agitation. For a brief ten months in 1834 a Grand National Consolidated Trades Union, with a membership of half a million, championed workers' rights, but in that same year six farmworkers at Tolpuddle in the south of England received savage sentences for union activity. The laboring classes soon sought other outlets for their accumulated indignation. From 1838 to 1842, for example, the popular radical movement known as Chartism pressed for annual parliaments, elected by universal

with a religious renaissance

male suffrage, as a panacea for Britain's ills. There were violent outbursts in 1839 at Birmingham and Newport, but Chartism was too weakly led and too confused in objectives ever to constitute a serious danger to entrenched interests. It declined in appeal during 1842 when splits developed between the North and Midland sections of the movement. In 1848 it stirred once more, but when its climactic spring demonstration ended in a rain-swept fiasco, Chartism was ridiculed into the scrap heap of good intentions.

Religion revived

Although the power of organized religion was declining in Europe, particularly in the large cities, where the antiquated parochial organization of the churches was unable to keep pace with the growth of population, the 1830s and 1840s saw a remarkable religious renaissance in many European countries.

In France, where religious life had been totally disrupted by the Revolution of 1789 and its aftermath, there was a rebirth of parochial life, which achieved its finest expression in Jean Baptiste Vianney (1786–1859), the saintly "Curé of Ars," whose piety and intense faith made such an impression upon his contemporaries that Ars became a place of pilgrimage in his lifetime. Religious houses—suppressed during the Revolution—were reopened. The most significant event in this field took place in 1833, when Dom Prosper Guéranger (1805–75) reestablished the Benedictine Order at the medieval priory of Solesmes; it soon became a center of liturgical studies. Little less important was the reintroduction of the Dominicans into France in 1843, the result of years of effort by the friar Henri Lacordaire (1802–61).

Not only did religious life at a parochial level show an unprecedented vigor, but the laity also expressed its restored confidence in the authority of the Church, and its interest in the relationship between Church and State. Perhaps because of dissatisfaction with Napoleon's Church policy, many of the faithful looked beyond the mountains (*Ultramontes*) to Rome as the seat of ecclesiastical authority. The spread of ultramontanist ideas in France was aided by the reestablishment of the Jesuits, who had always been directly under papal control, in 1814.

Ultramontanism, the source for many of the Roman Catholic Church's problems in the twentieth century, was founded by Félicité de Lamennais (1782–1845). He combined political liberalism with extreme papalism, a difficult combination in the years after the Congress of Vienna, and one that had little appeal even for the papacy. In 1832 Gregory XVI condemned Lamennais' social ideas, and, his faith in the papacy shattered, Lamennais left the Roman Catholic Church. Yet his ideas on papal authority found increasing acceptance within the Church and at the Vatican Council of 1870 were to triumph.

The medieval priory of Solesmes.

In England the principal storm over religious matters and dogma finally broke in the 1840s (although the issues at stake were not new and the debate continued for almost half a century). At the end of the Napoleonic Wars the Church of England accepted its privileged position as part of the established state without seriously considering pastoral obligations. The religious pacemakers in the new industrial towns were either dissenters following the Methodist doctrine of John Wesley (1703–91) or representatives of the evangelical minority within the established Church. It was from this group that such conscientious public servants and social reformers as William Wilberforce and Lord Shaftesbury emerged.

In the 1830s a movement developed at the University of Oxford that sought to make the Church of England more self-consciously aware of its pre-Reformation heritage and less dependent on its explicitly Protestant tradition. The Oxford Movement was led by John Keble (1792–1866), John Henry Newman (1801–90) and Edward Bouverie Pusey (1800–82), all of whom sought to revive belief in the Church of England as a divine institution rather than a department of state and to emphasize the Apostolic Succession of the Anglican episcopate. As a result of their series of ninety *Tracts for the Times*, their supporters were called Tractarians. A later generation of Tractarians enthusiastically adopted gothic revival architecture, and believed in reviving liturgical ceremonial (long ignored in the Church of England) and in establishing settlements in working-class districts, where the Church could bring both consolation and color into a drab existence.

The Oxford Movement aroused intense opposition from conservatively minded Protestants (ever vigilant against popery); this hostility drove many Tractarians into the Roman Catholic Church. Newman himself was received into the Church of Rome in 1845 (and was created a cardinal in 1879), but Pusey and Keble never seceded from the Church of England. Trivial as the issues may seem to the twentieth-century reader, many of the greatest minds in the country were focused on the Tractarian dispute; the great statesman William Ewart Gladstone (1809–98), for example, wrote twice as many books and articles on religious topics between 1838 and 1858 as he did on political matters. In the early days of the Oxford Movement, the statesman Lord Melbourne (1779–1848) complained that "things have come to a pretty pass when religion is allowed to invade the sphere of private life." That point of view had become totally out of date by the late 1850s.

Partly due to the Tractarians, but more as a result of the writings of the liberal theologian Frederick Denison Maurice (1805–72), there was growing interest in the Church's role in social questions. Although the "Christian socialism" of Maurice and his disciples had a less obvious influence than the work of Lamennais in France, it was at the root of most of the social and political concern later evidenced among English speaking Christians.

The Church of Scotland, too, was affected by religious controversy. A movement to disassociate Church and State, comparable in some ways to the Oxford Movement, was led by Thomas Chalmers (1780–1847), who sought to ensure that parish ministers were appointed by the people. His failure in this led to a major schism in 1843, when almost one-third of the ministers left the established Church of Scotland to set up a free church.

John Keble, "Tractarian."

Despite the importance of religion, however, material advance was close to the heart of the nineteenth century. The world of agriculture, revolutionized in the mid eighteenth century, experienced yet another revolution in the mid-nineteenth century.

McCORMICK'S PATENT VIRGINIA REAPER.

The above cut represents one of M'CORMICK'S PATENT VIRGINIA REAPERS, as built for the harvest of 1848. It has been greatly improved since that time, by the addition of a seat for the driver; by a change in the position of the crank, so as to effect a direct connection between it and the sickle, (thereby very much lessening the friction and wear of the machinery, by dispensing altogether with the lever and its fixtures;) by board ribs on the reel, (which operates more gently on the grain than the round ones;) by a sheet of zinc on the platform, (which very much lessens the labor of raking;) by an increase of the size, weight and strength of the wheels of the machine, and by improvement made on the cutting apparatus.

D. W. BROWN,

OF ASHLAND, OHIO,

Having been duly appointed Agent for the sale of the above valuable labor-saving machine (manufactured by C. H. McCormick & Co., in Chicago, Ill.,) for the Counties of Seneca, Sandusky, Erie, Huron, Richland, Ashland and Wayne, would respectfully inform the farmers of those counties, that he is prepared to furnish them with the above Reapers on very liberal terms.

The Wheat portions of the above territory will be visited, and the Agent will be ready to give any information relative to said Reaper, by addressing him at Ashland, Ashland County, Ohio.

***Ashland, March*, 1850.**

A Revolution in Agriculture 1834

From time immemorial, grain had been harvested by the slow, tedious, backbreaking use of sickle or scythe, limiting the acreage a community could plant to how much they could harvest in the brief interval in which the grain was appropriately ripe. No significant change was made until Cyrus Hall McCormick patented his mechanical reaping machine—and had the energy and acumen to publicize it, so that even the most stubbornly conservative farmer not only knew that it existed but that it worked. Agriculture would never again be the same.

The vastness of the acreage now occupied by the world's grainfields, and the relative ease with which they are harvested, contrasts sharply with the situation a little more than a century ago. Then the technique of reaping was not much different from that used by the ancient Egyptians. A strong man wielding a cutting implement—such as a sickle or scythe—would progress slowly through a field, hacking down the grain and laying it in bundles. He would be followed by two or three others who would tie it into sheaves that other workers would gather together prior to threshing. They would perhaps be followed by women and children with rakes to gather any stray stalks. A hardworking team of six might manage to cut two acres a day, and since the time factor was critical—the entire harvest had to be completed within about ten days, while the grain was ripe, but not over-ripe—the acreage a group could till was naturally limited. The harvest, romantically viewed in literature as a splendid time in the farming calendar, when communities came together and worked in sunlit fields, was in reality the most arduous time in the rural year. The farmer, at the mercy of the weather and the availability of a large temporary labor force, expressed his gratitude when this crucial period was over in the harvest festivals celebrated throughout the world.

Agricultural productivity was clearly greatly restricted by the persistence of these primitive methods. In the early nineteenth century, after the Industrial Revolution had begun to create an urban landscape, it still took nine men working a backbreaking year on the land to provide enough for their own needs and to support a single city dweller on the surplus. While machinery was altering industry and town life, on the farms of both the Old and New Worlds, man was still struggling with basically the same tools he had used for millennia. A few ingenious devices had been introduced: the plow had been improved and the seed drill was gradually more widely adopted, but reaping was still done with sickle or scythe, which had changed little over the centuries.

Some attempts were made from earliest times to mechanize reaping, the most tedious aspect of agriculture, but none were completely practical or far-reaching. Among the first recorded "mechanical" reapers was one used in Europe at the time of the Roman occupation, and described by the historian Pliny in the first century A.D.:

> In the vast domains of the provinces of Gaul, a large hollow frame, armed with teeth and supported on two wheels, is driven through the standing corn, the beasts being yoked behind it; the result being that the ears are torn off and fall within the frame.

The oxen that powered this primitive machine pushed from behind to avoid trampling the grain to be cut—a problem encountered by later inventors—but its major disadvantage lay in its only being able to operate as a "header"; it trimmed off the heads of the grain, but left the stalks that were required for animal fodder to be gathered by the slow, time-honored method of the sickle. After the fall of the Roman Empire, this device appears to have been forgotten, and only occasional references to attempts at mechanizing the reaping process occur during the subsequent centuries. In the late eighteenth century a number of clever, but still inadequate solutions were found, although the threshing machine, in various forms, had appeared and was being widely used.

About 1813, a Scotsman, James Smith, attempted to win a £500 prize offered by the Dalkeith Farmers' Club for a successful reaping machine. Although his invention, which cut corn at ground level by means of a circular blade powered from the wheels, was moderately effective, it was easily damaged on uneven ground, and had

A daguerrotype of Cyrus Hall McCormick, taken in 1848 when he was thirty-nine years old. McCormick became one of America's first industrialist millionaires, extending his business interests to mining, real estate and railroads.

Opposite Poster advertising McCormick's reaper; McCormick's singleminded persistence and promotional acumen helped ensure that his, rather than any other, model would revolutionize agriculture.

The McCormick Reaper factory on the banks of the Chicago River, before it was destroyed in the Great Chicago Fire of 1871. The following year work started on a bigger and better factory.

various other technical drawbacks. Neither Smith, nor any other would-be inventor, won the prize. A British schoolmaster, Henry Ogle, pioneered some important features later adopted by other inventors, such as a reel to sweep the grain toward a cutter, in a machine of 1825, but it was never extensively used. Inspired by a picture of Smith's machine, in 1826 another Scotsman, a minister, Patrick Bell, having worked in secret for two years, tested his reaping machine (that used shears instead of rotating blades) with marginally greater success than that of any of his predecessors. Some copies of his reaper were made and used in Britain and elsewhere for many years, but Bell, believing that to patent it would restrict its use by poor farmers, did not embark on any commercial exploitation of his invention, and, lacking widespread promotion, it was eventually forgotten. A factor to consider in those early days of mechanized agriculture was that most farmers tended to be cautious and wary of innovations.

At about the same time, in the 1820s, other inventors in Europe and in the United States were working on roughly parallel lines, and most of the basic features of the reaping machines of the future were established. But it still remained for one man to overcome the technical problems posed by mechanized reaping and to combine these essential elements into a workable machine. That man was Cyrus Hall McCormick.

Born in 1809 in a family of Scots-Irish descent that had settled in Rockbridge County, Virginia, Cyrus McCormick's father Robert McCormick was a moderately successful farmer, who tilled his land at Walnut Grove and was in addition a skilled worker in wood and iron, with a particular interest in the mechanical aspects of agriculture. On his farm he had a blacksmith's shop in which he made traditional implements and devised many new ones, some of which he patented, including a hydraulic machine, a threshing machine and a device for harvesting hemp. Cyrus worked with his father on a number of these projects, and himself possessed a craftsman's ability and an inventive inclination. At the age of fifteen he had perfected a lightweight scythe and grain cradle, and by 1831, at the age of twenty-two had invented and patented a hillside plow, and, later, a self-sharpening plow.

Robert McCormick, aware since before Cyrus was born of the need for a functional reaping machine, after twenty years of attempting to build one finally abandoned the effort and handed the quest over to his son. Cyrus set to work in 1831 and completely altered many of the basic principles of his father's unsuccessful machine, creating an entirely new one of his own design. Thus, in July, 1831, (the exact date is unrecorded), Cyrus McCormick and a slave, Joe Anderson, trundled out a curious contraption from the workshop, hitched it to a couple of horses, and successfully cut some ripe wheat at Walnut Grove. After modifying and rebuilding the prototype, McCormick proceeded to the field of a neighbor, John Steele, and, without assistance, cut with ease and in an unprecedented time six acres of oats. With subsequent modifications, this was the machine that was to revolutionize agriculture and thereby change the face of the world.

Most of the parts, except for the cutter, were made of wood. The machine, the first to combine all the essential features of a reaper in a single structure, consisted of the following: an adjustable platform, or grain deck, five or six feet long, to ensure that the machine rode smoothly over uneven surfaces; a reciprocating cutter, about four and a half feet long, to shear the grain off at ground level;

a rotating reel, with "bats," to sweep the grain toward the cutter; a main wheel, providing the drive—by gears to the cutter, and by a belt to the reel—and supporting the machine; a divider, to separate the grain to be cut from that to be cut on the next run; a series of fingers, to separate the grain as it approaches the cutter, to prevent tangling; and a side draft, so that the horses that pulled it walked alongside on the stubble of the previous run and avoided trampling fresh grain. (Previous experimenters had often been balked by this problem; when they tried to solve it by having the horses *push* the reaper, it was frequently forced to "nosedive" into the ground, and side draft—until McCormick solved the problem by using a single wheel to take the weight of the machine—often created the added difficulty of imbalance and misalignment.)

It seems likely, despite his rivals' claims to the contrary, that McCormick arrived at this total solution to the problem of mechanical reaping quite independently of any other pioneer, although most of these features were already established in earlier experimental models. The persistent work of his father in the same researches, and his own inventive genius clearly led him to this overall conclusion. It is highly doubtful, in the isolation of Walnut Grove, that he ever saw or was influenced by any earlier reaper, other than his father's attempts. However, there were other machines produced in subsequent years that satisfied the same fundamental requirements. The McCormick reaper was not unique, and its success was largely due to McCormick's singleminded persistence and promotional acumen.

McCormick, though naturally pleased with the success of his invention, was at first cautious, and continued to experiment with it, introducing a number of refinements. Probably he felt initially uncertain of its potential, a feeling later revealed by a contemporary witness of an early field trial who remarked that "nobody ever believed it would come to much." The reaper revolution then did not occur overnight. Cyrus made further tests in fields around Lexington, Virginia, in 1832 and excited some local interest. The announcement in 1834 of a patent on a reaper invented by Obed Hussey a year earlier prompted McCormick to patent his 1831 machine; the patent was granted on June 21, 1834. After 1836 he was involved with his father in an iron-smelting venture, which both believed was more likely to make their fortunes than the reaper. Instead, after the crash of the United States Bank in 1837, when the iron market collapsed, both Cyrus and Robert found themselves heavily in debt and were forced to close their Cotopaxi Iron Furnace.

The reapers, McCormick's dormant interest throughout the 1830s, at last occupied his full attention, and he began modifying and publicizing them. In his own words:

> No machines were sold until 1840, and I may say that they were not of much practical value until the improvements of my second patent in 1845. Up to this period, nothing but loss of time and money resulted from my efforts.

Production began in a modest way in the old workshop at Walnut Grove, and after several years of small-scale operation—under forty machines had been made by 1843—McCormick decided to expand by having his reapers made under license at workshops in Brockport, N.Y., and Cincinnati. Disappointed by the inferior quality of these machines, he withdrew the contracts and by 1847 was concentrating production in a newly built factory in Chicago, then at the beginning of its development as a major city. Production grew steadily and the Chicago factory produced and marketed reapers on a national basis. By 1861, McCormick had sold twenty-three thousand reaping machines.

Even in these early years, McCormick laid great stress on what have since become universal manufacturing and marketing techniques—applying mass-production methods, using field tests, guarantees and testimonials in extensive advertising campaigns and offering his product on a credit payment system. The field tests in particular aroused great interest. As one commentator wrote:

Bottom James Smith's reaping machine. Although moderately effective—cutting wheat at ground level by means of the circular blade, powered from the wheels—the machine was easily damaged on uneven ground and had other technical drawbacks.

Below A reconstruction of one of the first recorded "mechanical" reapers. Used in Europe at the time of the Roman occupation, it was described by the historian Pliny in the first century A.D.

Patrick Bell's reaper.
Bell was inspired by a picture of James Smith's machine to use shears instead of rotating blades.

"All were highly gratified, and many would linger and follow it around the field to admire and witness its neat, rapid and perfect performance."

Adding a seat for the operator to the basic design was the last modification McCormick himself made to the reaper. But ever aware of competition, especially in the 1850s and 1860s, he was always open to suggestions for improvements, purchasing the patents of such refinements as the wire-binder, twine-binder, and self-rake (which eliminated the need for a worker to rake the cut grain from the grain deck). He also fought numerous suits, warding off rivals both by threats and legal action. Most of them, tired of battling with so resolute a foe, withdrew from the struggle, leaving him virtually monopolistic control of the reaper market. The dispute over priority to the invention—still argued by students of agricultural history—raged particularly severely between McCormick and Obed Hussey (who had patented his machine shortly before McCormick, but he accepted after a legal wrangle McCormick's precedence by some two years). Hussey was a one-eyed Quaker sailor from Ohio who for no known reason had left the sea to invent a reaper. Both men showed their reapers at the Great Exhibition in London in 1851 (by which time McCormick had sold over a thousand machines). McCormick's machine of that year was a much improved version of the prototype of twenty years before. It was claimed that with two operators—one to drive the horses and steer the reaper, and one to rake the grain from the deck—it could do the work of forty men with sickles. It was not generally realized—even by Hussey—that his machine was better suited to mowing than true reaping. So it was McCormick's that captured the imagination of the formerly skeptical Exhibition judges and won for him the Council Medal (and subsequent fame and honor throughout Europe; he was made an officer of the Legion of Honor in 1879 for a contribution to agriculture that the French authorities regarded as greater than that of any living man). In England, the reaper was remarkably successful in difficult conditions, such as uneven fields and cutting wet grain, and presaged much for the future. As the British press, which had earlier called it "ridiculous" remarked:

> The success which attended the trials of Mr. McCormick's Reaping Machine (U.S.A.) has convinced English farmers that it can be economically employed; it is therefore probable that, within a very short time, similar improvements, or some improvement on the American invention, will be very generally used throughout the country. In agriculture, it appears that the machine will be as important as the spinning-jenny and power-loom in manufactures.

The subsequent worldwide spread of the McCormick reaper proved this prediction to be true.

The company that Cyrus McCormick founded, managed by his brothers Leander and William, prospered, despite often strained relations between Cyrus, notorious as a hard taskmaster, and Leander—especially when Leander later attempted to prove that their father was the real inventor of the reaper. Cyrus McCormick himself also prospered. He became one of America's first industrialist millionaires, extending his business interests to mining, real estate and railroads. He also became a pillar of the Democratic Party, and a philanthropic proponent of Presbyterianism, endowing the McCormick Theological Seminary, publishing the

The McCormick reaper. Displayed at the Great Exhibition, the reaper won McCormick the Council Medal and subsequent fame and honor throughout Europe as well as the United States.

Presbyterian Expositor, and purchasing the *Chicago Times* as a medium for expressing his political views. He married at the age of forty-nine, and died on May 13, 1884, his last words being, "It's all right. It's all right. I only want Heaven!" After his death, the company was merged with several others to form the giant International Harvester Company, which remains dominant in the world reaper market and is still controlled by the McCormick family.

The invention and patenting of the reaping machine marks not only a significant turning point in the history of agriculture but in the history of the world. It marked the beginning of a series of events that led to the use of mechanical reapers throughout the world, and meant that for the first time, huge tracts of grain could be harvested rapidly and by relatively few workers. The great prairies of the United States and Canada, now feasibly plowed by John Deere's newly invented steel plow, could be opened for grain production, and it has thus been estimated that after the mid-nineteenth century, the McCormick reaper in particular enabled the American frontier to be pushed westward at over thirty miles a year by extending the potential of cultivable land. In moving agriculture away from its total dependence upon labor, the reaper also proved an important instrument of social change, for it released farm workers from the land to work in industry and provided the grain surpluses that made possible the phenomenal development of urban America in the late nineteenth century. It also made grain for export.

The population of America in 1831 was about thirteen million, of which three-quarters lived on the land. Sixty years later, it was sixty-three million, with more than half living in cities. Even allowing for the growth of the demand for agricultural products, perhaps twenty million people became urban dwellers who would otherwise have been required to work on the land. Had the reaper and other less important mechanical advances not released them, the industrial prosperity of the United States would have been seriously reduced, since the demand for food in any economy is of overriding importance.

During the American Civil War—vociferously opposed by McCormick—the release of Northern farmers from the land, made possible by the widespread use of the reaping machine, provided both the manpower and food supply that enabled the Union to defeat the Confederate States. As Abraham Lincoln's Secretary of War, Edwin M. Stanton, remarked:

> By taking the places of regiments of young men in the Western harvest fields, it releases them to do battle for the Union at the front, and at the same time keeps up the supply of bread for the nation and the nation's armies. Thus without McCormick's invention I fear the North could not win, and the Union would be dismembered.

After the Civil War, the abolition of slavery speeded the further spread of the reaper as a replacement for slave labor.

The success of the reaper, and the conversion of so many conservative and thrifty farmers to mechanization also encouraged the production of other important agricultural machines and prompted a revolution in farming. By inventing the reaper, Cyrus McCormick ended for ever the ancient drudgery of harvesting by scythe and sickle and converted arable farming from a demanding chore to a profitable business.

RUSSELL ASH

Prussian power and Italian nationalism

The growth of Prussian power

The rapid growth of Prussian power held as much importance for the nineteenth century as the revolution in agriculture. The Napoleonic Wars had changed the face of Germany more than that of any other European region by sweeping away many of the smaller states and rationalizing the borders of those that remained; instead of the three hundred-odd states that had existed in 1790, there were now only thirty-eight. The largest German beneficiary of the Congress of Vienna was Prussia, which gained Swedish Pomerania, much of Saxony, Westphalia and the Lower Rhine. Between 1815 and 1848 Prussian influence on the Germanic Confederation increased rapidly. This was due in part to its military strength, but also to an effective bureaucratic system built up during the eighteenth century. The Prussian civil service was, in the words of the brilliant contemporary historian Leopold von Ranke (1795–1886), "a selection of the ablest of the whole nation." At a period when other national bureaucracies were ill-developed and corrupt, Prussia already saw itself as having the mission to unify—and to dominate—Germany. As the historian Barthold Niebuhr (1776–1831) wrote, "Prussia is the common fatherland of all Germans who excel in scholarship, arms or administration." But if she was to play such a role, Prussia would have to struggle and to make sacrifices: "Prussia is proud of the mission to defend herself and Germany; she must, however, be strengthened for this mission in order not to exhaust herself and to be bled white."

That Prussia was able to realize her ambitions—at least in part—during the 1830s and 1840s was, however, due more than anything else to economic strength. The Congress of Vienna had allowed Prussia to take over Germany's most industrialized regions, including the coal mines of the Ruhr valley and Essen, where the Krupp family were building up an important business. The decades after the Congress witnessed the rapid growth of north German industry in general, but Prussia developed particularly quickly. Above all Prussia was quick to see the potential of an efficient railroad system, and soon one of the largest networks in Europe was completed.

The Prussian government saw the need to modernize the old and highly inefficient tariff system that had grown up between the various German states. In 1818 the Director General of Customs had introduced a new law that swept away all tariffs between the different Prussian regions and allowed raw materials to be imported tax free—although the tax on luxury consumer goods rose as high as thirty percent of their value. But, because of the geographical division of Prussia's possessions and because of their relative lack of access to the sea, the full effect of the tariff changes would only be felt if neighboring states agreed to a similar measure. The two states of Hesse both joined in a customs union (*zollverein*) with Prussia in 1831, and other states rapidly followed their example. As a result, internal trade between the German states, which had previously been fairly small, grew rapidly. By 1843 the union covered seventeen states with a total population of over twenty-five million. Prussia—by far the largest producer—was also the largest beneficiary, and in the years ahead this economic power was to form the basis of Prussia's political supremacy. The failure of Austria to enter the *zollverein* was the main cause of her decline and eventual exclusion from a united Germany.

Friedrich Krupps' steelworks in Essen, 1819 with the original foundry on the left.

Austria

Although theoretically the dominant member of the German Confederation, Austria's influence was diminishing and she found herself fully occupied protecting her vast dominions. The fundamental internal problem facing Austrian ministers (Metternich was responsible only for foreign affairs) was the growth of nationalist ideas in many parts of the Empire. Almost everywhere—in Bohemia and the Slav lands, in Hungary and Austria and above all in Italy—there were problems so deep-rooted that they came close to destroying the whole Empire in 1848.

It was in Italy that Austria's problems were most intractable. Ostensibly Austrian power was unshakeable: the Kingdom of Lombardy–Venetia was part of Austria's Empire, as were the Grand Duchy of Tuscany and a few small isolated areas; in the Papal States and the Bourbon Kingdom of the Two Sicilies—Italy's largest kingdom—Austrian troops helped the governments to ensure that order was kept; the Duke of Modena was a Hapsburg; the small duchies of Parma and Lucca were theoretically independent but Austrian influence was strong, and in 1847, Lucca, too, became a Hapsburg possession. The only state in Italy that had retained more than nominal independence from the Hapsburgs was the Kingdom of Sardinia, but that was troubled by dynastic disputes.

Yet, in reality, the Austrian hold on Italy was weak, and desire for an independent united Italy was growing. Secret nationalist societies flourished, although their disagreements with each other were little less strong than their dislike of Austria; some hoped that Italy would be ruled by the Pope, while others hoped for a secular monarchy and a few wanted a republic. To meet this potential threat, the governments of Italy encouraged the formation of antirevolutionary societies. The largest and by far the most influential of the revolutionary societies was that of the Carbonari (charcoal burners). The Austrians were not, however, the first target of the Carbonari; after an abortive attempt to impose a constitution on the reactionary Kingdom of the Two Sicilies, the Carbonari scored their first success by forcing King Victor Emmanuel of Sardinia to abdicate in 1821, although subsequent Carbonari-inspired risings were suppressed with Austrian help. Under liberal pressure Sardinia introduced, before 1848, a fairly progressive civil and penal code, based on French models, and also established a broadly based system of primary education.

Giuseppe Garibaldi, Italian patriot.

Although it was not a liberal state, Sardinia won the support of most nationalists and became the focus for their hopes of a united Italian monarchy. The increasingly reactionary attitude of the papacy under the previously liberal Pius IX, who was Pope from 1846 to 1878, gradually lost it most nationalist support; the socialism of republicans such as Giuseppe Mazzini (1805–72) alienated middle-class and aristocratic nationalists; the brutality of the reactionary Bourbon kings of the Two Sicilies ensured that the House of Sardinia faced no competition for the leadership of the nationalists.

During the years before the 1848 risings in Italy there was little

undermine Austria's domination of Germany

open violence against Austrian rule; however, Austrian troops were so unpopular that they often had to be confined to barracks in order to avoid the danger of violent incidents. Despite the appearance of calm, Austrian Italy was close to revolution.

Spain

Although neither Spain nor Portugal had much in common with Italy, liberalism in both countries—as in Italy—found its home in revolutionary societies. The loss of their American colonies and the devastation caused by the Napoleonic Wars contributed to social unrest in the Iberian states. In 1820, King Ferdinand VII of Spain, who ruled in 1808 and again from 1814 to 1833, disregarding the constitution imposed by revolutionaries in 1812 sent troops to the American colonies to fight the rebels. He was at once faced with rebellion at home. It was not until 1823 that the Spanish rising was suppressed with the help of French troops under the reactionary Duke Louis of Angoulême, who would later (1836) be hailed by some of his compatriots as Louis XIX. For the next ten years, "the ominous decade," Ferdinand imposed a reactionary regime on his land and persecuted liberals vigorously. Despite this, the King was not authoritarian enough for all his subjects, and in Catalonia in 1827 there was an attempt to put his brother Don Carlos (1788–1855) on the throne. After Ferdinand's death in 1833, war broke out between the supporters of his three-year-old daughter Isabella and the Carlists, who claimed that the succession of a woman to the Spanish throne was illegal because of the Salic Law.

While the Madrid government sought to extend its power base by making concessions to the largely city-based liberals, Don Carlos, with the support of the northern provinces and most of the nobility, raised the standard of revolt. Civil war continued for five years, but although Don Carlos was defeated, Carlism did not die. A further political fragmentation occurred when the victorious establishment divided into two parties, the moderates (conservative) and the progressives (radicals), that struggled for power for the next forty years, frequently depending on military support to remove their rivals from office. Foreign and colonial interests played a secondary role, and interest centered on the Church's position and the continuing Carlist threat.

Portugal

Portuguese politics were fairly closely linked with those of Spain, and the outbreak of rebellion in Spain in 1820 was speedily followed by a rising in Portugal. The cause was, however, different. The success of Napoleon had caused the Portuguese royal family to flee to Brazil in 1807, and after Waterloo John VI (1769–1826) who took far more interest in his Brazilian empire than in his kingdom of Portugal, did not return. A

William, Viscount Beresford, British military ruler of Portugal during the King's absence in Brazil.

council of regency, supported by a British military force, led by Lord Beresford (1768–1854), governed Portugal. In 1820 the Portuguese garrison at Oporto mutinied and the British withdrew. The King reluctantly returned from Brazil, and a liberal constitution was passed. His return to Europe cost Portugal—although not the ruling House of Braganza—control of Brazil; John's eldest son, Dom Pedro (1798–1834), was made Emperor of an independent Brazil, although John retained the purely nominal title of "Supreme Emperor." The death of John led to conflict between Pedro and his brother Miguel (1802–66); civil war broke out and for a time it seemed that Portuguese colonialism was operating in reverse, with wealthy Brazil controlling impoverished Portugal. After Brazil became independent, economic links remained close—Brazil and Portugal continued to be each others' main trading partners, and Brazil benefited from massive immigration from Portugal during the nineteenth century. But neither economic links nor the common rule of the House of Braganza could prevent the gradual separation of the two countries; politically Brazil tended to be liberal, while Portugal reflected the success of the moderates in Spain.

Neither Spain nor Portugal was able to recover fully from the disruption caused by the Napoleonic Wars, and the economies of both countries were severely weakened by the loss of their American colonies. Obsessed by a vision of their past glories, Spain and Portugal faded further and further into a political and economic twilight, increasingly divorced from the problems and the opportunities of the rest of Europe.

The wedding of Pedro I, Emperor of Brazil, to Princess Amelia de Beauharnais.

Meanwhile in America the newly independent former Spanish colony of Mexico was having difficulties with its northern neighbor, the United States, and its land-hungry settlers. The Mexican border extended far to the north of the Rio Grande River, and under an 1819 treaty included the modern states of California, Nevada, Utah, Arizona, New Mexico and parts of Colorado as well as Texas. During the 1820s many Americans had settled in Texas, and the attempts of the Mexican dictator Antonio López de Santa Anna (*c.* 1795–1876) to close the border in 1830 met with little success. In 1836 the American settlers in Texas declared themselves an independent republic.

The knights entering the plaza; part of the celebration of the three-year-old Isabella's coronation on June 22, 1833, as hereditary Princess of Spain and the Indies.

1836 "Remember the Alamo!"

In the early nineteenth century Texas was nominally part of Mexico, but what few settlers were there came mostly from the United States. Disagreement was inevitable and sporadic fighting and uprisings were commonplace. When Antonio López de Santa Anna seized power in Mexico, Texans rose again, and Santa Anna gathered an army and moved north. He set siege to the Alamo, a fortress held by some hundred and eighty defenders. After several days he stormed it, and the entire garrison was annihilated. The incident gave Texans an issue to rally over and a slogan they would never forget.

General Antonio López de Santa Anna; an ardent admirer of Napoleon, he called himself the Napoleon of the West.

Opposite Stephen Austin's map of Texas in 1836, the year the Republic was established.

Just before dawn on Sunday, March 6, 1836, the 188 defenders of the Alamo fort, outside San Antonio, Texas, heard the bugles of the besieging Mexican army sound the notes of the *degüello*—the ancient call dating back to the Moorish wars in Spain, and signifying "no quarter." For, as General Antonio López de Santa Anna, commander of the two thousand or more besiegers, told one of his generals, "You know in this war there are no prisoners."

Three Mexican columns advanced on the fortified mission, which had withstood two weeks of siege and bombardment; troops poured through the breach in the northwest wall where shells had pulverized the crumbling eighteenth-century masonry. The defenders, strung out along a quarter of a mile of breastworks, fell back to the two-storied convent building, and made their last desperate stand. By dusk they were dead: the Texan commander, the hot-headed Lieutenant Colonel William Barret Travis; James Bowie, who perfected the Bowie knife; Davy Crockett, who had cheered the Texans with tunes on his violin in the anxious hours before the attack. As the Mexicans swarmed through ravaged, smoking buildings, they came across one American, the wife of a Lieutenant Dickinson, sheltering in the convent church. She was rescued by a Mexican officer; she was the sole survivor.

The Alamo was at once invested with that pride and emotive power reserved for desperate defeats and massacres.

Six weeks later, at the mouth of the San Jacinto River, Santa Anna and twelve hundred men made contact with Sam Houston and his army of eight hundred, the last defense of the young Republic of Texas. Santa Anna and his men, confident of victory, were at rest. Suddenly, the Texans broke out of the woods and, with cries of "Remember the Alamo," fell upon the unprepared army and slaughtered six hundred of the fleeing enemy. The Mexican second-in-command, Colonel Almonte, managed to stem the panic, and surrendered with the remainder of the troops; of the twelve hundred, barely forty escaped death, wounds or capture. Two Texans were killed and twenty-three wounded. Santa Anna himself was captured next day, skulking in the long grass, still wearing his red carpet slippers. Texas had won independence—on the battlefield if not on paper—and the legend of the Alamo had played its part.

The Alamo, and its sequel, San Jacinto, were crucial episodes in the drama of the Texas Revolution; and the Texas Revolution was a turning point in the emergence of the continental United States. To place the legend of the Alamo in its historical context, it is necessary to look at North America a generation after the Declaration of Independence.

In the 1790s the young Republic was confined to the Atlantic seaboard: treaties with Spain and Great Britain recognized American sovereignty as far west as the Mississippi, but Spain retained possession of Louisiana and the Floridas, while Spanish claims, if not control, stretched through the middle and southwest of the present United States, merging with British and Russian counterclaims in the virgin lands of the Oregon country. In 1802 Napoleon acquired Louisiana from Spain but, three years later, facing a renewal of war with Britain, he agreed to sell the province to the United States. By cutting off the Spanish territories in East Florida from West Florida, Texas and New Spain (later Mexico), American designs on these border provinces were encouraged. In 1810, when Spain was distracted by the Spanish American revolutions, American settlers at Baton Rouge revolted against the Spanish authorities, and gave President Madison the opportunity to occupy West Florida. Two years later the territory was

MAP OF TEXAS
With Parts of the Adjoining States
COMPILED BY STEPHEN F. AUST
PUBLISHED by H.S.TANNER PHILADELPHIA
Note. The Latitude and Longitude of Saltillo
Larede Bexar Nacogdoches and the Point where t
ary line leaves the Sabine are from the observations
General Teran of the Mexican Army.
1836.
OZARK DISTRICT
TERRITORY
RED RIVER
CAMERON'S GRANT
PRAIRIE
FELISOLA'S GRANT
AUSTIN & WILLIAMS
GRANT
BURNET'S GRANT
ZAVALL
WOODBURY & CO
GRANT
Granted to STEPHEN F. AUSTIN 1827
WHELIN'S GRANT
AUSTINS COLONY
DE WITT'S COLONY
McMULLEN & McGLONE'S GRANT
DE LEON'S GR.
GALVESTON BAY
SABINE LAKE
MATAGORDA B.
Aransas Bay
Corpus Christi
Galveston Inlet
Liberty
Harrisburg
Bolivar
Brazoria
NACOGDOCHES
STATE OF TAMAULIPAS
STATE OF
NUEVO LEON
MONTEREY
Matamoros
Brasos Santiago
Point Isabel
Laredo
Salt Lakes
NOTE.
SCALE OF MILES

formally annexed to the new state of Louisiana: it was, in effect, a dress rehearsal for the Texas Revolution twenty-five years later. A similar coup was attempted in East Florida, which Georgian planters coveted for the expanding cotton industry, but the War of 1812 with Great Britain intervened.

By 1819, however, Spain, racked by a decade of revolutionary upheaval in her American provinces, agreed to cede East Florida, recognize American possession of West Florida and renounce all claims north of the forty-second parallel. As a result the Adams-Onis Treaty was signed, by which the United States gained access to the Pacific, along the line of the present northern boundaries of California, Nevada and Utah. Hence its alternative title, the Transcontinental Treaty.

But some interests, particularly the Southern cotton interests, were not satisfied. The treaty did not include Texas; indeed, it recognized the old border along the Sabine River. In the prolonged ratification debates, House Speaker Henry Clay spoke out against the exclusion of Texas, while in the disputed area itself there was the usual resort to direct action which, in the case of East Florida, and nearby West Florida, had forced the hand of the United States government. After a public meeting at Natchez, the cotton capital on the Mississippi, James Long led a filibustering expedition into Texas, seized the frontier town of Nacogdoches, and proclaimed the new "Republic of Texas." The regime was shortlived. While Long went to Galveston Island to negotiate an alliance with Jean Laffite, uncrowned king of the last pirate colony in North America, Spanish troops attacked Nacogdoches, drove out the invaders, and put an end to the insurgent Republic.

But designs on Texas were only postponed, and

developments south of the border offered encouragement. In the twilight of Spanish rule in New Spain, the Viceroy in Mexico City granted Moses Austin, a Connecticut Yankee, permission to establish a colony of Americans in Texas. The offer was not taken up until 1821 when Stephen Austin, Moses' son, planted the first American settlement at San Felipe de Austin. By then, Spanish imperial rule had collapsed; New Spain had become the independent Empire (1821–24) and then Republic of Mexico, and Texas was included in the state of Coahuila. But American penetration only quickened. In 1823 a colonization law laid down the terms for immigrant settlement: farming families were to receive 177 acres, and cattle families 4,428 acres; *empresarios* (colonizing agents) like Stephen Austin were to receive additional holdings, to found towns, and to organize local militias. Fifteen *empresarios* other than Austin took advantage of the offer of cheap land, and the 1820s saw a flood of immigrants. Texas, which in 1823 had a white population of some three thousand, outnumbered by Comanches, buffalo and mustang, by the early 1830s had a white population of twenty to thirty thousand, plus a rising population of Negro slaves, imported to work the growing cotton fields.

The motives of the Mexican government in encouraging this immigration are questionable. Moses Austin's original grant was probably the result—as were many contracts and concessions in Mexico—of an influential contact at the viceregal court. But at the same time Mexican policy had a certain rationale, even if the succession of unstable and bankrupt administrations in Mexico City were unable to control the application of policy in the remote frontier regions. Inheriting the vast, virtually uninhabited northern provinces of New Spain, the rulers of independent Mexico sought to secure their possessions by encouraging settlement; and where the old regime had been able to rely upon the colonizing genius of the Church, particularly the Jesuits, the Republic had to fall back on secular methods. In offering lands for colonization, they anticipated a mixed response from Americans, Europeans and native Mexicans; they stipulated that Austin's immigrants were to be "Roman Apostolic Catholics . . . of steady habits"; they required that all public transactions be conducted in Spanish, and offered a bonus in land to any colonist who married a Mexican girl. But having laid down these rules, the distant central government failed to enforce them, just as it remained equivocal on the question of slavery, and allowed the settlers to import Negro slaves in defiance of Mexican practice.

As for the immigrants themselves, their attitudes were varied. Some, like Stephen Austin, while flouting the religious requirement, nevertheless took their obligation to Mexico seriously, and showed a persistent loyalty to their country of adoption. But others harbored designs for independence and union with the United States from the beginning, and took the example of West Florida as their prototype. In 1826, these designs, and the threat they presented to Mexican sovereignty, became starkly apparent with the revolt of Haden Edwards. Edwards was an obscure character; bold and reckless where Austin was steadfast and patient, he succeeded in becoming an *empresario* and setting up a colony near Nacogdoches—scene of the 1819 "Republic"—conveniently close to the Louisiana border. Edwards planted his colony on territory claimed by absentee Mexican landowners, and when the state and federal governments ordered him off the disputed land and out of the country, Edwards seized Nacogdoches and proclaimed the inde-

Opposite above The Battle of the Alamo, the memory of which spurred the Texans on to win the Battle of San Jacinto.

Opposite below Comanche Indians; in 1823 they outnumbered the three thousand Texan whites. By the early 1830s the white population had risen to nearly thirty thousand.

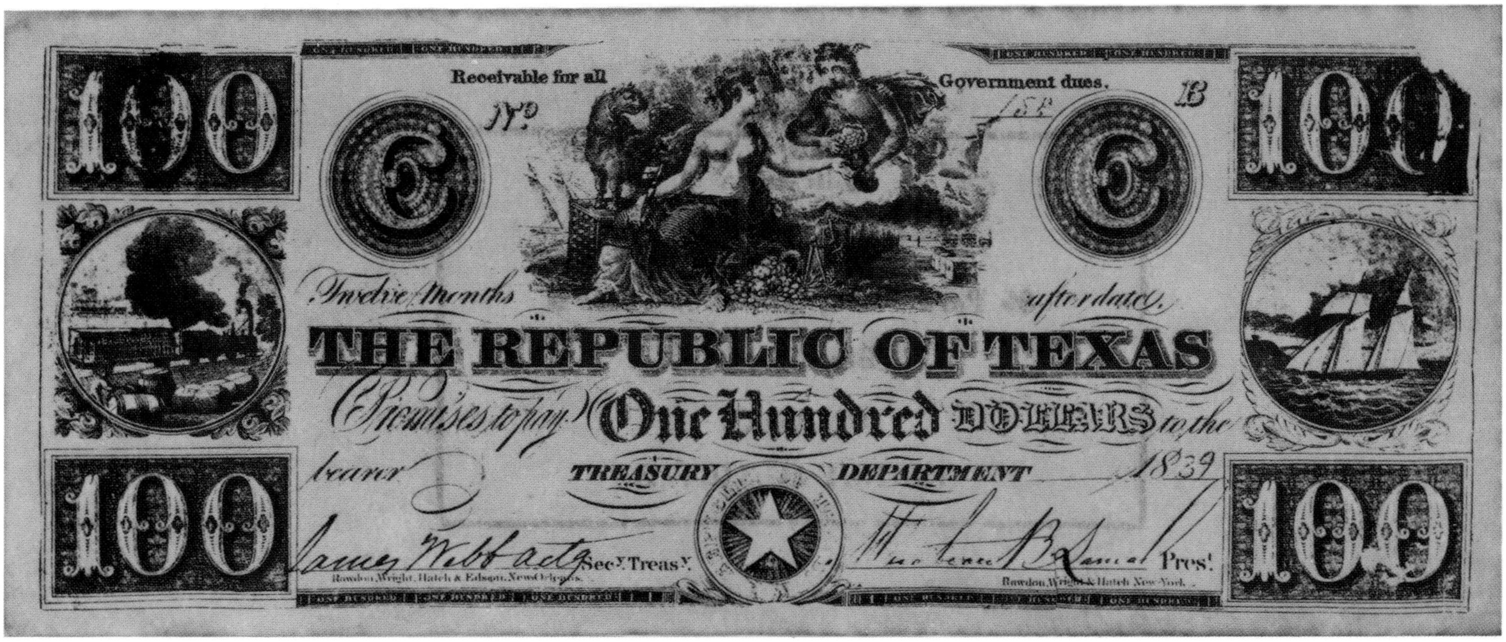

A hundred-dollar bill issued by the Republic of Texas. The annexation of the twelve-year-old Republic by the United States was a major cause of the Mexican-American War.

The Alamo floodlit. The Alamo withstood two weeks of siege and bombardment before falling to the Mexicans.

pendent Republic of Fredonia, complete with an American-style constitution. He raised an army of two hundred, appealed to the United States for support, and contracted an alliance with the Cherokee Indians. Public opinion in the United States—particularly in the Mississippi Valley—rallied to Edwards and the Fredonians. But within Texas, the American settlers were divided. Austin not only refused assistance, but even sent a force to cooperate with the Mexicans in an attack on Nacogdoches. By January, 1826, Fredonia no longer existed.

But the lesson remained. Furthermore, Mexican suspicion of United States' intentions was heightened by the tactless conduct of the first American minister to independent Mexico, Joel Poinsett. Poinsett believed that Mexico would be glad to relinquish Texas and the problems that the continued possession of Texas entailed; he also plunged into Mexican domestic politics, siding with the liberal freemason faction which, he claimed, stood for "our Republican principles." So, with rumors of his political involvement spreading through Mexico City, and the Fredonia revolt, fresh in Mexican minds, Poinsett transmitted an offer from President Adams of $1,000,000 in return for the territory of Texas down to the Rio Grande (1827). Mexico—still refusing to accept the 1819 Treaty, concluded by the Spanish government, and therefore claiming, in theory, the land right up to the Mississippi—rejected the offer outright, suspecting that the United States government was conniving with the Texan dissidents. Though incorrect, these suspicions were understandable.

In the wake of the Fredonia revolt a Mexican commission under Manuel Mier y Teran visited Texas and reported on the situation. He found the further north one traveled the more Mexican influence gave way to American; at Nacogdoches the Mexicans were outnumbered ten to one, and occupied only menial positions in society. The American settlers ran English schools and sent their sons back to the United States for further education. Most important, although Mexican laws forbade slavery, the state congress recognized contracts made between master and slave prior to entry into Texas; slaves could not be born in Texas, nor could they be imported wholesale, but they could be brought in by new settlers, thus perpetuating slavery and, argued Mier y Teran, ensuring the booming prosperity of Texas, which acted as a magnet for more immigration. "It could not be otherwise," he warned, "that from such a state of affairs should arise an antagonism between the Mexicans and foreigners which is not the least of the smouldering fires I have discovered. Therefore, I now warn you to take timely measures. Texas could throw the whole nation into revolution. . . ."

Promoted to military commander of the eastern states, Mier y Teran continued to urge policies that would strengthen Mexican control over Texas: a complete embargo on the supply of

Stephen Austin, Secretary of State for the Republic of Texas. The American colonization of Texas began in 1821 when Austin obtained a grant of land on condition that he establish a settlement.

slaves, the establishment of military garrisons and Mexican colonists to counterbalance the Americans.

The garrisons had to come first, and Mexican determination was heightened by a second inept attempt by the United States to purchase Texas outright—this time for $5,000,000. This offer, made through an acquaintance of President Andrew Jackson, Anthony Butler, met the inevitable, indignant refusal. In this atmosphere, the Mexican Congress approved Lucas Alamán's *Iniciativa* (April, 1830) which prohibited further immigration from the United States into Texas, and established customs posts along the Louisiana border. That summer, Mier y Teran led a Mexican army into Texas to garrison the major towns and enforce the new status quo.

From 1830, increasingly strained relations developed between the Texans and the Mexican government, represented by Mier y Teran's military garrisons. Conflict centered on the question of customs. In 1830 a seven-year exemption from customs duties came to an end, and the Americans found themselves subject to the Mexican tariff that prohibited the import of certain goods—notably agricultural machinery—which they had been used to importing from Louisiana. Henceforth, they could only get certain supplies from the Mexican trading posts far to the south, across Indian-infested desert, or, as a two-year concession, through two frontier ports, controlled by Mexican authorities. At one of these ports, Anahuac, conflict between smugglers and the authorities led to arrests, a riot and revolt (1832).

Texan troubles now merged with the endemic civil strife that had plagued independent Mexico since its foundation. The year 1832 also saw the fall of the tough, centralized, conservative administration of Anastasio Bustamante and Alamán, which had pushed through the "Mexicanization" policy in Texas. In its place, a coup, led by Santa Anna, established a liberal government. Santa Anna, then forty years old, was an ambitious soldier whose hero was Napoleon; he called himself the Napoleon of the West, and kept a Napoleonic veteran by his side for first-hand advice.

Inasmuch as Mexican political struggles concerned issues rather than personalities, patronage and power, the liberals whom Santa Anna led to power in 1832 stood for federalism, states' rights and a curtailment of clerical and military privileges. The Texans saw the opportunity for an alliance with the liberals, whereby they could pass off their recent revolt as a "liberal" *pronunciamiento*, and secure the benefits of federalist government. Stephen Austin therefore established close relations with the liberal commander, Colonel Mejia, who was advancing into Texas; Texan town councils announced their allegiance to the Santa Anna government; and at Nacogdoches, where the last Mier y Teran garrison held out, Texans led by Colonel James Bowie attacked the town and forced the garrison to change sides. Mier y Teran himself died in circumstances that suggested assassination or, more probably, suicide.

With the triumph of the liberals, the Texans expected to benefit. Conventions representing the Anglo-American population met in October, 1832, and April, 1833, and appealed to Santa Anna (now President) for a repeal of the customs laws and the right to exist as a separate state, distinct from Coahuila. Finally, they drew up a state constitution, virtually a replica of an American state constitution. Austin went to Mexico City to plead the Texan case, still hopeful that a settlement could be reached without a complete break, but prepared for more extreme measures if the Texan proposals were disregarded.

For a time, Santa Anna prevaricated. But Ambassador Butler was still scheming to secure the purchase of Texas, thereby antagonizing the Mexicans. Suddenly Santa Anna performed a dramatic about-face; he ousted the puppet liberal president, suppressed Congress and repealed the anticlerical legislation of the previous administration. This return to conservative government implied a return to conservative policy in Texas. Austin was jailed; Santa Anna's general in Coahuila, General Cos, ordered the reestablishment of an orderly customs house at Anahuac, and arrested the Governor of Coahuila. The Texans had no great affection for the state governor, but they did for "states' rights."

In June, 1835, another convention met to discuss the situation, and while a majority still favored a

Above The original design for the Texas flag, approved in 1839. Because of the flag's single star the Republic became known as the Lone Star Republic.

President John Tyler who annexed Texas to the Union, thereby virtually establishing the southern frontier of the United States and aggravating the question of slavery.

Reproduced by permission of The John Judkyn Memorial, Bath.

cautious policy, the activists were gaining support. One of them, William Barret Travis, later commander at the Alamo, took the matter into his own hands and with a force of forty men forced the surrender of the garrison at Anahuac. General Cos responded by sending more troops into Texas to arrest the ringleaders of this coup, and his refusal to negotiate with the Texan authorities helped aggravate the situation. Austin, recently returned to Texas after a two-year absence, found the state agitated and belligerent. A Committee of Safety was set up, with Austin as chairman, charged with organizing volunteer companies to resist the Mexican advance.

Conflicting opinions still prevailed and were evident in the Consultation, the Texan assembly, which met in November, 1835. This gathering, justifying its revolt against centralizing, military oppression, declared that Texas would remain loyal to Mexico so long as the government respected constitutional procedures and voted down a motion of secession. Nevertheless, it is significant that they chose Henry Smith, recognized leader of the "war party" and long-time campaigner for open defiance, as provisional president in preference to the more moderate Austin. They also appointed Sam Houston, another acquaintance of Jackson, as commander of the Texan forces.

The campaign which followed was decentralized, even anarchic. Cos was surrounded in San Antonio and the Texan council of war decided to raise the siege and go into winter quarters. But on December 5, 1835, the Texans suddenly attacked, battering their way through the adobe walls of the houses with twelve-foot logs. Cos surrendered and was allowed to return with his forces to Mexico. Now divisions and dissensions arose among the Texans over the strategy to be followed: some favored an expedition into Mexico to link up with prospective liberal allies, and part of the San Antonio garrison was detached for this purpose. Another part went home. Travis remained in command of a depleted force—about one hundred and fifty—in the Alamo. On February 24, he reported that a Mexican force had reoccupied the city across the river. The Mexican force was the main Mexican army under Santa Anna. The stage was set for the Battle of the Alamo.

After the Alamo and San Jacinto, Texas was independent, in fact if not in name, but it was a precarious, vulnerable independence. Santa Anna, in captivity, was prepared to barter his freedom for Mexican recognition of Texan independence, but the Mexican government refused, while making no move to reassert its authority. In Texas itself a plebiscite revealed a huge majority in favor of union with the United States. But, freed from the trammels of Mexican domestic politics, Texas found that its future was inextricably bound up with a live issue in American politics—slavery. With the 1836 presidential election out of the way, and Martin Van Buren replacing

Jackson in the White House, Congress passed resolutions recognizing the independent state of Texas;. but the debate over annexation, which the Texans had requested, soon produced bitter sectional divisions. Opponents of slavery argued that the admission of Texas into the Union was a plot engineered by slave interests to tip the political balance in their favor. In addition, the slump of 1837 made business interests anxious about the prospects of war with Mexico, which annexation would surely provoke. For six months Congress debated the question, and, finally, after a three-week filibuster by the Abolitionist leader John Quincy Adams, the annexation proposal was defeated.

Texas now faced twelve years of independence and isolation, punctuated by sporadic Mexican attacks, fruitless negotiations and diplomatic overtures by Great Britain, who hoped to effect a Texan-Mexican reconciliation based on a recognition of independence in return for the "moral triumph" of securing the abolition of slavery in the state—all in the interest of commercial stability. These British overtures had the effect of reviving the annexation issue and casting it in a new light. Abel P. Upshur, President John Tyler's Secretary of State, regarded British policy in Texas as part of a deliberate plan to undermine the "peculiar institution" of slavery, sabotage the American economy and further British commercial interests. Upshur, and his successor, the fervent proslaver John C. Calhoun, approached Sam Houston, now President of Texas, and secured his cautious approval for annexation, but Calhoun's treaty, incorporating a gratuitous eulogy of slavery, was defeated in the Senate. But annexation could now be regarded as a matter of national as well as sectional interest.

The victory of James K. Polk in the presidential election of 1844 was taken as a mandate for annexation, which Congress approved and outgoing President Tyler signed in March, 1845. Colonel Juan Nepomuceno Almonte, Santa Anna's old second-in-command at San Jacinto, was then Mexican Ambassador to Washington, and had made it plain that annexation would mean war. He was right. Although by 1846 Mexico was prepared to recognize Texan independence, annexation was regarded as a *casus belli*. Polk did not want war. But in addition to Texas, he had his eyes on California, another region of immense potential wealth, sparsely settled by American immigrants and a handful of Mexican landowners and supposedly coveted by Great Britain. Accordingly, Polk sent John Slidell as minister to Mexico, offering a settlement of American claims against Mexico in returr for Texas as far as the Rio Grande, and a further $25,000,000 for California and New Mexico; it was the last, and the largest, of several such cash offers, and as the previous ones was indignantly rejected. The Mexicans especially resented that Slidell had been sent as a minister rather than a special commis-

Sam Houston, first President of Texas. A strong believer in the Union, on the admission of Texas Houston became a senator.

sioner, for it implied that the United States regarded relations as normal and their conduct in annexing Texas as blameless. Polk meanwhile sent "Old Rough and Ready," Zachary Taylor, a veteran of forty years of Indian fighting, to the banks of the Rio Grande, and an American fleet to blockade the Gulf coast of Mexico. The Mexicans responded by attacking across the Rio Grande; the Mexican-American War had begun.

Its results were momentous. Thanks more to its superior artillery than to Zachary Taylor's generalship, the American army in northern Mexico defeated Santa Anna's larger forces at Buena Vista, near Saltillo (thereby securing Taylor the presidency in 1848), and in the south, General Winfield Scott landed at Veracruz and fought his way up to Mexico City, defeating Santa Anna en route. With the country approaching a state of anarchy, the Creole aristocracy were obliged to accept terms. By the Treaty of Guadalupe Hidalgo, ratified by the United States Senate in March, 1848, Mexico agreed to cede Texas, New Mexico and Upper California in return for $30,000,000 compensation, thus losing over half her national territory. The United States, adding Texas and the southwest to the Louisiana Purchase, acquired essentially the same southern frontier as exists today.

But, as the fourteen senators who opposed ratification realized, the question of slavery remained unresolved, and seriously aggravated by the acquisition of vast new territories, where the status of the "peculiar institution" had yet to be defined. The problems of definition therefore became the key political issues of the day, sectional interest solidified, and the stage was set for the Civil War.

ALAN KNIGHT

The ideals of nationalism and socialism

Canada

While the United States expanded to the south by annexing part of Mexico, the British colonies in Canada were developing rapidly. In the early nineteenth century, more British emigrants went to Canada than to any other colony. Some fifty thousand settlers—mostly from Scotland and Ireland—crossed the Atlantic in 1832, but a conflict between nominated legislative councils and popularly elected assemblies led to an armed rebellion in 1837, and for several years the number of settlers declined. In 1839, however, John Lambton, Lord Durham (1792–1840)—who had served as governor for six months the previous year—published his famous *Report on the Affairs of British North America*, in which he proposed that the Canadian provinces be granted responsible government.

Durham's concept was a revolutionary one, and its partial implementation in 1840 enabled the Canadians to boost their seaborne trade and avoid dependence on the far stronger American states to the south. Federation—an essential preliminary to opening up the interior by a transcontinental railroad—followed in 1867. Colonial problems such as these added to the preoccupations of the British government, already fully occupied by domestic affairs.

A pioneer camp in Canada, c. 1840. In the early nineteenth century many British emigrants settled in Canada.

Reform reaches the Continent

Many of the problems that confounded the parliamentarians of Westminster also affected their counterparts on the mainland of Europe. This was particularly true in France, where the reign of Louis Philippe had fallen short of the revolutionary expectations of July, 1830. The new franchise instituted by the July Monarchy was little broader than the one it replaced. Parliament was narrowly bourgeois in composition, obstinately hostile toward workers' demands and closely attached to protectionist tariffs.

The French government appeared to be extremely unstable during this period (which saw thirteen ministries in eighteen years). However, power remained in the hands of a small circle of men who moved from one ministerial post to another; there were only sixty different office holders within the thirteen ministries. The strongest political figure was François Guizot (1787–1874), whose narrow conservatism kept the franchise firmly in the hands of the "men of property," thereby excluding ninety-seven percent of the French male population.

Kossuth, leader of the Magyar rebels.

Radical insurrections in Lyons in 1831 and in Paris and Lyons in April, 1834, were suppressed with more severity than the contemporaneous riots in England, and press laws imposed in 1835 made it impossible for a movement comparable to the Anti-Corn Law League to develop in France. Both countries suffered from the bad harvests of the 1840s and a panic over rash mercantile investment. The collapse of railway booms in northeastern England and central France ruined thousands of small speculators in 1847. Uncertainties over the future development of industry thus made life insecure for capitalists and workers on both sides of the Channel.

By the mid-1840s Germany and Austria were also suffering from the growing pains of industrial capitalism (despite the basically agrarian nature of those countries' societies, which were almost feudal in their restraints on free labor). In Berlin, Frankfurt and Vienna, young agitators were demanding representation; in Hungary the brilliant orator and journalist Lajos Kossuth (1802–94) aroused the intense patriotism of his fellow countrymen, calling for a responsible government, independent of Vienna; and in four of the Italian states, liberals were putting pressure on their rulers in the hope of obtaining constitutions. There was unrest throughout Europe—most of it aimed at the conservative sterility of the Metternich System.

Indeed, the Austrian Chancellor was still at the center of affairs in Vienna, just as he had been each year since 1809. "If they throw me out, the whole structure will collapse," he remarked early in 1848, sublimely indifferent to the signs of the approaching storm.

During the last week of February, 1848, the storm did break—not over Austria, but in Paris. A campaign for extension of the suffrage was to culminate with a reform banquet in the capital, but the meeting was proscribed by the authorities. Barricades went up in the labyrinthine alleys of the old city. There was some shooting, and the mood of the Parisians turned ugly. Louis Philippe, who, in his seventy-fifth year, could well recall losing his father to the guillotine in 1793, thought it wiser to abdicate and seek refuge in England. Few dynasties have toppled more gracefully, but few have had such slender foundations.

When news from Paris reached St. Petersburg, Tsar Nicholas I thundered at the officers of his guard: "Gentlemen, saddle your horses. France is a republic!" It was a premature alarm, for with the Romantic writer Alphonse Marie de Lamartine (1790–1869) incongruously seated at Talleyrand's old desk in the French Foreign Office, the mood of the country was neither Jacobin nor Bonapartist. There was a danger to the Tsar's autocratic principles, however, for the reports that had stirred him to choleric wrath also sent quivers across the Rhine and the Alps and down the Danube to Vienna and Budapest. Within three weeks of Louis Philippe's abdication, rioting in the Austrian capital forced Metternich to resign, and Germany, Italy and Hungary resounded with nationalist sentiment. Before the end of the year barricades of revolution had gone up in twenty European cities—from Seville in southern Spain to Poznan in Prussian Poland.

Metternich's appraisal had been right: the structure had collapsed. But what would take its place? A confederation of European

find expression in a series of abortive uprisings

Proclamation of the restored French Republic on February 24, 1848.

republics, as Mazzini hoped for in Italy? Independence for the historic peoples of Europe, as Kossuth believed in Hungary? "Healthy national egoism," as a delegate of the German pre-Parliament in Frankfurt demanded? There were numberless suggestions, but most were impractical and the risings failed.

It would, however, be a mistake to dismiss the 1848 revolutions as no more than dramatic failures. The authority of absolute monarchy declined in each of the principal areas of insurrection. Louis Napoleon's France, for instance, was in many ways a negation of the ideals of the barricades, but its plebiscites did pay lip service to the principle of universal male suffrage. Frederick William IV of Prussia restored the position of the great landowners in local administration, but he retained a partially elected legislature in which, by 1859, liberals formed a majority. The Austrian statesmen Felix Schwarzenberg (1800–52) and Alexander von Bach (1813–93), the mentors of Francis Joseph, ruled the Austrian Empire through a centralized bureaucracy, but no one sought to reimpose feudal obligations on the emancipated peasantry.

Socialism was indeed discredited, and yet each of these countries tacitly accepted the notion that the state had obligations toward the teeming millions who were being drawn into the expanding factory system. Nationalism seemed a total casualty (partly as a result of its intolerance of the claims of other peoples), but the reputations of Garibaldi and Kossuth were so high outside their countries that the cause of nationalism in Italy and Hungary became a crusading cause of liberals everywhere, much as Greek freedom had been in the days of Lord Byron. In England enterprising manufacturers named a blouse and a biscuit after Garibaldi and brewers honored the Hungarian patriots on the signboards of public houses. Popular acclamation could hardly have gone further. Yet the 1848 risings had another importance; for the first time socialist ideas circulated widely.

Origins of Socialism

The most important social changes of the late eighteenth and the nineteenth centuries were caused by the growth of industrialization. Large-scale industrial enterprise required a large and effective labor market and led to the growth of huge cities, in whose slums the laborers lived. They were usually underpaid as the potential labor force was larger than the amount of work available. One effect of the Industrial Revolution was to turn capitalism into a fully fledged social, industrial and economic system. Another—ironically—was to create socialism, a system of thought antithetical to capitalism but closely linked to it.

Although the standard of living of the working poor had been severely reduced during the early years of the Industrial Revolution, it began to rise from about the beginning of the nineteenth century. The wave of industrial violence represented by the Luddites soon died away, and a new and more fundamental challenge to capitalism would be mounted.

In Britain the word "socialist" was first used in 1827 by Robert Owen (1771–1858). Owen, a successful businessman, tried to develop a system of cooperatives, that would eliminate the need for competition. Practical difficulties and the failure of the liberalizing legislation of the 1830s to produce any profound social change led Owen in his later years to adopt increasingly ill-formulated and doctrinaire views, that met less and less support as they grew more and more extreme. Partly as a result of Owen's failure to hold the interest of more than a tiny minority of working people, British socialism tended to be much more moderate than its continental counterpart.

Owen did, however, have a major effect at a practical level. His attempts to create "model villages" were successful, although not very long lived. His enthusiastic advocacy of trade unionism led to the foundation of the Grand National Consolidated Trades Union in England in 1833 and a general trade union in the United States. Although, largely as a result of governments' persecution of unionists, neither of these bodies survived, many of the smaller unions that had joined them did, and these provided the nucleus of the later trade-union movement.

It was, however, in France that socialist ideas found their real intellectual home, although at first they were marked by the same kind of eccentricity as Owen's. French socialism was encouraged by rose-tinted memories of the 1789 Revolution, which seemed to embody the ideals of freedom popularized by the Enlightenment. The disorganized ideas of Count Henry de Saint-Simon (1760–1825) provided the basis for later socialist ideas, in particular the idea of a class struggle. A more disciplined thinker and a man more aware of the real problems of the working class than the wealthy and aristocratic Saint-Simon was Charles Fourier (1772–1837). He drew attention to the basic problems inherent in an uncontrolled capitalist economy—that manufacturers seek to produce poor-quality goods in order to maximize their profits, and that profits are used neither for the benefit of the workers who made them nor for the benefit of the society in which they were made. Like Owen, Fourier advocated the development of cooperatives, which he called phalanxes. However, his ideas—like those of Owen—had little appeal for contemporaries, and—also like Owen—he got carried away into more and more unrealistic theorizing.

It is easy to dismiss the early socialists, Saint-Simon, Fourier and Owen, as mere utopians, whose ideas were totally divorced from reality. The element of fantasy in their theories derived largely from the hostility of the intellectual environment in which they lived. Until trade unionism found a wide acceptance and the working class was able to make society feel its needs and desires, it was almost impossible for individuals to express the unformulated aspirations of that class. It could only be done by imposing religious or high moral ideas on society, and since the clergy—the official guardians of religion and morality—tended to support the status quo, it was inevitable that the expression of socialist ideas would at first be somewhat eccentric.

In the years before the 1848 revolutions, socialist ideas became more realistic, and increasing efforts were made to define the means by which a just society could be brought into being. This was largely due to the work of two French authors, Louis Blanc (1811–82) and P. J. Proudhon (1809–65), but in 1848 the German political philosophers Karl Marx (1818–83) and Friedrich Engels (1820–95) published a short pamphlet that was to become the most influential document in the development of socialism.

Saint-Simon, radical French philosopher.

1848

A Manifesto for the Masses

"The proletarians . . . have a whole world to conquer" concluded the authors of the Communist Manifesto, *a succinct twenty-three-page document issued in London in February of 1848. The document's authors—Karl Marx and Friedrich Engels—were both exiles from their native Germany. The bold conclusion that they reached in the closing paragraph of the* Manifesto *was the result of months of collaboration and years of study. In the course of their research, Marx and Engels had considered (and then either incorporated or rejected) the overlapping tenets of Chartism, utopian socialism, and a dozen similar contemporary socialist movements. Their synthesis concluded with a phrase that was to become international Communism's clarion call, one that would inspire riots and revolution around the world: "Workers of the world, unite!"*

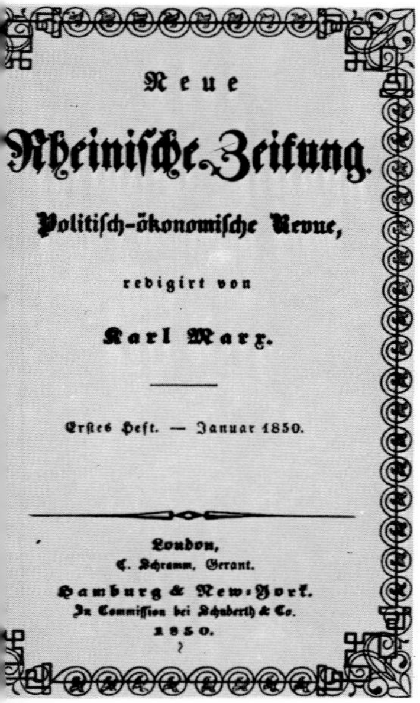
Neue
Rheinische Zeitung.
Politisch-ökonomische Revue,
redigirt von
Karl Marx.
Erstes Heft. — Januar 1850.
London,
C. Schramm, Gerant.
Hamburg & New-York.
In Commission bei Schuberth & Co.
1850.

Title-page of the first issue of the *Neue Rheinische Zeitung* to appear after the 1848 revolutions, edited by Marx.

Opposite Karl Marx, the father of Communism.

A specter haunts Europe—the specter of communism. All the powers of old Europe have entered into a holy alliance to hunt down and exorcise this specter: the Pope and the Tsar, Metternich and Guizot, the French radicals and the German police.

Thus begins the *Communist Manifesto*, a twenty-three-page document that first appeared in London at the end of February, 1848. Its German coauthors, Karl Marx and Friedrich Engels, were both excellent theorists as well as fiery agitators. They had been commissioned by the International Communist Federation to outline the concepts, characteristics and aims of the Communist movement. At that time the Federation was only one of the many socialist groups in existence. Its members were refugees and political outcasts of various nationalities, most of them workers and craftsmen living in several European capitals under the leadership of the German Communist cell.

Socialism, together with its Communist offshoot, had begun to appear in both France and England in the 1820s. It took the form of an intellectual and emotional protest against the paradoxical situation that the historian E. Halévy denounced as "pauperism engendered by the invention of machinery." Between 1820 and 1830, the progressive ideas of Marx' three great forerunners began to circulate. Those men—Robert Owen in England and the Count of Saint-Simon and Charles Fourier in France—were what one might term utopian socialists. They were indefatigable in their attempts to bring about social reform, and they dreamed of a perfect society in which the exploitation of man by man would no longer exist. They made little or no attempt, however, to deal with the vital problems of state, government or political power, and they reckoned on achieving their aims through persuasion rather than revolution.

The Communist movement in France, on the other hand, was fanatically republican, egalitarian and revolutionary. It represented a trend toward violent and direct action against the established order, and in both its ideas and its membership it had far more appeal for the working class. The leaders of this "working-class socialism" deliberately challenged utopian socialism, which had grown fashionable in the *salons*. They suspected, not without reason, that this form of socialism was more concerned with reforming the old capitalist structure of society than with replacing it with a brand new world.

The clandestine atmosphere of conspiracy and revolutionary violence that characterized the republican secret societies—especially the society known as the Seasons—during the reign of Louis Philippe was fertile ground for the growth of the spontaneous type of Communism that existed up to 1840. In May, 1839, an uprising inspired by the Seasons was crushed by the French Army and the National Guard. A German secret society called the Federation of the Just, which had taken part in the insurrection, was virtually wiped out. The members of this federation, whose motto was "all men are brothers," were craftsmen, workmen and a few progressive intellectuals. They had been steeped in the atmosphere of the Parisian Communist movement, but they still retained certain ideals and tendencies that were alien to it. The theorist and leader of the Federation of the Just was a tailor named Weitling, the son of a French officer and a German maidservant. His steadfast belief in revolutionary action was combined with a passionate longing for evangelical fraternity.

The 1839 uprising was followed by a decade of apparent calmness, but beneath the surface violent upheavals were going on. Paris, the great center of the European revolutionary movement, had become the cradle of social theories and ideals and the meeting place for exiles, revolutionaries and agitators from every country and from all levels of society. Theories varied widely: Etienne Cabet's nonviolent, idealistic version of Communism was based on dreams of future utopias; Louis Blanc's

THE RED REPUBLICAN:

EQUALITY, LIBERTY, FRATERNITY.

EDITED BY G. JULIAN HARNEY.

No. 21.—Vol. I.] SATURDAY, NOVEMBER 9, 1850. [Price One Penny.

German Communism.

MANIFESTO OF THE GERMAN COMMUNIST PARTY.

(Published in February, 1848.)

The following Manifesto, which has since been adopted by all fractions of German Communists, was drawn up in the German anguage, in January 1848, by Citizens *Charles Marx* and *Frederic Engels.* It was mmediately printed in London, in the German language, and published a few days efore the outbreak of the Revolution of 'ebruary. The turmoil consequent upon hat great event made it impossible to carry ut, at that time, the intention of translating into all the languages of civilized Europe. 'here exist two different French versions of in manuscript, but under the present opressive laws of France, the publication of ither of them has been found impracticable. he English reader will be enabled, by the llowing excellent translation of this importat document, to judge of the plans and inciples of the most advanced party of the erman Revolutionists.

It must not be forgotten, that the whole of is Manifesto was written and printed before e Revolution of February.

A frightful hobgoblin stalks throughout Europe. e are haunted by a ghost, the ghost of Commusm. All the Powers of the Past have joined in a ly crusade to lay this ghost to rest,—the Pope d the Czar, Metternich and Guizot, French Racals and German police agents. Where is the position which has not been accused of Commusm by its enemies in Power? And where the position that has not hurled this blighting accuion at the heads of the more advanced opposinists, as well as at those of its official enemies?

Two things appear on considering these facts. I. The ruling Powers of Europe acknowledge Communism to be also a Power. II. It is time for the Communists to lay before the world an account of their aims and tendencies, and to oppose these silly fables about the bugbear of Communism, by a manifesto of the Communist Party.

CHAPTER I.

BOURGEOIS AND PROLETARIANS.

Hitherto the history of Society has been the history of the battles between the classes composing it. Freemen and Slaves, Patricians and Plebeians, Nobles and Serfs, Members of Guilds and journeymen,—in a word, the oppressors and the oppressed, have always stood in direct opposition to each other. The battle between them has sometimes been open, sometimes concealed, but always continuous. A never-ceasing battle, which has invariably ended, either in a revolutionary alteration of the social system, or in the common destruction of the hostile classes.

In the earlier historical epochs we find almost everywhere a minute division of Society into classes or ranks, a variety of grades in social position. In ancient Rome we find Patricians, Knights, Plebeians, Slaves; in mediæval Europe, Feudal Lords, Vassals, Burghers, Journeymen, Serfs; and in each of these classes there were again grades and distinctions. Modern Bourgeois Society, proceeded from the ruins of the feudal system, but the Bourgeois régime has not abolished the antagonism of classes.

New classes, new conditions of oppression, new forms and modes of carrying on the struggle, have been substituted for the old ones. The characteristic of our Epoch, the Era of the Middle-class, or Bourgeoisie, is that the struggle between the various Social Classes, has been reduced to its simplest form. Society incessantly tends to be divided into two great camps, into two great hostile armies, the Bourgeoisie and the Proletariat.

The burgesses of the early Communes sprang from the Serfs of the Middle Ages, and from this Municipal class, were developed the primitive elements of the modern Bourgeoisie. The discovery of the New World, the circumnavigation of Africa, gave the Middleclass—then coming into being—new fields of action. The colonization of America, the opening up of the East Indian and Chinese Markets, the Colonial Trade, the increase of commodities generally and of the means of exchange, gave an impetus, hitherto unknown, to Commerce, Shipping, and Manufactures; and aided the rapid evolution of the revolutionary element in the old decaying, feudal form of Society. The old feudal way of managing the industrial interest by means of guilds and monopolies was not found sufficient for the increased demand caused by the opening up of these new markets. It was replaced by the manufacturing system. Guilds vanished before the industrial Middle-class, and the division of labour between the different corporations was succeeded by the division of labour between the workmen of one and the same great workshop.

But the demand always increased, new markets came into play. The manufacturing system, in its turn, was found to be inadequate. At this point industrial Production was revolutionised by machinery and steam. The modern industrial system was developed in all its gigantic proportions; instead of the industrial Middle-class we find industrial millionaires, chiefs of whole industrial armies, the modern Bourgeois, or Middle-class Capitalists. The discovery of America was the first step towards the formation of a colossal market, embracing the whole world; whereby an immense developement was given to Commerce, and to the means of communication by sea and land. This again reacted upon the industrial system, and the developement of the Bourgeoisie, the increase of their Capital, the superseding of all classes handed down to modern times from the Middle Ages, kept pace with the developement of Production, Trade, and Steam communication.

We find, therefore, that the modern Bourgeoisie are themselves the result of a long process of developement, of a series of revolutions in the modes of Production and Exchange. Each of the degrees of industrial evolution, passed through by the modern Middle-class, was accompanied by a corresponding

The "Communist Manifesto" in *The Red Republican,* a magazine that idolized the republicans of the French Revolution. In the bleak years after 1848, when it was first published, republication of the *Manifesto* encouraged socialists not to abandon their ideals.

socialism was based on the organization of work and called on the state to subsidize the "national workshops." Then, in 1840, Pierre Joseph Proudhon, a typographer and self-educated man, made his appearance on the scene, attracting the shocked attention of the public with his pamphlet *What is Property?* Proudhon condemned private ownership, arguing instead that property should be in the hands of those who actually do the work. According to his theory, voluntary associations formed by these workers eventually would replace tyrannical state governments.

It was in the Paris of the 1840s, the Paris of Proudhon, Louis Blanc, and Cabet, that foreigners burning with revolutionary ideals gathered together. And it was to Paris that Karl Marx, a native of the Rhineland, came toward the end of October, 1843. Marx was an extremely talented twenty-six-year-old Hegelian philosopher. Because his left-wing beliefs excluded him from an academic or journalistic career in Prussia, he was condemned to a life of exile—first in Paris, later in Brussels and finally in London, where he remained until his death in 1883.

In Paris, he became friendly with the Russian Mikhail Bakunin, a dedicated agitator and anarchist and a sworn enemy of the state who at a later date was to become Marx' archenemy. Marx, with his prodigious passion for reading, plunged into the study of the French Revolution. He became conscious for the first time of the problem of classes, and of the proletariat and the working-class movement. He showed a marked preference for Communism over socialism, which was too middle class for his liking. Communism, he believed, was far more suited to the needs and hopes of the working-class proletariat, the class in bondage. Unfortunately, the Communism of that time, as taught and disseminated by its supporters, was doctrinally far too simple for Marx. Nor had he reached the stage of realizing the vital importance of economics. That importance was to be revealed to him by his compatriot Friedrich Engels.

Engels was also a left-wing Hegelian philosopher, two years younger than Marx. He came from a family of rich textile manufacturers, and his father had sent him to England to learn the business. Engels was shocked at the sight of so much misery and poverty among the working classes. He was profoundly interested in Chartism, the movement of the British industrial working class for political reforms, notably universal male suffrage. He compared the movement to the utopian socialism of Owen, became engrossed in the study of the classical economists, and was haunted by the phenomenon of periodic crises of overproduction. It was just at the time that Engels was about to publish his remarkable work, *The Condition of the Working Classes in England* (1845), that he established the close intellectual and emotional relationship with Marx that was to last until Marx' death. The two men were convinced that with their combined knowledge and experience they held all the keys to social evolution, and they set themselves the task, between 1845 and 1847, of working out their doctrine. That doctrine was to be unmistakably proletarian in character as well as strictly scientific in concept and expression. The emancipation of the proletariat would be the work of the proletariat itself—a radical new approach to Communism.

Marx wanted to collaborate with Proudhon, for whom he had the greatest respect. They had long discussions on the subject of Hegel's philosophy during the winter of 1844–45, but Proudhon ultimately refused to work with him, having no wish for another new dogma or religious intolerance. Even worse, Proudhon would not accept the necessity for action, professing that he no longer believed in the virtue of revolution. In May, 1846, there was a complete break between them, and in June of the following year Marx published a pamphlet with the ironic title of *Misère de la Philosophie* (*Poverty of Philosophy*), reversing the title of Proudhon's *Philosophie de la Misère.*

A far more serious and definitive break, which affected the immediate plans of Marx and Engels, had already occurred with the blond tailor Weitling, the theorist of the Federation of the Just. Since the disastrous uprising of 1839 in Paris, the Federation of the Just had gone through a difficult time. In order to avoid punishment, it had broken up and scattered to Switzerland, Belgium and England. A group eventually re-formed in Paris, but by that time London had become the main center of the movement. Dutch, Hungarian, Slavic and Scandinavian exiles in the English capital grouped themselves together around a central German contingent. When the leaders of the London-based movement invited Marx and Engels to become active members of the Federation, they agreed—but only on the condition that Weitling's theory, tainted with utopianism, be replaced by their own political philosophy.

In March, 1846, a stormy meeting took place in Brussels between Weitling, who had come there to justify his opinions, and his two powerful adversaries. A Russian delegate's eyewitness account of this meeting describes Engels as tall, upright and distinguished, "like an Englishman"; Marx, looking like a lion under his mane of thick black hair, was revealed by the dictatorial, cutting tone in his voice. Marx accused Weitling of deceiving the people by inciting them to revolt without having any solid foundations on which to base his action. His reply to Weitling's moving defense was to strike the table with his fist, causing the lamp to shake, and comment: "Ignorance has never helped anyone yet!"

Marx and Engels emerged victorious from the confrontation in Brussels. During the summer of 1847 the Federation of the Just accepted their doctrine and changed its name to the International Communist Federation. Their slogan "all men are brothers" was replaced by "workers of the world, unite," and the task of drawing up a manifesto presenting the views and aims of these new-style Communists was given to Marx in collaboration with Engels. The latter's first draft took the form of a catechism with twenty-five questions and answers, but that format was soon abandoned in favor of a straightforward narrative, presented almost as a historical drama. Because of the exceptional talent of the authors, there is an extraordinary mythical quality and feeling of enchantment about their analysis, even though it claims to be completely scientific in its approach.

Marx and Engels' fundamental premise in the *Manifesto* was that "the history of all human societies up to the present time has been the history of the class struggle." From this premise sprang the inescapable laws governing historical developments. The first prehistoric societies almost certainly had been classless, with goods belonging to all. But that Communist condition had disappeared when certain men seized control of the land, forcing others to work for them. Thus society became divided into the exploiters and the exploited. This feudal agricultural system was itself replaced when an emerging commercial class, the capitalists, established a manufacturing economy through a series of revolutions in methods of production and means of communication. Later on, manufacture was in turn replaced by the infinitely superior methods of large-scale industry. As a result of the expansion of trade and the establishment of world markets, the industrial middle class, or capitalists, had to make way for industrial magnates, owners of huge industrial complexes—the modern bourgeoisie. In this way, the bourgeoisie itself played an extremely revolutionary role in the course of history.

Such praise, however, was more in the nature of an obituary, since Marx saw the destruction of the modern bourgeoisie as a necessary stage in the historical development of society. According to his theory, every economic system that is based on exploitation carries within it the seeds of its own destruction. In the capitalist system, the bourgeoisie had created "its own gravediggers"—the modern working class, the proletariat. Marx felt certain that at a given stage in history the proletarians, who were constantly growing in numbers, would become conscious of their growing strength. Forced to sell themselves day after day like bales of merchandise, and totally enslaved by capital, they would come to look upon law, ethics and religion as bourgeois prejudices concealing bourgeois interests. Moreover, while all earlier historical movements had been minority movements, or carried out on behalf of minorities, the working-class movement would be a spontaneous surging forward by the vast majority in the interests of that vast majority. The proletariat, the lowest stratum of contemporary

Friedrich Engels, who co-authored the *Manifesto*.

François Guizot, the French Prime Minister, whom the *Manifesto* accused of joining in an unholy alliance with Pope Pius IX, Tsar Nicholas I of Russia and the Austrian Prime Minister, Prince Metternich, to crush the specter of Communism.

Dudley Street, Seven Dials, London, by Doré. Marx's concern with class may in part have sprung from his knowledge of London's slums. Dudley Street was very close to Dean Street where Marx lived for a time in London. Both Marx' sons and his daughter died of privation.

society, could raise itself and stand erect on its own feet only by smashing to pieces the superstructure of that society.

This despotic domination by the proletariat, however, would bear no resemblance whatsoever to dominations in the past. It would serve merely as a period of transition, a stage in the process leading to the eventual dissolution of all classes and all states. It would represent a transitory historical necessity, for the exploited oppressed class would be able to free itself only "by, at the same time, freeing the whole of society from exploitation, oppression and class struggles, once and for all." The *Communist Manifesto* finished with a call to action:

> The communists . . . openly proclaim that the only way they can achieve their aims is by the violent destruction of the old order of society. The ruling classes may well tremble at the thought of a communist revolution! The proletarians have nothing to lose in the struggle apart from their chains. They have a whole world to conquer—workers of the world, unite!

When the *Manifesto* was first published in London at the end of February, 1848, Paris was in a state of revolution and that revolution spread like an epidemic all over Europe to Sicily, Tuscany, Lombardy, Venice, Naples, Rome, Vienna, and Prussia. It was only in France, however, that a socialist (or partially socialist) revolution took place, with socialist theorists such as Louis Blanc, Pierre Leroux, Philippe Buchez and Proudhon all trying to impose their particular policies. The situation ended tragically: the violent uprising of the Parisian working class during the historic June Days of 1848 was suppressed with considerable difficulty after a battle that raged for four long days in the barricaded streets of the capital.

When the forces of reaction gained total victory after 1850, it seemed as if the working class had been permanently driven back into its original hopeless situation. The socialist theorists returned to their utopian dreams of the years preceding 1848, and it was not until 1864 that the passionate call to action of the *Communist Manifesto* encouraged them to fresh efforts. The International Working Men's Association—which later on was to change its name

Right The British Museum, where Marx wrote *Das Kapital*, as it was in the 1850s.

Robert Owen's institution at New Lanark, Scotland. In his social ideas Owen was a precursor of Marx, but unlike Marx his social attitudes were translated into action.

The view from the Place de la Bastille during the Paris Commune of 1871, when workers erected barricades in the streets.

to the First International—was founded. Within the space of ten years, however, Marx himself had put an end to the First International, after clashing first with Proudhon's supporters and then, far more seriously, with Bakunin and his devotees. Bakunin was a volcanic giant of a Russian whose concept of anarchism rejected any form of temporary dictatorship by the proletariat, or any provisional administration by the state.

Meanwhile, the uprising of the Commune in Paris in 1871—a violent, bloody offshoot of the Franco-Prussian War—had served as a rousing inspiration to the working-class movements in every country. It lacked a realistic basis entirely, however, and achieved very little; moreover, French socialism suffered a severe setback as a result of it. On the other hand, the victory of the Prussians over France, which led to German unity, had a very beneficial effect on German socialism. Marx and Engels took advantage of the opportunity to impose Marxism on the German Social Democratic Party, which was to enjoy a remarkable success in the years to come. At the same time, the *Communist Manifesto* emerged from its state of semiretirement. Its circulation in German, the language in which it had originally been written, led to its being translated into English, French, Russian and many other languages as new socialist parties were created both within and outside Europe in the 1880s. This growth gave rise to the idea of a new International, more powerful and more permanent than the first—and the Second International was founded in Paris in 1889. On May 1, 1890, militant workers demonstrated in both America and Europe and demanded the establishment of an eight-hour working day.

After several years of internal struggle for power, the Second International finally eliminated all the non-Marxist groups, especially the anarchists. Taking as its model the superbly organized German branch of the party—which some thought was too bureaucratic in its structure—the new International described itself as "social-democratic." The former qualification of "communist"—the word that had been deliberately chosen by the authors of the *Manifesto* to emphasize the proletarian violence and the defiance toward the bourgeois world adopted by "scientific socialism"—had apparently been dropped in the course of the organization's development. It was not until the first abortive Russian Revolution of 1905—which momentarily shook the tsarist regime, encouraged the formation of *soviets,* or councils of worker delegates, brought Trotsky to the fore and provided Lenin, the Bolshevik leader, with valuable experience—that violence and defiance were reinstated.

The social-democratic International was swept out of existence by the catastrophic world war of 1914–18; it was totally unable to prevent the war's outbreak or the vast majority of the socialist leaders and members from supporting their own countries. But during the war, Lenin set about founding a new body that was genuinely dedicated to world revolution; in his eyes, the Russian Revolution would be by no means the most important. He intended that this new International, which he would rebuild on the ruins of the second, should be efficient, highly disciplined and controlled by professional revolutionaries. He would call this Third International "Communist" in memory of the original *Communist Manifesto,* the historic document out of which the modern Communist movement had developed.

JEAN JACQUES CHEVALLIER

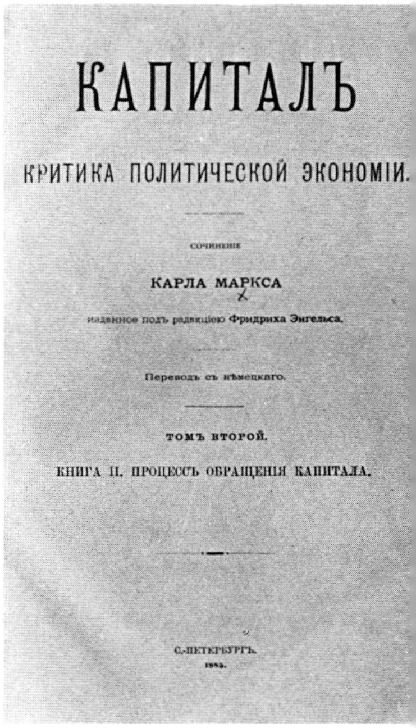

КАПИТАЛЪ

КРИТИКА ПОЛИТИЧЕСКОЙ ЭКОНОМІИ.

СОЧИНЕНІЕ

КАРЛА МАРКСА

изданное подъ редакціею Фридриха Энгельса.

Переводъ съ нѣмецкаго.

ТОМЪ ВТОРОЙ.

КНИГА II. ПРОЦЕССЪ ОБРАЩЕНІЯ КАПИТАЛА.

С.-ПЕТЕРБУРГЪ.

1885.

The title-page of the second volume of the Russian edition of *Das Kapital,* published in 1855. This translation has played an important role in subsequent European history as a result of the Communist Revolution in Russia.

Public unrest

By the end of 1848 it was clear that the old order would withstand the impact of revolution. The Hohenzollern dynasty still reigned in Berlin and the House of Hapsburg still ruled in Vienna (under the eighteen-year-old Emperor Francis Joseph). No radical movement threatened the Romanov throne in Russia, and although the Pope had been forced to flee to the fortified seaport of Gaeta, north of Naples, the governments of Roman Catholic Europe were all but competing with each other for the honor of restoring his Holiness to Rome. Even the French had eschewed socialism; caught up in the "Napoleonic legend," they had elected Napoleon I's nephew, Charles Louis Napoleon Bonaparte, as President of the Second Republic. The new President's lack of enthusiasm for the Republic soon became apparent. His election campaign had shown that he was prepared to make almost any promise in order to gain the presidency—but he soon made it clear that he was not satisfied with the presidency. In 1851 he organized a coup d'état that gave him absolute power and the imperial title. But as Emperor, Napoleon III showed that his ambition was not only personal. The rapid industrialization of France during the next three decades was largely due to his impetus and enthusiasm.

The radical tide was on the ebb throughout Europe by Christmas of 1848, but it had deposited clusters of determined rebels who were still gasping for survival among the flotsam of the barricades. The Roman Republic of Giuseppe Mazzini (1805–72) and Giuseppe Garibaldi (1807–82) successfully defied the forces of repression until it was crushed by an army of the French Republic in July. The Venetians, led by liberal patriot Daniele Manin (1804–57), retained their independence until August, 1849, despite a cholera epidemic and a long siege by the Austrians.

The lying-in-state of the Berlin victims of March, 1848.

Peace had returned to Germany by 1849, but the federal constitution written by the all-German assembly that had met in Frankfurt the winter of 1848 proved unacceptable to the German princes. In the spring those deputies were dismissed by Prussian soldiers. In Hungary by contrast there was no peace that Christmas. A grim civil war dragged on in the featureless steppeland of the middle Danube as the Magyars of Lajos Kossuth (1802–94) resisted attempts by Austrians and Croats to restore the united Hapsburg Empire from which Hungary had sought its freedom. In August, 1849, the Hungarian will for national unity and independence finally broke, and the last Magyar militia surrendered to the Russian troops that Tsar Nicholas I, an ever-vigilant gendarme of autocracy, had put at the disposal of the young Francis Joseph. By the late summer of 1849 counterrevolution was triumphant throughout Europe.

American population growth

While Europe was plunged into revolution in 1848, the United States continued its rapid development and expansion. Between 1790, the year of the first American census, and 1860, when the election of Abraham Lincoln as President brought America to the brink of civil war, the population rose from just under four million to over thirty-one million, an eightfold rise in seventy years. As by 1820 the population had not yet reached ten million, the bulk of this growth took place in-between 1820 and 1860. The growth was due both to a rapid natural increase and to massive immigration, although it was only gradually that immigration became the major factor in America's population growth.

Broadway, New York, in the 1850s.

Immigration was due in most cases more to conditions in Europe than to those in America, and it is not surprising that it was in the decade that saw both the great famine in Ireland and the 1848 risings that immigration really began to grow. By 1860 fourteen percent of the population had been foreign born, a percentage that was to stay fairly constant for the rest of the century. The Irish, of whom there about a million and a half, were the largest immigrant group—indeed there were already far more Irish in America than there were in Ireland. Germans and Austrians made up a group that was little smaller (1,300,000), and like the Irish most of them arrived between 1846 and 1856. The Italians, who were later to dominate the immigrant community, were not yet emigrating to America; in 1860 they numbered less than twelve thousand.

America benefited enormously from the wave of unrest that swept across Europe in 1848. The growth in immigrant numbers provided the cities of the East Coast with a ready labor force for industry and railroad construction. Over four thousand German-speaking refugees—the vanguard of an invasion that made Milwaukee virtually a German city within ten years—settled in Wisconsin. The contribution of these ardent idealists to American life was considerable. The influential Carl Schurz (1829–1906), the best-known German to live in Wisconsin, supported the Republicans so effectively in the 1860 election that he was instrumental in helping to put Lincoln in the White House. The 1848 revolutions did indeed have far-reaching ramifications.

American territorial expansion

Little less dramatic than the expansion in America's population was the growth in the territory of the United States. The speed with which the Western Territory was settled suggests that as early as the 1790s there was a need for further expansion to satisfy land-hungry settlers. In the early years of the Republic, the government's attempts to sell land had been unsuccessful; the minimum price—$2 per acre—charged by the government was higher than that charged by many individual states. In 1820 the government had reduced the price to $1.20 per acre, and land sales had grown rapidly as a result. The first immigrants to the west and southwest had not really been settlers; they were pioneers—trappers, hunters and adventurers—who took little interest in settling on the land. It was only gradually that permanent settlements grew up and that land was cultivated.

The purchase of the Louisiana Territory was unable to satisfy the land hunger that engulfed the United States during the early decades of the nineteenth century, particularly as so much of it was inaccessible. The result was that by 1835 the only parts of the newly acquired region that had become states were Louisiana (formerly the Territory of Orleans) and Missouri. But the search for new land continued. Farther west, Jefferson had ordered exploration of the Pacific Territory to the north of

discovery of gold fuel American expansionism

Spanish California, and this came to be known as the Oregon Country. Much of this territory was disputed by the United States and Britain's Hudson's Bay Company, which in practice administered the area. However, in 1846, after substantial American immigration, Britain's claims were abandoned. Settlement in the far west was encouraged by many factors: missionary zeal; difficulties in the already-settled regions of the midwest; good climatic conditions and rich land; generous land grants. Prospects had to be good to justify the long and dangerous journey

A pioneer family resting before their covered wagons on the westward trek.

from the east coast or the Mississippi Valley.

War with Mexico

More important than the aquisition of Oregon was the growing hostility with Mexico as America colonized areas claimed or controlled by Mexico. At first the United States government showed little enthusiasm for a war with its southern neighbor, thereby causing considerable presidential reluctance to stir up the Mexicans by admitting independent Texas to the Union. It was not until 1845 that Texas finally became one of the United States.

The myth of the American frontiersman encouraged many to enter Mexico's other northern provinces, New Mexico and California. The new President, James Polk, elected in 1844, was more favorable to a militant line than his predecessor, John Tyler, had been. Polk showed no concern for legality; he wanted New Mexico and California and was prepared to fight if need be. There were already more Americans than Mexicans in California, and when war broke out in January, 1846, California was quickly annexed, to be followed by New Mexico within a few months.

But, before Mexico would recognize the loss of the sparsely populated but potentially rich north, an American army had to be sent into Mexico itself. It was only after the fall of Mexico City that the Mexicans were willing to accept defeat. By 1848 the war was over and the United States had grown by a million square miles.

Gold

The newly conquered lands were settled more quickly than anyone had expected, largely as the result of the discovery of gold. The California Gold Rush began in December, 1848, after gold was discovered at Sutter's Mill thirty miles from Sacramento. In the new trading post of San Francisco, rumors rapidly caused excitement to rise to fever pitch. Within a month of President Polk's confirmation to Congress that gold had been discovered, more than sixty vessels crammed with fortune-seekers were on their way around Cape Horn. As soon as the winter snow receded, thousands of wagons set off westward along the trail from Santa Fé. Many died along the route from cholera, picked up at contaminated waterholes in the Great Plains, or in the Rockies from a mysterious "mountain fever." Some were attacked by Indians and others perished from starvation in the awesome desolation of the Sierra Nevada. Yet more than eighty thousand people arrived at the ramshackle mining camps before the end of the year, and San Francisco became a city of over twenty-five thousand inhabitants (larger than Boston had been at the start of the century). Vigilante committees and lynch law—both common forms of frontier justice—proved to be ineffective means of maintaining law and order, and even the admis-

A gold digger at work in Colorado

sion of California as the thirty-first state in 1850 failed to assure ordered government.

During the late 1840s and the 1850s countless fortunes were made and lost in the shanty towns of the Mother Lode. The discovery of silver in Nevada eventually tempted moves eastward to Mount Davidson, and soon after that gold was found in Colorado. From the 1850s on, wealth came to those not "with a washbowl on my knee," but to the engineers who could afford expensive machinery. The true "miners' frontier," a crudely vigorous society of retributive democracy, was a phenomenon of the 1850s.

Other areas benefited from the Gold Rush less directly. The increase in the number of travelers brought wealth to the Mormons who had trekked to the Great Salt Lake the year before, and provided them with funds to build a temple and a tabernacle below the Wasatch mountains.

But the expansion of American society did not prevent political and social quarrels between North and South. The desire of Californians to ban slavery became an issue that threatened to destroy the United States. The compromise reached in 1850 only delayed the deeply rooted disagreements between those who favored and those who opposed slavery from clashing headlong.

A southwestern view of the rapidly growing town of San Francisco in 1850.

The Compromise of 1850

The question whether to admit California to the Union hinged on the concept of slavery. To the industrial North it was unthinkable to extend slavery to places where it had never been—and sentiment for its total abolition was growing. Slavery was an essential part of the way of life of the agrarian South, and admitting more antislavery than slave-holding states promised disaster. Henry Clay's compromise brought California into the Union but begged the real question. It did, however, stave off for ten years the moment when North and South would take up arms to settle once and for all whose view would prevail.

At the end of 1819 Missouri, part of the Louisiana Territory purchased by Thomas Jefferson in 1803, applied for admission to the United States as a slave state. "This momentous question," Jefferson wrote from his retirement, "like a fire-bell in the night awakened and filled me with terror. I considered it at once as the knell of the Union." Jefferson's forebodings were well founded. Once America had thrown off the British yoke and established herself as the United States, the dominant political theme in American history resolved itself into a struggle for power and influence between the North and the South. That struggle was partly one between competing economic systems, between the plantation agriculture of the South and the urban industry and commerce of the North. But above all it was a struggle over the future of slavery in the new nation.

In the territory of the Louisiana Purchase the American government had done nothing to disturb slavery as it existed under French and Spanish law, and in the westward rush of settlers after the War of 1812, several thousands of slave owners pushed into Texas and Missouri with their slaves. In 1821 Missouri was admitted to the Union as a slave state—a state in which slavery was legal. But as part of what became known as the Missouri Compromise, the northeastern state of Maine was admitted as a free state—in which slavery was outlawed. That left the balance of free and slave states at twelve each. In addition, it was enacted that henceforth slavery was to be prohibited north of 36° 30′.

That compromise put the question to rest for a time; but in 1836, when Texas won independence from Mexico, it was stirred up again. When American settlers had first gone to Texas there were no Indian peons and the soil offered such a rich opportunity for the culture of sugar and cotton that Southern planters refused to settle unless allowed to take their slaves with them. Hence slavery had developed despite the abolitionist decrees and laws of the Mexican government.

When Texas broke away from Mexico and declared itself an independent republic, it adopted a slave constitution. John C. Calhoun, Senator for South Carolina and the most articulate of the Southern defenders of slavery, called for the annexation by America of the Lone Star Republic (Texas had adopted a flag with a single star). The North was alarmed by the threat to the North–South political balance that Calhoun's suggestion posed. In 1837 the Vermont legislature "solemnly protested" against the entry into the Union of any state in which slavery was not banned. Calhoun's reply was that any attempt to exclude a state because of its "peculiar institution" would lead to the dissolution of the United States.

The Southern states were already beginning to realize that they had received the short end of the bargain made in 1820. Since then, Arkansas and Michigan had come into the Union, making thirteen free and thirteen slave states. Waiting in the wings were four more territories: Florida, Wisconsin, Iowa and Minnesota. They would soon be demanding statehood and only Florida was a slave territory. Even more free lands would be clamoring to enter if the Indiana barrier to the Great Plains were broken. The issue, then, was finely poised; could a formula be found for admitting new states that would satisfy both the North and the South on the question of slavery and so preserve the Union?

In 1844 the presidential election was won by the little-known former governor of Tennessee, James Polk. Polk was the nominee of the Democratic Party, the old Southern party of Jefferson under a new name. He won the election on the cry of the annexation of Texas and Oregon. Polk wanted both and he also wanted California, a golden land with every variety of climate and soil, forests of

Detail of prayer-meeting in Uncle Tom's cabin from *Uncle Tom's Cabin.* The book became an important factor in solidifying Northern sentiment against slavery.

Opposite President Zachary Taylor, "Old Rough and Ready." His sudden death removed one of the major opponents to Clay's compromise.

giant redwoods, broad valleys suitable for wheat farming, extensive pasture, rich minerals and the magnificent natural harbors of San Francisco and San Diego. So badly did Polk want California (and so much did he fear that France or Great Britain might seize it) that he baited Mexico into war in order to get it.

In 1845 the United States annexed the Republic of Texas, which Mexico still regarded as a rebellious province under her authority. The ensuing war between the United States and Mexico ended in February, 1848, with the signing of the Treaty of Guadalupe Hidalgo. Mexico ceded Texas, New Mexico and Upper California to the United States. Upper California included what were to become the states of California, Utah and Nevada, large sections of New Mexico and Arizona and parts of Colorado and Wyoming. With that treaty the United States had rounded out her continental territory almost to its present limits. (The process was completed in 1853 when the "Gadsden Purchase" transferred the Gila River Valley in southern Arizona and a portion of southern New Mexico from Mexico to the United States.)

The acquisition of so much new land brought the antagonism between proslavery and antislavery interests, an antagonism which had been smoldering for a decade, out into the open.

On August 8, 1846, about three months after the outbreak of the Mexican War, an obscure Democratic congressman from the manufacturing state of Pennsylvania, David Wilmot, speaking in the debate on President Polk's request for a secret appropriation of $2,000,000 with which to bribe the Mexican government into surrendering California, remarked that although he had no objection to the purchase of California, he did not believe it to be compatible with the principles of democracy to extend slavery into a free territory. He therefore proposed as an amendment to the appropriation bill the qualification that in any lands bought by the United States "neither slavery nor involuntary servitude shall ever exist." That amendment became known as the "Wilmot Proviso."

Cotton-picking in the South. With the spread of the cotton culture, Southern sentiment turned increasingly toward slavery.

Southern California, with its hot climate and rich soil, was a natural home for slavery, once introduced, to thrive and multiply. Indeed it was there that Chinese and Mexican labor was later callously exploited. For the South, however, the blocking of slavery in California itself was not really the issue. Most Southerners believed that the geography of the West erected a barrier against the spreading of slavery to California. They looked upon the Wilmot Proviso, nevertheless, as a slur upon their "peculiar institution." More important, they were concerned about the future balance of power in the nation.

In 1789 the population of the country had been about equally distributed between North and South. By 1820, in a population of about ten million, the North had a majority of 667,000. And by the 1840s the stream of European immigration was increasing the Northern preponderance, since immigrants were drawn by jobs in Northern industries and were repelled by the prospect of working in a slave economy. The Southern planters were therefore fighting against the census returns and against the development of the American economy. The rapid growth of Northern industries, the extension of railways, the expansion of foreign trade and the growing attachment of farming regions in the West to the centers of finance through transportation and credit facilities were making a dynamic thrust too powerful for the planters, operating in a limited territory on soil of diminishing fertility, to resist. For the South the time had come when it had to expand or die.

That was why the South, unconcerned about California itself, was aroused by the Wilmot Proviso. The American Constitution provides for two Houses of Congress. The size of a state's representation in the House of Representatives is proportionate to its population. There the North already had control. In the Senate each state has two members, and there the balance was still even. But if the admission of new states gave the North control of the Senate, too, then the day when Congress would pass a constitutional amendment outlawing slavery *everywhere* might not be far off. Wilmot's proposal would effectively seal off the South, confine it to its existing size, while opening up the possibility of a flood of free states entering the Union.

The North, whose conscience was being stirred by the mounting Abolitionist campaign, took the line that it was monstrous to introduce slavery into

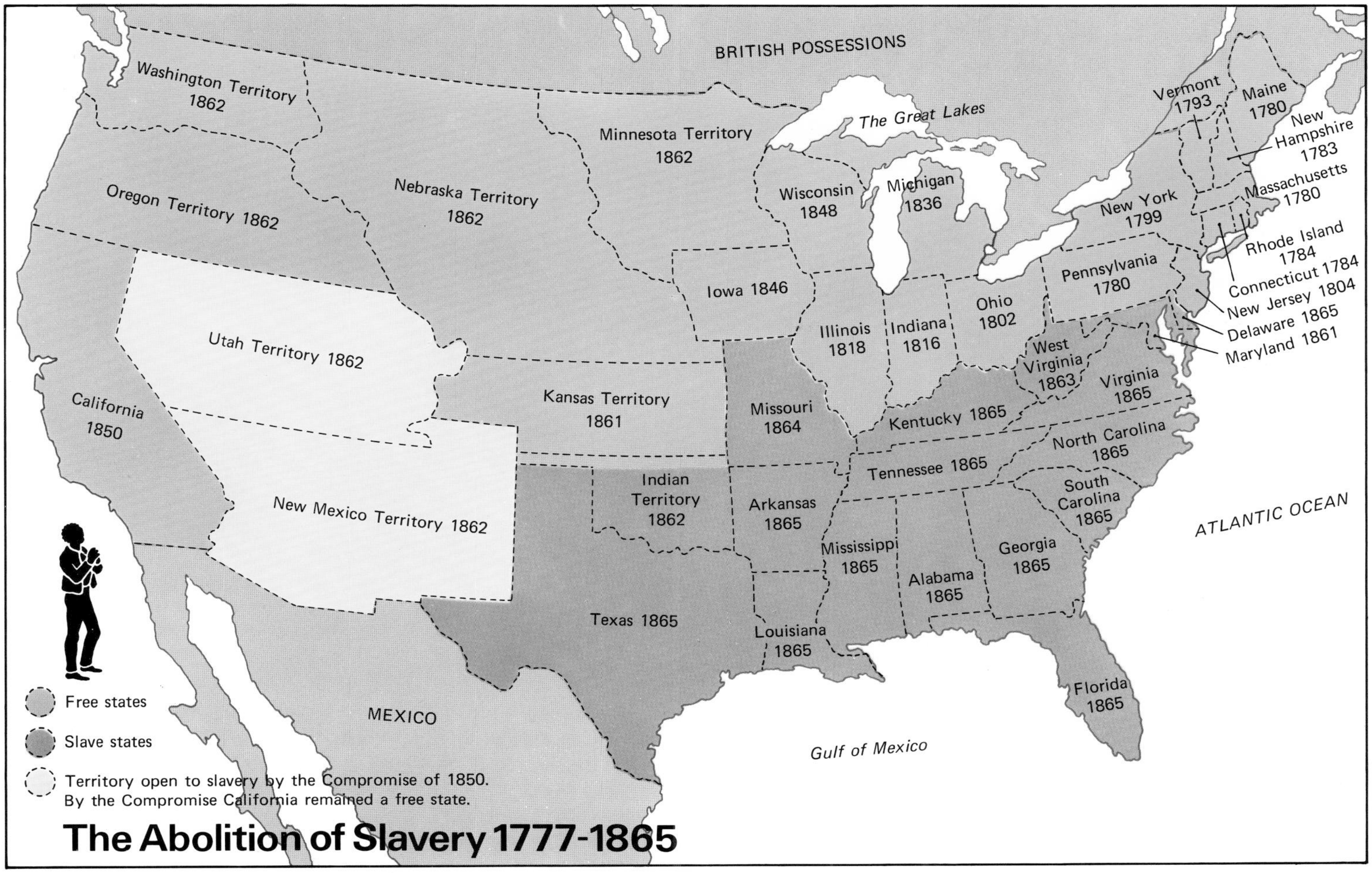

The Abolition of Slavery 1777-1865

territories where it had never before existed. In previous territorial acquisitions—Louisiana and Florida—slavery had already been accepted before the areas became part of the United States. But in California and future free territories the North, by and large, supported the principle of the Wilmot Proviso.

President Polk suggested an obvious compromise: that the 36° 30′ line established in 1820 for the area acquired by the Louisiana Purchase be applied to the territories won in the war with Mexico. This was a solution that failed to satisfy either side. Wilmot's amendment was not passed; nor was any other solution found. There the matter rested. Polk's term of office ended in March, 1849, without anything having been done about the status of California, Utah or New Mexico.

A long time might have passed before Congress broke the deadlock had it not been for a fortuitous event of signal importance. In January, 1848, the world was startled to learn that gold had been discovered in the millrace of John Sutter in the Sacramento Valley. By the end of the year everyone in America, Europe and Australia had heard of the overnight fortunes that were being made by gold panners in California, fortunes made simply by separating the grains of gold from the sand of river beds in a common washbowl. In 1849 the great Gold Rush began. In all, eighty thousand prospectors made the trek to California, either by routes via Cape Horn or Panama or overland from the eastern seaboard.

The Gold Rush brought the slavery crisis to a head. Hitherto little had been done by the deadlocked Congress about the government of California. It was still, in theory, under military government; in practice, government scarcely existed. Officials appointed by the military government administered any sort of law they wished—including lynch law. The sudden spurt of population led California to bypass the dithering Congress and set up its own government. With the blessing of Polk's successor in the White House, General Zachary Taylor, a convention met at Monterey in September, 1849, and drafted a state constitution that prohibited slavery. Without waiting for approval from Congress, California elected a governor and a state legislature that convened in 1850. All that remained to be achieved was admission into the Union. On that issue the Union was nearly split.

Ever since the Constitutional Convention had convened in 1787, the Southern states had been jealous guardians of the doctrine of "states' rights." Suspicious of a distant, bureaucratic, central power, they had stuck to a strict interpretation of the Constitution, which gave to the

Sailing to California in search of gold. Following confirmation that gold had been discovered more than sixty vessels rounded Cape Horn.

federal government narrow, defined fields of authority and left everything else to the state governments. They had, therefore, all along admitted the right of a state to prohibit or legalize slavery according to its own lights. But if California were admitted as a free state the slave states would lose more than half of the new conquests from Mexico. Throughout 1849 Southern anxieties deepened. From all sides—New England, Great Britain, Mexico and now California—slavery was under attack. For Southerners the choice now before them was either expansion in order to survive within the Union or secession from the Union in order to survive as a separate slave-holding republic. When Congress reassembled in December, 1849, California applied for admission to the Union as a free state and, in order to apply pressure to the Representatives, the South began to prepare for a Southern Convention, intended to be a stepping stone to the formation of an independent confederacy if necessary.

President Taylor, the fourth soldier to have become President, was a man of no political experience. A professional soldier for forty years, he had never, before assuming office, even voted in a presidential election. His view of politics was simple. He was himself a slave owner, but he was devoid of proslavery sentiment. In addition he was under the influence of a rising young Abolitionist politician, Senator William Seward of New York, the rival from whom Abraham Lincoln was to wrest the presidential nomination of the newly formed Republican Party in 1860. Taylor saw no reason why California should not be a free state if that was what it wanted to be; and he saw no reason why the South should have to be bribed to admit California as a free state. He therefore recommended the immediate admission of California and the organization of Utah and New Mexico as territorial governments without reference to slavery. To Southerners who protested against this proposal he promised to crush secession, even if he had to lead the army himself to accomplish his purpose.

That was a naive approach to the crisis. Henry Clay, the wily and experienced Senator from Kentucky, knowing that however bravely Taylor talked, the Union was not yet ready to meet the threat of secession, drafted for Congress a compromise settlement. It consisted of five main proposals: the admission of California as a free state, the organization of Utah and New Mexico as territorial governments free to decide the slavery question for themselves, a new, stringent fugitive slave law, the abolition of the slave trade in the District of Columbia and the assumption by the federal government of the Texan national debt.

Those resolutions were the occasion of one of the most memorable Senate debates in American history, in an age when votes in Congress were still often swayed by oratory. The debate was dominated by a triumvirate of men now near the end of famous careers, men who for more than a generation had been the chief molders of Senate opinion: Clay, Calhoun and Daniel Webster.

Clay, now haggard in appearance and faltering in voice, opened the debate with a passionate defense of his proposals and of the Union. He appealed to the North for concession and to the South for moderation and peace. The North had

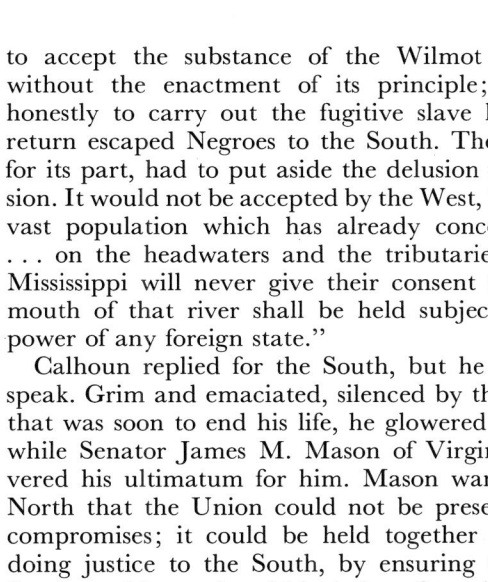

John C. Calhoun, champion of states' rights, slavery and the Southern cause.

to accept the substance of the Wilmot Proviso without the enactment of its principle; it had honestly to carry out the fugitive slave law and return escaped Negroes to the South. The South, for its part, had to put aside the delusion of secession. It would not be accepted by the West, ". . . the vast population which has already concentrated . . . on the headwaters and the tributaries of the Mississippi will never give their consent that the mouth of that river shall be held subject to the power of any foreign state."

Calhoun replied for the South, but he did not speak. Grim and emaciated, silenced by the illness that was soon to end his life, he glowered at Clay while Senator James M. Mason of Virginia delivered his ultimatum for him. Mason warned the North that the Union could not be preserved by compromises; it could be held together only by doing justice to the South, by ensuring that the South could remain within it in safety. And that meant ending the agitation over slavery, conceding to the slave states an equal portion of the new lands by allowing slavery in California and New Mexico, and returning to the Southern states an equal voice in the federal government (by which was implied a dual executive, one president elected by the North, one by the South, each with a veto power). In

Procession in San Francisco in celebration of California's admission into the Union as a free state. Before admission the people of California had drafted a state constitution prohibiting slavery.

Right Daniel Webster who strongly supported the compromise measures and persuaded Northerners to accept the fugitive slave law.

effect Calhoun delivered to the North an ultimatum: "justice" to the South or the breakup of the Union.

Three days later Daniel Webster made his last great Senate speech. It was not very different from Clay's. Attacking both the Abolitionists and the Wilmot Proviso, he pleaded for the preservation of the Union. Webster represented Massachusetts and his last great service to the nation was to persuade the Northerners that they must accept the fugitive slave law if they wanted to reach a settlement with the South.

By the time that Webster spoke the debate had been going on for six weeks. For all Clay's efforts, the two sides were still hopelessly stalemated. Tempers were rising—senators exchanged body blows on the Senate floor, and one Senator was threatened by another with a cocked and loaded revolver. Two events broke the deadlock. In July the sudden death of President Taylor removed one of the major opponents to Clay's compromise and elevated to the presidency Millard Fillmore, a New York Whig who was favorable to it. Before that, in June, the Southern Convention—which met at Nashville, Tennessee, deprived of the leadership of Calhoun, who had died in March—adjourned without taking any action. Secession had been avoided. The Southern bluff had been called. In

Crossing the Rockies. In the Gold Rush many fortune-seekers died in the Rockies from a mysterious "mountain fever."

September the five proposals of Clay were at last enacted into law as the Compromise of 1850.

It was a compromise that was to last for ten years. As a temporary expedient it was successful. Certainly if California had not been admitted as a free state, separatist movements would have rapidly developed on the west coast. Yet the settlement had serious weaknesses. One was the fugitive slave law. On that issue, it is true, the South had a real grievance. Over a thousand slaves had been escaping yearly to the North, at an estimated annual loss to slave owners of $200,000, and the Northern states showed little interest in arresting and returning them. But the new law was severe. It ran counter to the old Roman maxim that a man was presumed to be free until he was proved to be a slave; it lay on the captured Negro the burden of proving his free status. And by an extraordinary provision the commissioner who decided the case received $10 if he judged a man a slave, only $5 if he found him a freeman. The real purpose of the law was to satisfy Southern pride by irritating the North, not to recover runaway slaves. To that end it was admirably designed and became one of the minor influences leading the North to its final, resolute opposition to the extension of slavery. Another weakness, necessary at the time, was leaving slavery open to Utah and New Mexico. That provision provided the precedent for Kansas' demand for similar action four years later.

Indeed the Compromise of 1850 was successful for a time only because the South was not yet ready—as the breakdown of the Nashville Convention revealed—for secession. What was evident, underneath Clay's patchwork, in 1850 was that slavery had become a problem that could no longer be settled by the methods of constitutional democracy. Symptomatic was Calhoun's demand that the North cease to discuss the slave question; in effect he was asking for a ban on free speech. Men cannot live together under the same government, even on federal principles which allow for sectional diversity, unless they are agreed on first principles. And on the fundamental question of whether all men, not just white ones, were equal, endowed with certain "inalienable rights," the North and the South were, by 1850, absolutely incapable of agreement.

ROBERT STEWART

Above left Henry Clay who hoped that his compromise would avert civil war forever.

Above The independent gold-hunter on his way to California. Numerous fortunes were made and lost during the California Gold Rush.

In science a spate of discoveries extends

Biology, medicine and the population problem

While the frontiers of the United States were pushed forward by the admission of California to the Union, the frontiers of knowledge too were being pushed rapidly forward. Although the first half of the nineteenth century produced no great men comparable to such towering, if different, scientists as France's Louis Pasteur (1822–95) or England's Charles Darwin (1809–82), it laid the key foundations for their discoveries. In all fields of science, pure and applied, important discoveries were being made.

Although the full implications were not yet realized, the research of English physiologist Erasmus Darwin (1731–1802) and the French naturalist Jean-Baptiste de Lamarck (1799–1829) and the ideas of the English economist Thomas Malthus (1766–1834) provided all the ideas that Darwin and his somewhat younger contemporary, the English naturalist Alfred Wallace (1823–1913), needed to put forward the theories of natural selection and evolution.

No less significant was the development by the Italian astronomer Giovanni Battista Amici (*c.* 1786–*c.* 1863) of an efficient lens for microscopes, which made possible the research of scholars such as Germany's Matthias Schleiden (1804–81) and Theodor Schwann (1810–82) into cellular structure. The idea—closely linked with the belief that man was created in God's image—that man's life was based on some indefinable "vital force" was fading rapidly; the work of François Magendie (1783–1855) on experimental pharmacology and the nerve system showed that bodily functions followed observable rules and dealt a death blow to vitalism.

Medicine was advancing rapidly, too. It benefited to some extent from advances in biology but even more from the general improvement in standards of hygiene and from the use of improved drugs and other aids such as the stethoscope, invented about 1816 by the French physician René Laënnac (1781–1826). As a result, life expectancy, which had already been increasing in the later eighteenth century, rose rapidly. In the two and a half centuries from 1700 to 1950, the life expectancy of a typical child born in Germany rose from about twenty-eight to sixty-six years, and most of the increase took place during the nineteenth century. Despite the huge increase in population during the late eighteenth century the death rate in England, which had fallen rapidly from 3.34 percent in 1730 to 1.99 percent in 1810, scarcely rose between 1810 and 1840.

Francis Place, English reformer.

A multiple-tube microscope allowing simultaneous viewing by a number of observers. From Amédée Guillemin's *Les Applications de la Physique,* 1874.

Improved life expectancy during the nineteenth century was due largely to better sanitary measures encouraged by governments and to social measures reducing the use of child labor. In Britain, in 1842, a royal commission under the reformer Sir Edwin Chadwick (1800–90) recommended the introduction of adequate plumbing and drainage measures in large towns, where their lack encouraged the spread of typhoid, cholera and other diseases. The government had begun even earlier to pass a series of factory acts. In 1825 an act restricting children under sixteen years of age from working for more than twelve hours a day (excluding meal breaks) was passed, and measures taken over the next two decades further reduced hours both for children and for women. Although legislation of this sort was initiated in Britain, it spread rapidly to other countries, and had a major effect on public health generally and on childhood mortality in particular. But the growth of population was not an unmixed blessing and demographers began to worry about overpopulation. Thomas Malthus in his *Essay on Population*, published as early as 1801, pointed out the dangers that could arise for a country that was unable to feed itself, and suggested that famine and epidemic would be nature's answer to overpopulation. The argument was in many ways deficient, and the suggestion that nature would act as a *deus ex machina* was a crude oversimplification, but the book had an immense appeal. Although Malthus himself was resolutely opposed to any form of contraception other than self-control, other "neo-Malthusians," of whom the radical politician Francis Place (1771–1854) was the most prominent, caused a storm in the 1820s by recommending the use of crude protectives. In reality, however, since increased population at that time was caused more by increased life expectancy than by an enlarged birth-rate, contraception would not have had a major effect on population growth.

Chemistry and electricity

Interest in chemistry during the first half of the nineteenth century concentrated particularly on the study of air. In England, Joseph Priestley (1733–1804) showed that air, far from being an "element" as had previously been supposed, was made up of a mixture of different gases. Later study produced far less of interest, and chemistry became the neglected science during much of the nineteenth century.

Electrical knowledge on the other hand advanced rapidly. This was largely due to the American statesman Benjamin Franklin (1706–90). Although Franklin's ideas were often undeveloped—he thought that electricity was a material substance—he saw that lightning was electrical and that it was made up of positive and negative forces. He also helped found America's first scientific society.

Franklin's pioneering work, interrupted by his political activities, was soon overtaken by that of a more thorough scientist, Italy's Alessandro Volta (1745–1827), inventor of the voltaic pile, a primitive forerunner of the electric battery. Volta lent his name to the unit of electrical potential difference, and another early nineteenth-century electrical scientist, France's André Ampère (1775–1836), was similarly immortalized. It was he who synthesized contemporary knowledge of electricity

Alessandro Volta, Italian scientist.

and his name was used to express the practical unit of electrical current. But there were many others working on electricity. The most notable were the Danish Hans Christian Oersted (1777–1851), who studied the relationship between electricity and magnetism, and England's Michael Faraday (1791–1867). Through his study of fields of force the latter posed a major scientific problem. His invention of "ether," as a substance that could exist in a vacuum, seemed at the time to be a useful solution to the difficulty posed because it was thought that electricity must exist in something. Speculations about ether were, however, to hold up the advance of electrical knowledge and of physics until the discovery of the electron and advanced research on electrodynamics in the early twentieth century.

Russia and Britain avoid the 1848 revolutions

The revolutions that upset so much of Europe were not felt everywhere. On Europe's geographical fringes—Russia, Greece, Portugal and Spain, Britain and Scandinavia—the effects of the risings were felt only marginally. Difficulties of communication and a largely oriental autocratic system of government account for the failure of any rising in Russia or Greece; Spain and Portugal were obsessed with their own political difficulties to the point where nothing that happened elsewhere had any real interest for them; in the Scandinavian countries the governments were able to disarm the worst of the opposition by making political concessions; in Britain, too, special factors were operating.

Yet, despite the local peculiarities of the countries that escaped revolution, there was a more general reason. There were in reality two Europes: the countries in the geographical center—France, Germany, Austria-Hungary, Denmark, Switzerland and Italy—whose primary political interests were European, that is with each other, and were as a result easily influenced by each other; and the countries on the periphery, which were either self-absorbed or had largely extra-European interests. It is doubtful how far these peripheral countries can be considered European in interest at all.

The 1848 revolutions had little effect on Britain other than isolated riots in Ireland and disorder caused by the Chartists (working men's associations whose petition, or charter, calling for parliamentary and electoral reforms had been rejected by Parliament). This lack of influence may also have been due in part to the extensive social legislation that had been passed by Parliament during the 1830s and 1840s.

There was a more fundamental reason for the failure of Chartism than merely its apparent imperfections. Throughout the nineteenth century the British people had responded far less readily to general ideas than their counterparts on the Continent. It was almost as if the collective mind of the English populace could comprehend only a particular problem for which there seemed a practical solution. At no time was this more clearly shown than in the "hungry forties." After the bad harvests of 1839, 1840 and 1841, the principal worry of the middle classes and the laborers was the price of food. They flocked to meetings of the Anti-Corn Law League, founded in Manchester in 1839 by Richard Cobden (1804–65) and John Bright (1811–89) to advocate the abolition of all duties upon imported grain. The simple clarity of the League's purpose and the personal magnetism of its two leaders made it the most formidable pressure group a democratic society had ever known. The Tories, who had come into office in 1841 under Sir Robert Peel (1788–1850), repealed the Corn Laws in June, 1846. Prices were stabilized and grain imports rose so rapidly that within five years a quarter of England's bread supply depended on overseas grain. But starvation continued to take its toll in Ireland.

Cobden and Bright had won a victory for free trade. As the British found that they could sell more manufactured goods by admitting food and raw materials without import duties, all protectionist tariffs were swept away. The Tory Party was hopelessly split. The Peelites, of whom William Gladstone (1809–98) was the most eminent, made common cause with the Liberals; the Tory rump, shocked and dismayed, sought a new philosophy of conservatism under Benjamin Disraeli (1804–81). The year 1846 proved a truer watershed in British politics than 1832, the year in which the Reform Act, part of whose effect was to help avert the danger of violent revolution in 1848, was passed.

"Pam's" England

In England the man of the hour in 1848 was Lord Palmerston (1784–1865), who had first held ministerial office in October, 1809 (two months before his eventual colleague, William Ewart Gladstone; was born). At the age of sixty-one "Pam" returned as Foreign Secretary in the ministry of Lord John Russell (1792–1878), formed when Peel's government broke up in the summer of 1846. He was to dominate the cabinet for all but twenty-eight months of the next nineteen years, in more than half of which he served as Prime Minister.

Lord John Russell, later Earl Russell.

Palmerston's robust and cavalier temperament won him affection and acclaim from the British people, who admired his colorful waistcoats and jauntily tilted hat, envied the excellence of his racing stables and delighted in the patriotic bluster of his diplomacy. He shared their liking for Garibaldi and Kossuth and their suspicion of all foreign sovereigns. In 1850 he sent a naval squadron to blockade Greece in order to obtain compensation for Don Pacifico, a moneylender born in Gibraltar—and therefore a British subject—whose house in Athens had been ransacked by an angry crowd. Such highhanded behavior led to protests from the French and the Russians, and it shocked Queen Victoria. But it delighted her subjects!

Lord Palmerston, Britain's popular, if highhanded, premier.

Lamentably, Palmerston's judgment on foreign affairs, astute in the 1830s, became increasingly wayward as he grew older. Yet his popularity never waned. "He is Mama England's spoilt child," a Tory opponent acidly observed some two years after the Don Pacifico affair, but there were many both at home and abroad who saw him as John Bull incarnate (an image that pleased his constituents but aroused disquiet among foreign statesmen).

Palmerston was by no means typical of Victorian England. He lacked its earnest desire for self-improvement and its prim concern with the virtues of hard work. The principal festival of the age, the Great Exhibition of 1851, was essentially alien to all that he represented.

17613.
Lithographed Printed & Published by VINCENT BROOKS 421 Oxford St London.

Queen Victoria's Crystal Palace 1851

Great Britain in the nineteenth century led the world in manufacturing and trade. What could be more appropriate than an international trade fair, where all nations could display their wares and compete for prizes? After some discussion—one critic called it "the greatest fraud"—and with the assistance of Prince Albert, a vast building of metal and glass, the Crystal Palace, was built in Hyde Park and the Great Exhibition was held, with the Queen herself in constant attendance.

By the middle of the nineteenth century Great Britain was the most important economic power in the world. She controlled a lion's share of world trade and her early lead in industrialization had made her the "workshop of the world." To contemporaries this triumph was based not only upon the skill and enterprise of British merchants and inventors, but also upon the beneficial effects of free trade, heralded by the repeal of the protectionist Corn Laws of 1846.

Consequently it was believed that trade would continue to expand to the benefit of all nations, but that Britain would continue to improve her wealth and position because of her natural advantages. With a manufacturing capacity that outstripped any of her rivals. Britain welcomed the opportunity to show off her achievements and to promote further commerce between nations. She had overcome the domestic problems of the 1840s and was confident of her supremacy. Thus the concept of a great international exhibition on a scale never seen before was born; an exhibition that would mark the progress and expansion of the nineteenth century and harness science to national prestige for the first time.

In 1845 Henry Cole joined the Council of the Society of Arts, a society which encouraged art, manufacturing and commerce by awarding prizes to potential inventors otherwise unable to finance themselves. The appointment was of singular importance, for the Society had fallen into a state of virtual inactivity and Cole was a man of great energy and influence. He was a civil servant—an assistant keeper at the Record Office—and the editor of a popular art-journal, but his main interest was the improvement of industrial design.

Under his influence the Society of Arts soon began to show more life; it caught the interest of Albert, the Prince Consort, who, as President of the Society, procured for it a charter naming it the Society for the Encouragement of Arts, Manufactures and Commerce. As a foreigner Albert was faced with a daunting task in fulfilling the role generally expected of him as the Queen's husband. He was regarded as a rather humorless foreigner. However, his interest in the economic and intellectual life of the country was recognized as serious and sincere; here he had found a part he could play with some success. The presidency of the Society of Arts was one in a long line of public appointments that covered many educational and charitable organizations.

In 1847 the Society of Arts held the first of three annual exhibitions of art manufactures. The impetus came from Cole, whose enthusiasm was shown to be well founded when the attendance of twenty thousand for the first exhibition soared to seventy thousand the following year. The 1849 exhibition was even more successful. Although trade exhibitions were not new, they seemed, of a sudden, to capture the imagination of manufacturers and public. That same year, for example, a large show was held at Birmingham by the British Association, to which the Prince once again lent his patronage.

The success of his exhibitions encouraged Cole to further efforts. In 1851 he considered inaugurating a series of triennial exhibitions of British industry. This plan, however, changed dramatically when Cole visited the eleventh Quinquennial Exposition at Paris in the summer of 1849. There was little doubt that the French goods on display were of a higher quality than many British products. Cole was a firm believer in free trade and it seemed to him that, if he were to display British and French products side by side, he would give British—and French—manufacturers the impetus to produce finer quality goods and encourage trade. Indeed, why only French and British goods; why should his 1851 Exhibition not contain the very

One of the more fanciful exhibits: a sportsman's knife with a carved mother-of-pearl handle and eighty blades and other instruments, on one of which the Crystal Palace is engraved.

Opposite The elegant arched transept that Joseph Paxton added to his original design in order to enclose three giant elm trees. The central fountain of crystal glass is surrounded by sculptures in differing moods.

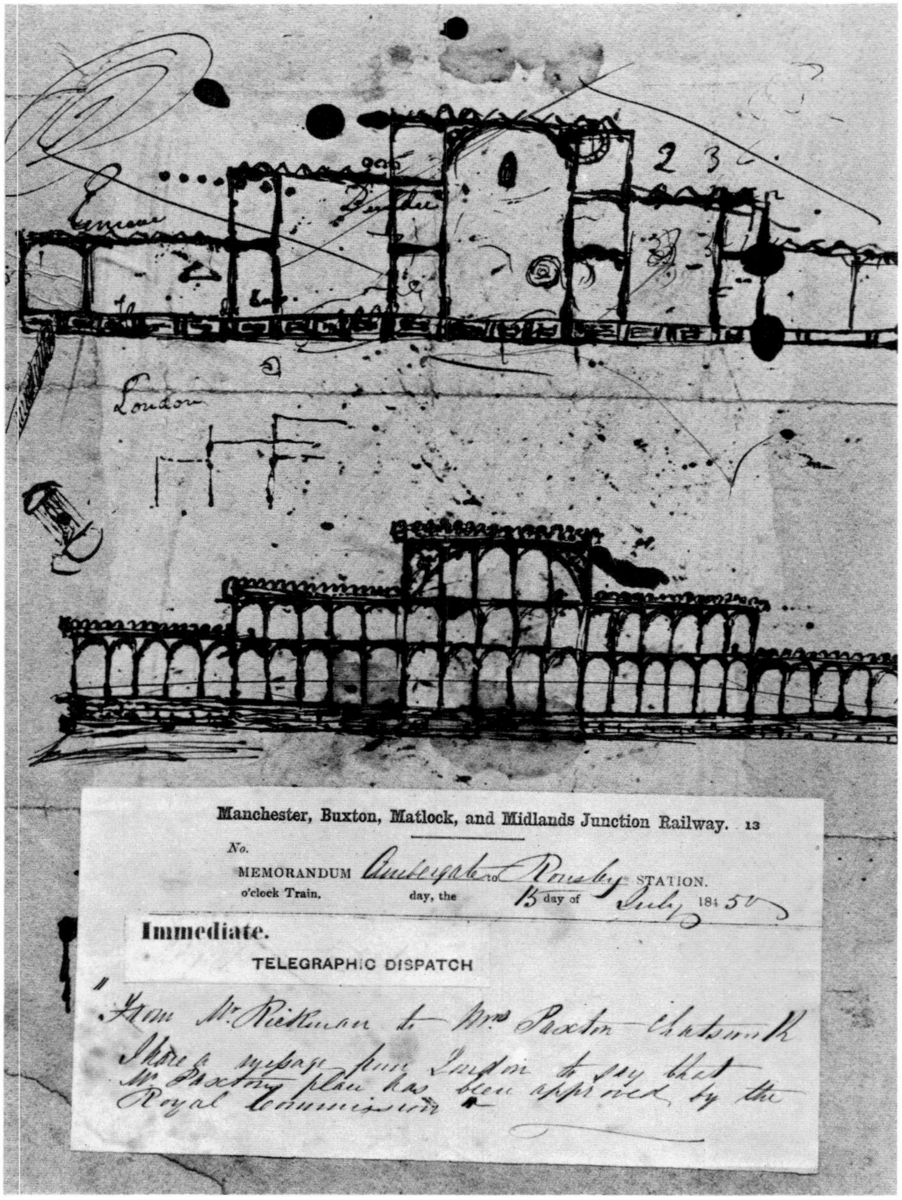

The original sketch by Paxton for the Great Exhibition and the telegram approving it. Paxton had scribbled his design upon blotting paper while attending a meeting of the Midland Railway Company in Derby.

best manufactured work from the entire world?

By the end of June, 1849, Prince Albert had been persuaded that an international exhibition should be planned and, enthusiastic for the idea, he had suggested the section of Hyde Park just opposite the Knightsbridge Barracks as an ideal site.

Cole set to the task of organizing an exhibition with prodigious energy. He raised interest for it in enough quarters for the scheme to become secure financially. As a viable proposition, the Exhibition could now enjoy royal support and so, early in 1850, Albert appointed a royal commission to organize the event. He was joined by many of the most prominent men of the day, but it was upon Cole and Lord Granville, the Vice President, that the bulk of the work was to fall.

While the task of gathering potential contributions and subscriptions was proceeding, the commissioners turned to the problem of housing the vast collection of international exhibits. A building committee was appointed from among eminent architects and engineers, including Charles Barry, designer of the Houses of Parliament, Robert Stephenson, son of the inventor of the *Rocket*, and Isambard Kingdom Brunel, architect of the Great Western Railway. By February they had agreed that Hyde Park was the ideal site for the Exhibition and invited designs for the exhibition building to be submitted. Two hundred and forty-five sets of plans were received and the committee retired to deliberate.

The committee's decision, when it came in April, was surprising. Eighteen of the entries were considered to be of high distinction, but none worthy of adoption. Consequently the committee itself had produced a design that, in its view, combined the best points of all the submitted entries. The design was of a large, low brick building, entered under enormous false arches and flanked by long verandahs. Surmounting this edifice was a vast dome, more than twice the height of the rest of the building, two hundred feet in diameter and made of sheet iron.

The design, mostly the inspiration of Brunel, was published in the *London Illustrated News* on June 22, 1850. Its appearance at once provided a focus for the largely unspoken opposition to the entire scheme that had been building up over the previous months. Arguments against the Exhibition came from many quarters, including those who feared free trade and thought that the introduction into the country of foreign goods would undermine British industry. Among these, the most vociferous was a Member of Parliament, Colonel Charles Sibthorp. His opposition to the Exhibition never wavered; it is this implacable obstinacy which has rescued his name from obscurity. The Exhibition, Sibthorp ranted to the House, would be:

> The greatest trash, the greatest fraud, and the greatest imposition ever attempted to be palmed upon the people of this country. The object of its promoters is to introduce amongst us foreign stuff of every description—live and dead stock—without regard to quantity or quality. It is meant to bring down prices in this country and to pave the way to the establishment of the cheap and nasty trash and trumpery system.

Less extreme but more widespread opposition to the plan was the fear of attracting all kinds of people to one of the most exclusive areas of London, and the greater fear that the Park would be disfigured permanently. The commissioners had promised that their building would be removed when the Exhibition closed, but few who looked at the design in the *London Illustrated News* believed them. It looked far too solid. "The erection of this huge structure on such a site," declared *The Times*, "is equivalent to the permanent mutilation of Hyde Park."

Meanwhile Prince Albert, seeing once more the specter of his unpopularity threatening to overwhelm him, wrote gloomily to his brother Ernst:

> Now our Exhibition is to be driven from London; the

Patrons who are afraid, the Radicals who want to show their power over the crown property, *The Times* whose solicitor bought a house near Hyde Park, are abusing and insulting . . . . We shall probably be defeated and have to give up the whole Exhibition. You see we do not lie on a bed of roses.

It is ironical that, at the time Albert was writing to Ernst, the problem of the building and its popularity had been resolved. The story reads like a fairy tale.

In 1850, Joseph Paxton was a prosperous and influential man, with interests in many areas, including the expanding network of railways; but his main concern was the running of the Duke of Devonshire's estates. He was the Duke's bailiff, stockbroker, adviser and close friend. He had been in the Duke's service since 1826 when, as a gardener at Chiswick, a village to the west of London, he had first met the Duke, who had a villa there. Young Paxton, who had taught himself botany and horticulture since leaving school, so impressed the Duke that he was offered, in 1829, the post of head gardener at Chatsworth, the Duke's estate in Derbyshire. Paxton transformed the gardens, laying out new walks, creating a lake, a canal and a fountain 269 feet high. He sent expeditions all over the world to find rare plants unknown in Europe. In 1837, Paxton began the construction of an enormous conservatory at Chatsworth, and the following year he was commissioned to redesign and rebuild the Duke's estate village of Edensor. He also edited several horticultural magazines and even founded the popular newspaper, *Daily News*, which Charles Dickens edited for a time.

Early in June, 1850, Paxton was visiting the newly rebuilt House of Commons with Mr. Ellis, Chairman of the Midland Railway Company, when the conversation turned to the Exhibition and its building. The design had not yet been published, but Paxton had heard the outlines of the plan. He told Ellis that he "had a notion in his head" for the building and wondered whether it were too late to submit it. Ellis took him immediately to see Henry Cole, who suggested that a new plan might be considered, but there was little time as a decision had to be made very soon. A day or two later, while attending a meeting of the Midland Railway Company at Derby, Paxton, unable to concentrate on anything else, doodled a rough sketch of his exhibition building on the blotting paper in front of him. He took the blotter back to Chatsworth and in little over a week produced, with the help of his staff, the first complete plans of his design.

Paxton had dreamed up a three-tiered palace of glass on a framework of slim iron pillars and girders. Within this vast, lucent hall a gallery would run at the level of the first tier. The building was clearly inspired by the conservatories Paxton had designed at Chatsworth and he drew heavily on the knowledge he had gained from their construction. As the building would be constructed in standardized prefabricated sections, there would be no difficulty in

Design for converting the Crystal Palace, called so by the humorous magazine *Punch,* into a tower a thousand feet high.

Right Displayed at the Exhibition, an envelope-making machine invented by the British astronomer and inventor Warren de la Rue.

Below Queen Victoria opening the Great Exhibition. For three months after the opening the Queen visited the Exhibition informally almost every day.

finishing it in time and it would be comparatively easy to remove, leaving Hyde Park untouched. But the use of glass as a main building material was unheard of; in fact, until 1845 there had been a prohibitive tax on glass. How safe the building would be remained an unanswered question.

Stephenson, to whom Paxton showed his plan, was enthusiastic. Prince Albert, who knew and admired Paxton's work at Chatsworth, was delighted. Only the building committee hesitated to support such a visionary and, perhaps, dangerous project.

While the building committee were deciding what to do, Paxton appealed directly to the public. He sent his design to the *London Illustrated News*, which published it on July 6. The response was so laudatory that Paxton's contractors, Fox and Henderson of Smethwick, immediately offered to execute the work. Their terms were so reasonable—as to eliminate any competition—that the building committee had no choice but to accept the plan.

There were a few small changes of plan before building could start. Three giant elm trees on the site, which had become something of a *cause célèbre* among the Exhibition's opponents, were to be enclosed by the building. To achieve this, Paxton added an elegant arched transept to his original box-shaped design. In addition an extra gallery was added, thus increasing the total floor

space of the building to well over twenty acres.

By the end of July, the royal commissioners had secured possession of the site and the contractors began work. Throughout the autumn and winter of 1850 a popular diversion for Londoners was a visit to the Park to watch Paxton's building take shape and marvel at the speed and ease with which it was erected. It was at this time that Douglas Jerrold of the topical humor magazine *Punch* dubbed the building "the Crystal Palace," an apt title it never lost.

Colonel Sibthorp and others continued to criticize, but by its completion the following February, the Palace had survived at least one violent hailstorm as well as a stringent test of its strength when a corps from the Royal Engineers had marched to and fro along the gallery. As opening day approached the criticisms lessened and the preparations became more hectic. Exhibits had to be arranged and cataloged and the building had to be decorated inside and out. The Customs Board helped by allowing foreign exhibits into the Exhibition duty free, and the architect and historian (who had published the first architectural study of the Alhambra) Owen Jones designed a bold color scheme of bright red, yellow and blue for the ironwork.

Preparations were just completed by 9:00 A.M. on May 1, when the Great Exhibition opened "to present a true test and a living picture of the point of development at which the whole of mankind has arrived." Only the Russian exhibits arrived late. To the first day were invited the twenty-five thousand season-ticketholders, who had paid three guineas each for the privilege; outside in the Park were a further half million or so waiting for the Queen to arrive and watching the comings and goings of the other eminent personages. The Queen arrived at midday and, after an elaborate opening ceremony, proceeded along nearly a mile of red carpet on a tour of the exhibits. Her pride and pleasure were boundless. She wrote in her diary:

> The great event has taken place, a complete and beautiful triumph, a glorious and touching sight, one which I shall ever be proud of for my beloved Albert and my country. . . . The tremendous cheers, the joy expressed in every face, the immensity of the building, the mixture of palms, flowers, trees, statues, fountains, and my beloved husband the author of this "Peace Festival," which united the industry of all nations of the earth,—all this was moving indeed, and it was and is a day to live for ever. God bless my dearest Albert, God bless my dearest country, which has shown itself so great today!

From the first day the Exhibition was a resounding popular success. It was open every day except Sunday at varying admission prices. Paxton had wanted to let people in gratis but the idea was greeted with horror. Instead, entrance cost five

The British nave; the leading economic power in the world, Britain welcomed the opportunity to show off her achievements and promote further commerce between nations.

London's Piccadilly during the Great Exhibition. By the time the Exhibition closed over six million people had visited the Crystal Palace.

shillings a day until May 26, when cheap days were introduced—one shilling from Monday to Thursday and two shillings and six pence on Fridays. Four and a half million people bought shilling tickets and, by the time the Exhibition closed, over six million visitors had seen the Crystal Palace and its contents.

The critic and artist William Morris considered the show "wonderfully ugly"; indeed, ingenuity and invention seem to have been valued above beauty and some of the more bizarre exhibits included "an alarm bedstead, causing a person to arise at a given hour" and an expanding figure of a man which could be made to change from life size to gigantic proportions at the turn of a handle. But such oddities, popular though they were, like the tableaux of stuffed animals from Germany that so enchanted the Queen, were only a small proportion of the whole collection, which contained more than a hundred thousand exhibits. The area west of the transept was allocated to Britain and the Empire, while the slightly smaller eastern nave was allotted to foreign nations. Entries were grouped roughly under the headings, raw materials, machinery, manufactures and fine arts.

The most impressive exhibits must have been the machinery and inventions featured on the British section. There were models of the Conway and Menai bridges by Stephenson; a model of the Bell Rock Lighthouse and a full-size lighthouse reflector; new precision tools from Whitworth and Armstrong; self-acting cotton mules from Bradford; steel knives from Sheffield and the telegraph cable that was to be laid under the Channel that very year. There was even a forty-foot model of the Liverpool Docks with sixteen hundred ships complete in every detail. A special boiler-house was incorporated in a corner of the Palace to provide power for the working machinery on display. Steam presses and pumps, ships' engines and steam threshers all hissed and bumped away before the delighted gaze of visitors. The Folkestone Express was on show to represent the growing railway network. Foreign products almost equaled those from

Britain, and visitors could see power looms and labor-saving devices from America, women's fabrics from France, glassware from Bohemia, and —inconspicuous among the thousands of exhibits— some steel cannon manufactured by a Herr Krupp of Essen, Germany. On each side, exhibits proclaimed the twin ideals of Work and Peace, the latter implicit in the international nature of the goods displayed. At the center of the Exhibition was a fountain of crystal glass surrounded by sculptures—sentimental, like *The Greek Slave*, from the United States, or melodramatic, like *Amazon Mounted on Horseback Attacked by a Tiger*, from Prussia.

Largely as a result of the already widespread railway system, the Exhibition won national popularity. Excursions were organized from all parts of the country; on one occasion the Great Western Railway carried five thousand visitors on a single train. A frequent visitor was the aging Duke of Wellington; he adored the Exhibition and had taken a keen interest in it from the beginning. The Queen herself visited the display almost every day for the first three months, working her way conscientiously round the exhibits. She would wander informally among the visitors as the Exhibition opened each morning. Fears that the crowds would prove to be a dangerous liability to the inhabitants of Kensington proved groundless.

The closing ceremony was held on a very wet October 18. Medals were awarded to winning exhibits, many of which seem to have been chosen less for their merit than because the commissioners were anxious to reward as many foreign entries as possible. It was hoped that the Exhibition would help an insular nation understand its neighbors a little better, and inaugurate an era of international peace. Yet the "Peace Festival," as the Queen called it, could not avert the Crimean War three years later—but perhaps the British found it a little easier to accept the French as allies.

After the Exhibition Paxton's building was moved south of London to Sydenham Hill where, greatly enlarged, it settled down to life as a pleasure palace, until it was destroyed by fire in 1936. However, two towers survived to be demolished in 1940; they were too large a landmark for the Luftwaffe.

In all, the project made a profit of £186,437, £5,000 of which was immediately bestowed upon Paxton. The rest was used to promote the educational schemes dear to Prince Albert. The museums and colleges that surround the Victoria and Albert Museum in South Kensington were all founded on the proceeds of the Great Exhibition and to this day a trust fund still gives away many thousands of pounds each year to promote the arts and sciences.

The success of the Great Exhibition encouraged ever greater and more expensive international exhibitions to give testimony to the rise of other industrial powers—France, Germany and the United States. The famous Paris Exhibition of 1867 was evidence that Britain would soon give up her position as the sole "workshop of the world." Nonetheless the Great Exhibition had provided the foundation for a tradition of international exhibitions that marked the progress and achievements of mankind seeking to overcome national barriers peacefully.

JOHN STEVENSON

Top The so-called aeronautic view of the Crystal Palace. Paxton had dreamed up a three-tiered palace of glass on a framework of slim iron pillars and girders.

Above The Crystal Palace in Hyde Park. Throughout the autumn and winter of 1850 a popular diversion for Londoners was a visit to the park to watch the building take shape.

Tsarist Russia, Europe's backward giant,

Russian expansion

During the 1850s the massive and cumbersome Empire of the tsars began to consolidate the gains of earlier centuries. Isolated Russian outposts had been established on the bleak coasts of the northern Pacific as early as 1650, but for two centuries the powerful Chinese Empire had restricted these settlements to icebound wastes, frequented only by trappers and seal hunters. In 1847 the Russians inaugurated an eastward sweep. The Tsar appointed a young and enterprising colonialist, Nikolai Nikolaevich Muraviëv-Amursky (1809–81), as Governor-General of Eastern Siberia, and for the next fourteen years every effort was made to secure Russian control of the mouth of the Amur River and to strengthen Russian influence over the Chinese government at the capital, Peking.

Count Muraviëv-Amursky's policy reached a climax in 1858 with the establishment of an imperial city at the head of a natural harbor on the Pacific. Significantly, Muraviëv-Amursky named this Russian counterpart to San Francisco Vladivostok (Domination of the East). Its very name seemed a challenge to nations whose vessels had long traded in Far Eastern waters (although the next half century was to reveal that Russia's greatest rival in the Far East was neither Britain nor the United States but Japan).

Russia's eastward expansion and America's westward expansion almost coincided in time, and yet there were few major nations in the world that were as dissimilar in character as the autocratic tsarist Empire and the vigorous Republic. It is true that the economies of large areas in both countries depended on forced labor, and it is also true that the institution of slavery in the southern United States was no more morally defensible than the bonds of serfdom in Russia, but industrial capitalism was far more advanced in America than it was in the predominantly agrarian society of the Tsar's semifeudal Empire.

Although the Russian flag flew over more than a sixth of the world's land surface in the mid-1850s, Russia had only fifteen towns with more than fifty thousand inhabitants (their combined population was almost the same as that of New York, Philadelphia, Baltimore and Boston). Russia also lagged behind the major European countries and the United States in communications and industry: it was only in 1851, after nine years of construction, that a railway linking the principal cities of Moscow and St. Petersburg was completed—and even this undertaking was financed and supervised by American engineers. In 1855 Russia had only one-fifth as many miles of railways as the United States.

Russian industry was still largely unmechanized at the turn of the century. Cotton spinning, for example, was largely carried out in homes rather than factories—and in 1850 there were four times as many spindles in New England alone as in the whole of Russia. Where factories did exist, working conditions were grim; as late as 1860, serfs constituted more than four-fifths of the labor force in textile factories and about three-quarters of the labor force in steel and iron foundries.

Yet, for all its industrial backwardness, Russia remained one of the great powers throughout the century. The Tsar's Empire seemed an almost limitless wasteland, capable of mobilizing hundreds of thousands of ruthless warriors and thrusting them deep into Europe—as the Hungarians had discovered in 1849. The Russian "bogey," with its Cossack raiders and its endless columns of infantry clad in long yellowish-gray greatcoats that almost swept the ground, was a very real apparition in the 1840s and 1850s. After the failure of the 1848 revolutions, Tsar Nicholas I acted so boldly in Europe that his power appeared to menace the security of the whole Continent. It was for this reason, more than any other, that the British and French governments drifted into war with Russia.

Russia and Turkey

The origins of the Crimean War lie far back, in old clashes of outlook and interest. To some extent, it can be argued that Louis Napoleon committed French troops to the conflict in the hopes of recovering the prestige that France had lost through his uncle's disastrous campaign in 1812. Anglo-Russian dissension, on the other hand, was caused by the "Eastern Question," the series of problems raised by the apparent inability of the Turkish Sultan's government in Constantinople to hold the Ottoman Empire together. The Russians, who had long been aware of the feebleness of their Turkish neighbor, had begun to move south around the Black Sea as early as 1790, and they had fought largely indecisive wars against Turkey from 1806 to 1812 and in 1828–29.

Each Russian move was regarded with suspicion by the British, who believed that the Tsar's army and navy were a danger to the stability of the Middle East and a threat to the overland route between Europe and India. The bolstering of the Turkish Empire became a canon of British foreign policy, for the British were anxious to prevent the Russian fleet sailing through the narrow straits of the Bosphorus and into the Mediterranean. The principal instrument in interpreting this policy was the British Ambassador in Constantinople, Viscount Stratford de Redcliffe (1786–1880), a diplomat who spent almost a quarter of a century in the Turkish capital. During

Emperor Napoleon III. France like Britain feared Russian domination in the East.

those years, Stratford de Redcliffe's sympathy and patience stood in marked contrast to the bullying arrogance of a succession of Russian representatives.

The immediate cause of war between Russia and Turkey in 1853 was the Sultan's refusal of a Russian demand that the Tsar be recognized as protector of all Christians living within the Ottoman Empire. The Turks would

A British cavalry camp during the Crimean War.

presents a threat to the European balance of power

Hagia Sophia in Constantinople. Despite its ill-treatment of religious minorities, the Ottoman Empire was always able to count on Western support.

never have dared to declare war on Russia had they not felt assured of French and British support—and in 1853 they had reason to feel assured. Franco-Russian relations had been severely strained by a dispute over the

Florence Nightingale, who created modern nursing on the battlefields of the Crimea.

custody of the holy places in Palestine, and in Britain distrust of the Tsar had been intensified by his proposals for the eventual partition of "the Sick Man of Europe," as he called Turkey.

When the Russian navy caught and destroyed the Turkish fleet in the harbor at Sinope, the British and French became genuinely alarmed. There was no other force capable of protecting the approaches to the Bosphorus and Constantinople, and the British and French squadrons were moved into the Black Sea. In March, 1854, an ultimatum was sent to the Tsar from London and Paris, and at the end of the month war broke out. The conflict had been caused not so much by deliberate aggression as by fear, misunderstanding and confusion. There are few conflicts that could have been so easily avoided. Russia was not alone in her expansionist interest in Asia in the 1850s.

The Mysterious Orient

During the early years of the nineteenth century there was increasing interest in the two great independent empires of the Far East, China and Japan. The Dutch and Portuguese had traded along the China coast since the sixteenth century. English ships had sailed up the Pearl River to Canton as early as 1637, and from the end of the sixteenth century until 1833, the East India Company retained a virtual monopoly of Chinese seaborne trade, carrying silks and tea back to its docks along the Thames River. American ships had broken the monopoly as early as 1785, but trade with the United States never reached substantial proportions until the second half of the nineteenth century. The narratives written by eighteenth-century travelers of their journeys in the Orient made Chinese ornamental gardens and hand-painted wallpapers fashionable from the 1760s. Chinese porcelain and furniture designs were much prized—and pirated—by Westerners. The philosophers of the Enlightenment admired all that they heard of Chinese customs. But however much Chinese customs and art might be admired by intellectuals and the *cognoscenti*, many merchants, including the governors of the East India Company, were convinced that the Chinese was a quaint but distinctly inferior animal. The reason for the development of this attitude during the early nineteenth century was the alleged susceptibility of the Chinese to opium, which had been smuggled from India into China by unscrupulous merchants. In 1839 the attempts of the Chinese authorities to stamp out the opium trade led to a disgraceful war between Britain and China.

The 1842 Treaty of Nanking, which ended the First Opium War, stipulated that five treaty ports (Amoy, Canton, Foochow, Ningpo and Shanghai) should be opened to foreign trade at reasonable tariffs. The Chinese also agreed to compensate merchants for the loss of revenue from the opium trade. Other concessions, to the French and to the United States, which benefited particularly from the right to induce coolies to cross the Pacific and labor in California in conditions hardly better than slavery, followed. Collectively these measures gave Westerners a stranglehold on the primitive Chinese economy. They also showed up the extreme weakness of the Chinese government and army—encouraging Europeans and Americans to make further demands.

The weakness of the Chinese government led to the Taiping rising of 1852. The "Heavenly Kingdom" of the Taipings, a neo-Christian Chinese sect, was able to rule much of the earthly Kingdom of China. The movement's followers captured Nanking, which became its capital, and were only suppressed in 1855 with the help of Western troops.

A year later China was again at war, this time with both Britain and France. The result of the Arrow (or Second Opium) War was that China was forced to grant further privileges to the Western powers. But far more serious, at least in Chinese eyes, than the loss of Hong Kong, which had been annexed by Britain in 1841, or the trading rights wrung from the Emperor, was the recognition that China would have to treat the foreigners as equals.

Nor was Japan able to escape China's fate. For centuries the shoguns had rigorously guarded their country's isolation by stamping out all the attempts of European nations to establish trading posts and by carefully building up a flourishing native economy. But, with the Chinese coast wide open to foreign trade, it became increasingly difficult for the Japanese to maintain their policy of deliberate seclusion.

American warships entered Japanese waters in 1846 and again in 1849, and a forceful descent on the islands could not long be delayed. It remained to be seen if Japan would submit—as China

Street scene in Hong Kong, which has been a British colony since 1842.

had done—to foreign mastery or if she would use her tightly knit authoritarian system to bridge the gap between her culture and that of the industrialized West. Either solution was possible in July, 1853, when Commodore Perry's steam frigates anchored in the great bay below Mount Fuji.

Panorama of Tokaido at Yokohama. Panel of a triptych by Kunitsuma, 1862.

Perry Opens Japan 1854

One of Millard Fillmore's last acts as President was to entrust Commodore Matthew C. Perry with the task of delivering a highly important official communiqué to the Emperor of Japan. In mid-July of 1853—four months after Fillmore was turned out of office—Perry delivered two letters to the Emperor. The first—Fillmore's—was diplomatic and conciliatory; the second, written by Perry himself, was somewhat more specific and far more threatening. It virtually commanded the Japanese to open their country to foreign trade. To underscore the gravity of his request, the Commodore announced that he would return the next year—with a larger fleet—to hear the Emperor's reply. Unhappily for the insular Japanese, Perry was as good as his word—and on March 31, 1854, the Japanese were induced to sign a treaty opening two harbors to foreign shipping. After centuries of self-imposed isolation, Japan had finally accepted membership in the family of nations.

On July 8, 1853, four ships of the United States Navy, two of them steamers, dropped anchor off the harbor of Uraga at the entrance of Edo (now Tokyo) Bay. In command of the squadron was Commodore Matthew C. Perry, a large and formidable martinet of fifty-nine who was popularly known as "Old Bruin" or "The Old Hoss."

Perry had with him a letter to the Emperor of Japan from President Millard Fillmore. That letter began by pointing out that Oregon and California lay directly opposite Japan and that steamships could cross the Pacific in eighteen days. The President declared that it would be profitable for Japan and the United States to engage in mutual trade, and he asked the Emperor to change the ancient laws that prohibited foreign trade except with the Chinese and the Dutch. Fillmore then proffered a half-promise that can only be described as insincere:

> If your imperial majesty is not satisfied that it would be safe altogether to abrogate the ancient laws which forbid foreign trade, they might be suspended for five or ten years, so as to try the experiment. If it does not prove as beneficial as was hoped, the ancient laws can be restored. The United States often limit their treaties with foreign states to a few years, and then renew them or not, as they please.

The American President's letter went on to appeal for good treatment of American mariners shipwrecked on Japanese shores and concluded with a request that American vessels be allowed to stop in Japan for coal, provisions and water.

Fillmore's letter breathed conciliation from start to finish, and its courteous phraseology seemed to imply no hidden threat. Commodore Perry had composed his own letter to the Emperor, however, and his missive, while repeating the main points made by the President, contained certain passages that conveyed an unmistakable warning to the Japanese. Perry observed that no friendship between his country and Japan could long exist "unless Japan ceases to act toward Americans as if they were her enemies." He expressed the hope that the Japanese government would "see the necessity of averting unfriendly collision between the two nations, by responding favorably to the propositions of amity, which are now made in all sincerity." Then he added:

> Many of the large ships-of-war destined to visit Japan have not yet arrived in these seas, though they are hourly expected; and the undersigned, as an evidence of his friendly intentions, has brought but four of the smaller ones, designing, should it become necessary, to return to Edo in the ensuing spring with a much larger force.

Perry refused Japanese demands that he sail to Nagasaki, the only port where foreigners were officially received, and he adamantly declined to meet any but the highest officials. He was equally firm in resisting Japanese procrastination, asserting that the President's letter must be accepted with due formality within three days. And less than a week after his ships dropped anchor the redoubtable Commodore disembarked with a bodyguard of just under three hundred sailors and marines. After delivering his messages, Perry announced that he would be back the following year—with a larger squadron—to accept a reply to his President's requests. Before heading out to sea the Commodore sailed farther up the Bay of Edo to within sight of the shogun's capital. (The shoguns were hereditary military dictators who had been the real rulers of Japan since the twelfth century.)

When the "black ships," as the Japanese called them, returned in February, 1854, there were eight of them instead of four. The Americans and the Japanese began negotiations immediately, and it soon became clear that the latter, although bargaining all the way, were ready to bow step by step to superior force. The Japanese fought hard against proposals for a trade treaty, however, and in the end

A Japanese Prefect with his two attendants. This portrait was drawn in the year Perry arrived in Japan.

Opposite Perry's "black ships," which caused a sensation when they appeared in Edo Bay in 1853.

Matthew Perry; a pioneer advocate of naval steamships, he is sometimes called the father of the steam navy.

Perry did not insist upon their signing one. But he did secure the opening of two harbors, Shimoda and Hakodate, as ports of refuge, and he did extract the reluctant promise that after eighteen months an American consul would be allowed to take up residence at Shimoda. Furthermore, Perry obtained for his country that invaluable concession known as "the most favored nation clause":

> If at any future day the government of Japan shall grant to any other nation . . . privileges and advantages which are not herein granted to the United States ... these same privileges and advantages shall be granted likewise to the United States and to the citizens thereof without any consultation or delay.

Perry's treaty, signed at the fishing hamlet of Yokohama on March 31, 1854, marked the end of Japan's long seclusion from the world. Perry had put his foot in the door; others were soon to open it further. Indeed, if Perry had not forced it open, a Russian or British naval commander certainly would have done so. Japan was not to be left alone—the very idea of doing so would have appeared

Commodore Perry meeting the Imperial Commissioners at Yokohama.

whimsical to the confident American or European businessman of that day. Within five years the British, Russians, Dutch and French had persuaded the shogun's government to sign commercial treaties, and the first American consul, Townsend Harris, had obtained the same benefits for the United States. The treaties, which forced the Japanese to accept a low scale of import duties and to concede extraterritorial rights to the nationals of eighteen countries, were regarded by the Japanese as unequal. But foreign pressure seemed irresistible, and by 1860 a community of European and American merchants was well established along the waterfront at Yokohama.

For most Westerners all this represented the attainment of a dream. After gold was discovered in California in the 1840s the Orient developed a new lure for Americans. China and Japan seemed to be not only potential markets of great value, but also fruitful fields for the missionary, the engineer, the educator and the doctor. Moreover, Britain's victory in the Opium War and her subsequent annexation of Hong Kong had left Americans both fearful and jealous of British commercial competition in the Far East. (There was, in addition, the menace of Russian expansion which threatened to engulf the Japanese islands.) It is not surprising, therefore, that lobbies representing both businessmen and missionary boards pressed Congress to promote America's Manifest Destiny in the Orient. The outcome was presidential authorization of the Japan expedition under Commodore Perry.

For Americans the consequences of Perry's mission were almost wholly beneficial for many years. However, the Civil War, which broke out seven years after Perry's treaty, restricted American expansion during the 1860s. But in succeeding decades trade between the United States and Japan flourished, America becoming Japan's largest single market, especially for silk. Before World War II, America's commerce with Japan was worth a good deal more than its trade with China. Yet long before that war began, Japan had become America's Oriental bogey—a supposed threat to California,

The Port of London, England, by Yoshitora, from the series *A Complete Mirror of Famous Places in Barbarian Countries.* Since the seventeenth century Japan had followed a policy of strict seclusion and regarded the Western powers as barbarians.

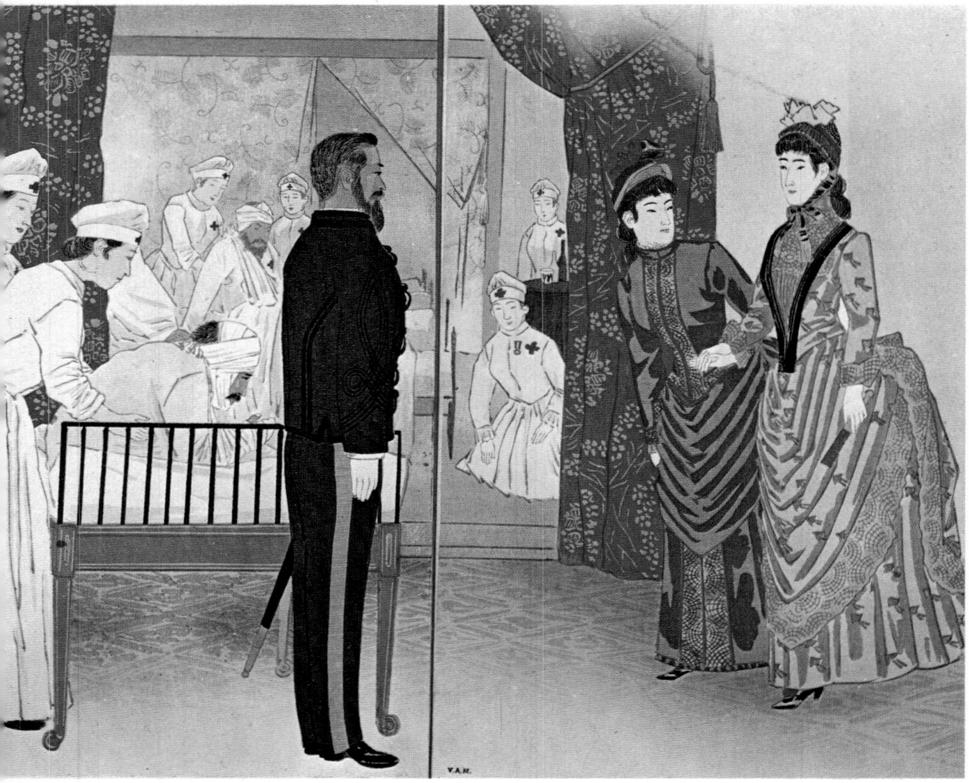

Japanese print showing Russian officers visiting wounded soldiers during the Russo-Japanese War of 1904–5. By the end of the century Japan had adopted Western customs in peace and war.

Right Trade soon followed as a result of Perry's expedition. A Japanese illustration of 1861 showing a visiting American businessman.

a shadow over the Philippines and a genuine menace to America's "sister republic," China.

For the Japanese the immediate consequences of Perry's visit and the subsequent treaties were generally unpleasant. The commercial benefits were small; the cultural shocks were intense. Whatever they thought of it in later years, the Japanese who greeted Perry in 1853 undoubtedly resented what amounted to an invasion of their territory. It is true that long before Perry's arrival, one or two scholars and officials had openly questioned the wisdom of the policy of strict seclusion that had been bequeathed to Japan in the seventeenth century by Iyemitsu, the third shogun of the Tokugawa line. They argued that there was much to be learned from Western nations and that only by intercourse with them could Japan make itself strong enough to hold its own in the world. But those who advocated the opening of the country to foreign commerce did so precisely because they saw a potential menace to Japan's independence in the activities of the Western powers in the Far East. Closer contact with "barbarians" might be inevitable; it was nonetheless regrettable. Further, the instinctive sentiment of the samurai class—the warrior elite—was decidedly antiforeign, and for some years after Perry's arrival powerful elements in Japan remained basically unreconciled to the opening of the country.

At the time of Perry's first visit in 1853, the Japanese government took the unprecedented step of seeking the advice of provincial lords, leading scholars and certain important merchants as to the answer to be given to President Fillmore's letter. The replies received in Edo varied. Some wanted to fight Perry as soon as he reappeared. Some warned that granting Perry's concessions would only encourage the Westerners to demand further concessions later on, and they urged that the policy of national isolation be firmly maintained. Others advocated temporary concessions to the Americans to enable Japan to build up its defenses. One widely expressed view was that Japan should study and master the technical skills of the foreigners in order to turn the tables on them in future years.

In other words, in their reaction to foreign interference the Japanese were divided into two broad categories. Some were fanatical isolationists; others were pragmatic. But all were patriotic in the sense that they believed in the special virtue and destiny of their land, ruled "from ages eternal" by a line of monarchs descended from the Sun.

Politically the country was thrown into growing confusion. Perry's treaty indeed was a deadly blow to the prestige of the shogun's government in Edo. The very word *shogun* was a contraction of a longer title meaning "barbarian-suppressing generalissimo." If the shogun failed in this fundamental duty, the respect due to his office must necessarily diminish. And in fact the shogunate's reaction to Perry's visit—seeking outside advice—suggested a loss of nerve. The Emperor's court at Kyōtō, long powerless, began to assert itself, nagging at the shogun's government in Edo for its failure to stand up to the foreigners. Certain provincial lords attempted to expel the intruders by firing on their vessels, but such ventures proved ineffective and merely demonstrated the superior armaments possessed by the Western powers. Gradually, even the

Japanese troops fighting the Chinese. Within a few years of Perry's arrival Japan had brought her armies up to Western standards.

Left Mihorabashi railroad station. By the end of the nineteenth century Japan had an advanced railway system.

most die-hard patriots were forced to recognize that the foreigners had come to stay. Curiosity began to conquer prejudice; and among younger Japanese especially, admiration struggled with dislike. The loser in all the welter of emotional confusion was the Tokugawa shogunate, for here was a government that seemed both incompetent and out of date. And as the shogunate lost face, the prestige of the monarchy rose.

The collapse of the shogunate and, in 1868, its replacement by a new regime—the turn of events known as the Meiji restoration—was the prelude to a process of modernization that would astonish the world. The slogan of the Meiji oligarchy, accepted with enthusiasm as a national ideal, was "a rich country with strong armed forces." The second part of that phrase was the more important. In the development of industry and communications, the needs of the army and navy were given priority. In the new system of state education, obligations took precedence over rights. There was nothing novel in all this. A warrior society, homogeneous, ethnocentric and impregnated by Confucian concepts of duty, was adapting itself to the power politics of the contemporary world and was girding itself for two prime tasks: first, to remove the "unequal" treaties, and second, to join the great imperial powers in the struggle for markets, spheres of influence and overseas colonies. Young samurai who had taken up arms when Perry landed at Uraga ("effeminate-looking Japanese," the expedition's historian called them) would see these goals achieved in their lifetime. By the twentieth century Japan had become a power in the world: a modern,

Perry delivering his letter from President Fillmore to the Imperial Commissioners.

militarily strong and advanced industrial state.

Thus, insult and humiliation—for that is what Western intrusion meant to the nineteenth-century Japanese—proved to be a challenge, a stimulus to effort. The twentieth century had scarcely begun before Japan was allied, on terms of formal equality, with Great Britain (an association that restored to the people of Japan the pride that had been lost half a century earlier). An apt pupil of the West, Japan then proceeded to demonstrate to the East that the West was not invincible. Victory over the Russians in 1905 made Japan, for a time at any rate, the hero of all Asia from the Yellow Sea to the Red Sea.

There are Japanese historians—controversial figures who presage an academic fashion of the 1970s—who claim that the era from the twilight years of the shogunate to the national surrender in 1945 should be seen as a kind of Hundred Years War against the West, in which Japan led Asia to eventual freedom and independence. According to this interpretation, the struggles for national freedom in India, Ceylon, Burma, Southeast Asia and, indeed, China itself were inspired by Japan's example.

The argument is that Japan demonstrated that an Asian country could modernize itself and become an industrial power with a minimum of foreign help. Then, by defeating Russia in 1905, Japan demonstrated that white men could be beaten in war by Asians. Those historians see Japanese intervention in China as the stimulus that awakened the Chinese to the threat of imperial aggression. Thus, as the agent of fate or of historical necessity, Japan was the rough midwife of Mao's revolution and of the rise of China as a great power. That process of obtaining Asiatic independence, which began with victory in the Russo-Japanese War, was completed in World War II when Japan's conquests during the early engagements destroyed the remaining prestige of the white colonial powers and its grant of nominal independence to their colonial territories made the postwar independence of these territories inevitable.

Such a remarkable and, at first sight, bizarre theory cannot be dismissed out of hand. It deserves serious consideration, for there can be no doubt that Japan was a catalyst in the growth and eventual triumph of Asian nationalism. But for Japan to claim exclusive credit for that triumph—and to ignore the profound influence of forces such as Marxism and the Russian Revolution—is absurd. That Japanese aggression in China, particularly from 1937 on, brought chaos and, as a consequence of that chaos, Communism to that country can hardly be denied. In that negative and destructive sense Japan was perhaps the midwife of Mao's revolution—but that was never the role in which Japan saw itself. In any case, Mao's success is not something on which the Japanese can fairly congratulate themselves.

There is somewhat more substance to the claims

An American sketch of a business session in progress between Perry and the Japanese.

Sumo wrestlers carrying bundles of rice ashore in the harbor of Yokohama.

made for Japan's role in Asia during World War II. The first shattering blows (symbolized by the collapse of Singapore) meant a final loss of prestige for Westerners in Asia—a loss that later successes never completely effaced. There is no question that the false independence granted to European colonies occupied by the Japanese meant that real independence could not be denied these territories by their Western rulers in the postwar years. Here the Japanese played what could be described as a constructive role in Asian affairs, although the cost at the time to many of those concerned tended to be expensive in terms of human life and dignity.

The phoenix that has risen from the rubble of the ruined and prostrate Japan of 1945 has astonished the Western world. By the year 2000, Japan—which is already the third greatest economic power on earth—may conceivably have a standard of living that is higher than that of any other nation. Enormous industrial energy was released by the opening of Japan, but its potential dates from an earlier age. The closing of the country by the shogunate in the seventeenth century forced a stopper into a barrel that effervesced with vitality. Had seclusion not been imposed upon them, the Japanese—notable seafarers—would undoubtedly have discovered and probably have colonized areas of the globe such as Australia and New Zealand well ahead of any European power. Perry, and those who hastened to follow his lead, withdrew the stopper from the barrel and released a new and remarkable political force, one that was destined to be both the scourge and the liberator of Asia.

RICHARD STORRY

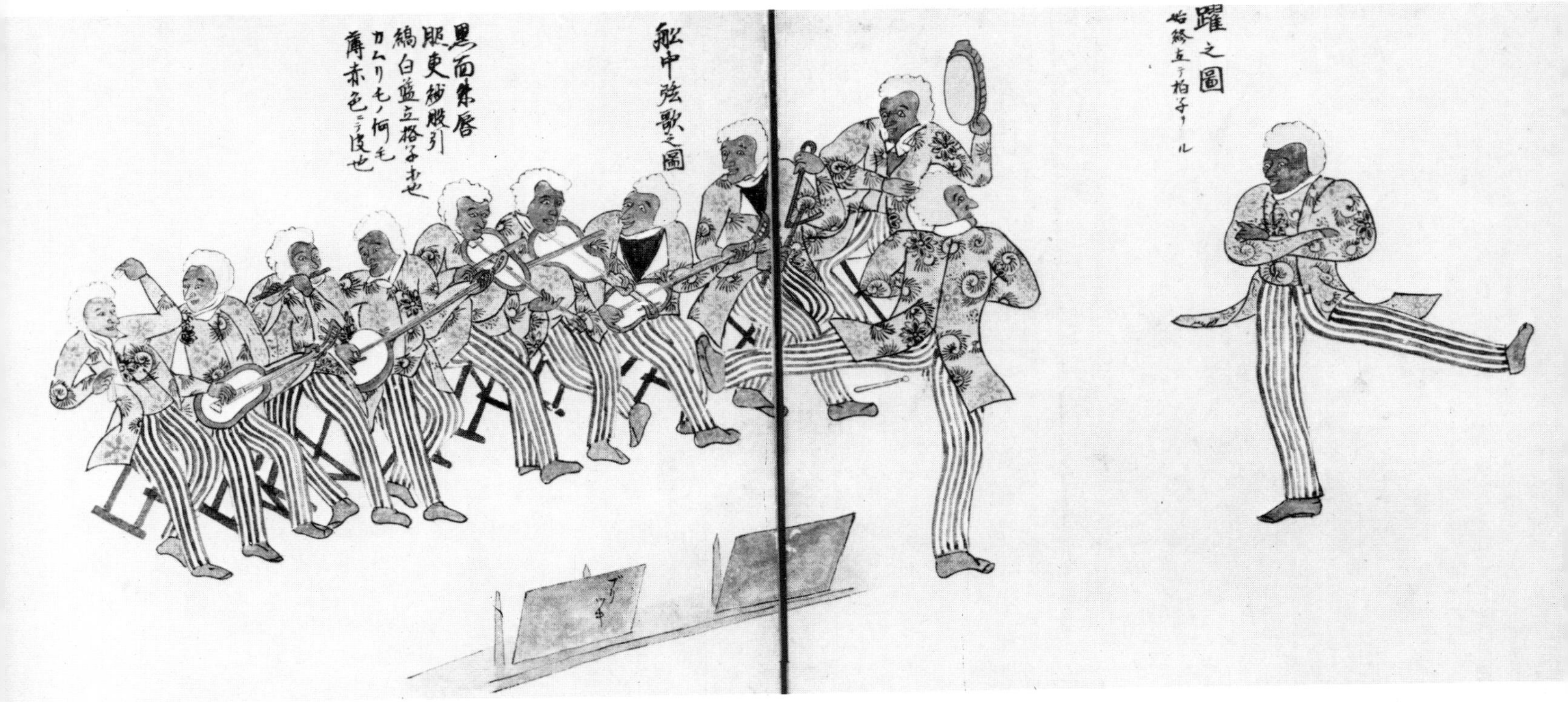

A contemporary Japanese sketch of a group of minstrel performers.

1740 1760 17

Thomas Jefferson 1743–1826
U.S. President

Francisco Goya 1746–1828
Spanish painter

Jeremy Bentham 1748–1832
British philosopher

Charles James Fox 1749–1806
British statesman

Francisco de Miranda 1750–1816
Venezueluan patriot

Charles Maurice de Talleyrand 1754–1838
French statesman

Louis XVIII 1755–1824
King of France

William Blake 1757–1827
British poet and artist

Horatio, Lord Nelson 1758–1805
British admiral

James Monroe 1758–1831
U.S. President

William Pitt the Younger 1759–1806
British statesman

William Wilberforce 1759–1833
British statesman

Claude Henri de Saint-Simon 1760–1825
French philosopher and social scientist

George IV 1762–1830
King of Great Britain and Ireland

William Cobbett 1763–1835
British political writer

Charles, Earl Grey 1764–1845
British statesman

Robert Fulton 1765–1815
U.S. engineer and inventor

John Quincy Adams 1767–1848
U.S. President

Michel Ney 1767–1815
Marshal of France

Joachim Murat 1767–1815
King of Naples, Marshal of France

Andrew Jackson 1767–1845
U.S. President

Francis I 1768–1835
Emperor of Austria

Napoleon Bonaparte 1769–1821
Emperor of the French

Lord Castlereagh 1769–1822
British statesman

Mohammed Ali 1769–1849
Pasha of Egypt

Arthur Wellesley, Duke of Wellington
1769–1852 *British statesman and soldier*

Alexander von Humboldt 1769–1859
German explorer and scientist

Ludwig van Beethoven 1770–1827
German composer

George Canning 1770–1827
British statesman

Georg Hegel 1770–1831
German philosopher

Frederick William III 1770–1840
King of Prussia

William Wordsworth 1770–1850
British poet

Walter Scott 1771–1832
Scottish writer

Robert Owen 1771–1858
British socialist

Samuel Taylor Coleridge 1772–18
British poet

Charles Fourier 1772–1837
French social scientist and reforme

Chaka 1773–1828
Zulu chief

Louis Philippe 1773–1850
King of France

Klemens von Metternich
1773–1859 *Austrian statesma*

Jane Austen 1775–181
British novelist

J. M. W Turner 17
British painter

Alexander I
Tsar of Rus

Nathan
London

Henry Cl
U.S.

Bernar
Chilean

José
South

780 | 1800 | 1820

The Louisiana Purchase **1803**
One of the best bargains in history doubles the size of the United States, provides a foothold on the Gulf and gives control of the central river system

1812
Retreat from Russia
Cossack raiding parties and an awesome Russian winter combine to decimate Napoleon's Grand Army as it retreats from Moscow

1815
The Reshaping of Europe
The rulers of Europe attend a glittering assembly at Vienna that, despite its autocratic and arbitrary agreements, helps keep the peace for half a century

1807
The Voyage of "Fulton's Folly"
Robert Fulton demonstrates to a skeptical world the feasibility of steamboat navigation

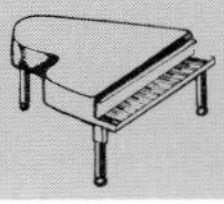

Beethoven's Rededicated Masterpiece **1803**
A brilliant young German composes a vast new symphony that both fascinates and bewilders its first audiences

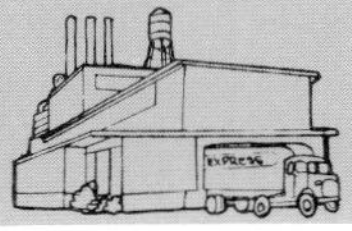

1811
"General" Lud's Army
Roving bands of jobless English textile workers vandalize the labor-saving machines that have robbed many of them of their livelihood

851

'77–1825

othschild 1777–1836
anker

'77–1852
atesman

Higgins 1778–1842
atesman and soldier

n Martín 1778–1850
nerican revolutionary

rd Melbourne 1779–1848
itish statesman

arl von Clausewitz 1780–1831
russian military theorist

ean Ingres 1780–1867
rench painter

George Stephenson 1781–1848
English inventor and engineer

John C. Calhoun 1782–1850
U.S. statesman

Martin Van Buren 1782–1862
U.S. President

Simón Bolívar 1783–1830
South American revolutionary

Stendhal (Henri Beyle) 1783–1842
French writer

Lord Palmerston 1784–1865
British statesman

Alessandro Manzoni 1785–1873
Italian writer

François Guizot 1787–1874
French statesman and historian

Lord Byron 1788–1824
British poet

Robert Peel 1788–1850
British statesman

Pius IX 1792–1878
Pope

Percy Bysshe Shelley 1792–1822
British poet

Sam Houston 1793–1863
U.S. soldier and political leader

Matthew C. Perry 1794–1868
U.S. naval officer

John Keats 1795–1821
British poet

James Polk 1795–1849
U.S. President

Antonio López de Santa Anna *c.* 1795–1876
Mexican revolutionary

Thomas Carlyle 1795–1881
British essayist and historian

Frederick William IV 1795–1881
King of Prussia

Leopold von Ranke 1795–1886
German historian

Nicholas I 1796–1855
Tsar of Russia

Franz Schubert 1797–1828
Austrian composer

Adolphe Thiers 1797–1877
French statesman

William I 1797–1888
King of Prussia, Emperor of Germany

Auguste Comte 1798–1857
French philosopher

Eugène Delacroix 1798–1863
French painter

Alexander Pushkin 1799–1837
Russian poet

Honoré de Balzac 1799–1850
French novelist

Felix Schwarzenberg 1800–52
Austrian statesman

Cetewayo ?–1884
Zulu chief

Helmuth von Moltke 1800–91
Prussian field-marshal

Victor Hugo 1802–85
French writer

Lajos Kossuth 1802–94
Hungarian statesman

Ralph Waldo Emerson 1803–82
U.S. man of letters

Richard Cobden 1804–65
British statesman

Benjamin Disraeli 1804–81
British statesman

Giuseppe Mazzini 1805–72
Italian statesman

Ferdinand de Lesseps 1805–94
French engineer and diplomat

Isambard Kingdom Brunel 1806–59
British engineer

Benito Juarez 1806–72
Mexican statesman

John Stuart Mill 1806–73
British political philosopher

1804 French *Code Civile* instituted

1804 Coronation of Napoleon as Emperor

1805 Napoleon defeats Russians and Austrians at Austerlitz; British defeat French at Trafalgar

1808–14 Peninsular War in Spain

1812 Spencer Perceval, British Prime Minister, assassinated

1812–14 Anglo-American War

1815 Prussia initiates a German Confederation, including Austria-Hungary

1820 Liberia founded

1820 Missouri Compromise: no new slave states in U.S.A. north of 36° 30′ latitude

End of an Empire 1824
As Simón Bolívar unites the rebel movements, Spain's South American Empire crumbles

1829
The People's President
American voters overwhelmingly endorse Andrew Jackson, populist candidate and hero of the Battle of New Orleans, for the nation's highest office

1824
Death of a Poet
England's foremost Romantic poet dies in Greece attempting to aid insurgent natives in the struggle against their Ottoman oppressors

1834
A Revolution in Agriculture
Cyrus Hall McCormick converts arable farming from a demanding chore to a profitable business

1830
The Age of Steam
In an effort to restore domestic tranquility, an unpopular Tory Prime Minister inaugurates Britain's first railway amid considerable fanfare

1836
"Remember the Alamo!"
The annihilation of the Alamo's defenders inspires Texans to overcome the Mexicans in a bid for independence

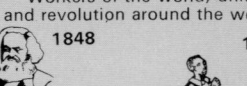

A Manifesto for the Masses
The last line of Marx and Engels' *Communist Manifesto*—"Workers of the world, unite!"—sparks riot and revolution around the world

1848

1851

185

1850
The Compromise of 1850
Henry Clay's compromise delays for ten years the moment when North and South meet to answer the question of man's "inalienable rights"

Robert E. Lee 1807–70
U.S. Confederate general

Giuseppe Garibaldi 1807–82
Italian patriot

Louis Napoleon Bonaparte (Napoleon III) 1808–73 *King of France*

Abraham Lincoln 1809–65
U.S. President

Pierre Joseph Proudhon 1809–65
French anarchist

Charles Darwin 1809–82
British naturalist

Cyrus Hall McCormick 1809–84
U.S. inventor

Alfred, Lord Tennyson 1809–92
British poet

William Ewart Gladstone 1809–98
British statesman

Frederic Chopin 1810–49
Polish composer

Camillo Cavour 1810–61
Italian statesman

William Thackeray 1811–63
British novelist

Louis Blanc 1811–82
French socialist

Charles Dickens 1812–70
British novelist

Alexander Herzen 1812–70
Russian revolutionary writer

Søren Kierkegaard 1813–55
Danish philosopher

David Livingstone 1813–73
British missionary and explorer

Richard Wagner 1813–83
German composer

Giuseppe Verdi 1813–1901
Italian operatic composer

Mikhail Bakunin 1814–76
Russian anarchist and writer

Otto von Bismarck 1815–98
German statesman

Charlotte Brontë 1816–55
British novelist

Henry Thoreau 1817–62
U.S. man of letters

Alexander II 1818–81
Tsar of Russia

Karl Marx 1818–83
German political philosopher

Gustave Courbet 1819–77
French painter

George Eliot (Mary Ann Evans) 1819–80 *British novelist*

John Ruskin 1819–1900
British art critic and sociological writer

Victoria 1819–1901
Queen of Great Britain and Ireland

Victor Emmanuel II 1820–78
King of Sardinia, then Italy

Friedrich Engels 1820–95
German political philosopher

Herbert Spencer 1820–1903
British philosopher

Florence Nightingale 1820–1910
British nursing reformer

Charles Baudelaire 1821–67
French poet

Gustave Flaubert 1821–80
French novelist

Fyodor Dostoevsky 1821–81
Russian novelist

Ulysses Simpson Grant 1822–85
U.S. President

Heinrich Schliemann 1822–90
German archaelogist

Louis Pasteur 1822–95
French chemist

Nana Sahib (Dandhu Panth) *c.*1825–60
Leader of Sepoy mutiny

Ferdinand Lassalle 1825–64
German socialist

Paul Kruger 1825–1904
South African statesman

Francisco López 1827–70
President of Paraguay

Joseph Lister 1827–1912
British surgeon

Hippolyte Adolphe Taine 1828–93
French philosopher and critic

Henrik Ibsen 1828–1906
Norwegian poet and dramatist

Leo Tolstoy 1828–1910
Russian writer

Porfirio Diaz 1830–1915
Mexican statesman

Francis Joseph 1830–1916
Emperor of Austria

Maximilian of Hapsburg 1832–67
Emperor of Mexico

Edouard Manet 1832–83
French painter

Charles Gordon 1833–85
British general

Alfred Nobel 1833–96
Swedish inventor and philanthropist

Johannes Brahms 1833–97
German composer

Sitting Bull 1834–90
American Sioux Indian leader

William Morris 1834–96
British poet and artist

James Abbott McNeill Whistler 1834–1903
American painter

Andrew Carnegie 1835–1919
U.S. industrialist and philanthropist

Léon Gambetta 1838–83
French statesman

George Armstrong Custer 1839–76
U.S. soldier

Paul Cézanne 1839–1906
French painter

John D. Rockefeller 1839–1937
U.S. industrialist and philanthropist

Peter Ilich Tchaikovsky 1840–93
Russian composer

Emile Zola 1840–1902
French novelist

Anton Dvořák 1841–1904
Czech composer

Pierre Renoir 1841–1919
French painter

Georges Clemenceau 1841–1929
French statesman

The Mahdi (Mohammed Ahmed) *c.* 1843–85
Sudanese rebel leader

William McKinley 1843–1901
U.S. President

Robert Koch 1843–1910
German bacteriologist

Henry James 1843–1916
U.S. novelist

Friedrich Nietzsche 1844–1900
German philosopher

Alexander III 1845–94
Tsar of Russia

Charles Stewart Parnell 1846–91
Irish statesman

Alexander Graham Bell 1847–1922 *U.S. inventor*

Thomas Edison 1847–1931
U.S. inventor

Paul Gauguin 1848–1903
French painter

Crazy Horse *c.* 1849–
Sioux Indian chief

Meiji
Emperor o

Vince
Dutch

Brazilian independence from **1822** Portugal

1823 Monroe Doctrine: no European interference in the Americas tolerated by U.S.A.

1825 Decembrist Revolt in Russia

1830 July Revolution in France; uprisings in Germany, Italy, Belgium, Poland (till 1831)

Reform Act enfranchises middle-class men in Britain **1832**

1835–37 Great Trek by Boers of Cape Colony

1840 Representative of Sultan of Oman establishes his capital at Zanzibar

1840 New Zealand becomes British colony

1839 Mohammed Ali's revolt in Asia Minor checked by European powers

1839–42 Sino-British Opium War: Hong Kong and trade concessions to Britain

1845 Republic of Texas annexed to U.S.A., leading to U.S.-Mexican War (1846–48)

1846 Irish Famine

Victoria gold rush in **1851** Australia

Thomas Cook organizes trip to Paris **1855**

1848 California gold ru

1850–64 Taiping Rebellion in China: Ch'ing dynasty retains powe with aid of British under Gordon

1855 Napoleon III's Universal Exhibition

)ueen Victoria's Crystal Palace
he Great Exhibition lays the foundation for
uture international fairs and festivals that seek
o overcome national barriers peacefully

'erry Opens Japan
bold U.S. naval commander all but single-
andedly forces the isolationist Japanese to
pen their country to international trade

ecil Rhodes 1853–1902
itish statesman and colonialist

Alfred Dreyfus 1859–1935
French soldier

William II 1859–1941
Emperor of Germany

Theodor Herzl 1860–1904
Austro-Hungarian founder of Zionism

Anton Chekhov 1860–1904
Russian writer

lutsuhito) 1852–1912
apan

n Gogh 1853–90
ainter

1857–65 First transatlantic cable laid

1864 War over Schleswig-Holstein: Prussia and Austria against Denmark

1859 War of Austria against France and Sardinia concluded at Solferino

1859 John Brown's raid on Harper's Ferry

1860–70 Maori Wars

1861 Liberation of 20 million serfs open Alexander II's program of reform in Russia

1870 Paris Commune; shortlived attempt by radicals to revive the spirit of 1792

1867 Alaska purchased by U.S.A. from Russia

1866 Prussians defeat Austrians at Sadowa

1867 Dual monarchy of Austria-Hungary created

1867 Canadian Federation

1865 President Lincoln assassinated

1869 Suez Canal opened

1865–70 Paraguayan War against Argentina, Brazil and Uruguay

1871 Compulsory primary education in Japan

1875–78 Eastern Crisis; Treaty of Berlin (1878) destroys Pan-Slav Greater Bulgaria

1870 Vatican Council pronounces on papal infallibility

1871 Trade Unionism legalized in Britain

1870 Unification of Italy completed

1879–91 Tariff walls erected by U.S.A. and Europe except Britain

1886 American Federation of Labor founded

1886 Gladstone's Irish Home Rule Bill splits the British Liberal Party

1882 British occupation of Egypt and Sudan

1885 The Mahdi's revolt in Sudan

1885 Indian National Congress founded

1882 Triple Alliance between Germany, Austria-Hungary and Italy

1887 Secret Russo-German "Reinsurance Treaty"

1889 Second International founded in Paris

1889 Interparliamentary Union founded

1887 Bloody Sunday; troops break up demonstration in Trafalgar Square

1893 Women gain vote in New Zealand; first instance of female suffrage

1894–1906 Dreyfus Affair discredits French monarchists and clericalists

1894 Sino-Japanese War

1898 Kitchener defeats Khalifa at Omdurman

1899–1900 Boxer Rebellion in China

1899 Hague Conference on arms limitation: establishment of International Court of Arbitration

1899–1902 Boer War

1896 First Olympiad held

Acknowledgments

The authors and publishers wish to thank the following museums and collections by whose kind permission the illustrations are reproduced. Page numbers appear in bold, photographic sources in italics.

12 Missouri Historical Society: *Orbis Publishing Ltd*
13 *Mansell Collection*
14 Louisiana State Museum
15 *Radio Times Hulton Picture Library*
17 (1) Louisiana State Museum (2) *Mansell Collection*
18 Louisiana State Museum
19 (1) *Mary Evans Picture Library* (2) National Portrait Gallery of America, Smithsonian Institution. Washington, D.C.
20 Gesellschaft der Musikfreunde, Vienna
21 *Mansell Collection*
22 (1) *Giraudon* (2) *Scala*
23 *Mansell Collection*
24 *Mansell Collection*
25 *Mansell Collection*
26 (1) *Mansell Collection* (2) *Radio Times Hulton Picture Library*
27 (1) National Maritime Museum, Greenwich, London (2) Minet Library, Lambeth Public Library, London (3) National Portrait Gallery, London
28 Musée de la Marine, Paris: *Mansell Collection*
29 British Museum, London: *R. B. Fleming*
30 Webb Institute of Naval Architecture, Long Island
31 From the Collections of the New Jersey Historical Society
32 Science Museum, London
33 *Weidenfeld and Nicolson Archive*
34 (1) Courtesy of the Mariners Museum, Newport News (2) Science Museum
35 New-York Historical Society
36 (1) *John R. Freeman*
37 (1) British Museum (2) Guildhall Museum, London: *Su Gooders*
38 *Mansell Collection*
39 *Mansell Collection*
40 *Mansell Collection*
41 (1) *Mansell Collection* (2) National Portrait Gallery, London
42 (1) British Museum: *John R. Freeman* (2) *Mansell Collection*
43 *Mansell Collection*
44 (1) National Portrait Gallery, London (2, 3) *Mary Evans Picture Library*
45 (1) *Mansell Collection* (2) National Maritime Museum, Greenwich
46 *Mansell Collection*
47 Musée des Beaux Arts, Liège
48 *Mansell Collection*
49 (1) Musée de l'Armée, Paris: *Giraudon* (2, 3) *Mansell Collection*
50 *Giraudon*
51 (1) Victoria and Albert Museum, London (2) *Mansell Collection*
52 Musée de l'Armée: *Snark International*
53 (1) Musée de Versailles
54 (1) *Novosti Press Agency* (2) National Portrait Gallery, London
55 (1) British Museum: *R. B. Fleming* (2) *Photo Bulloz*
56 By permission of the Master and Governors of Wellington College
57 Marquess of Anglesey Collection: *Cooper-Bridgeman Library*
58 *Mansell Collection*
60 Victoria and Albert Museum
61 (1) Guildhall Museum: *R. B. Fleming* (2) A. E. Haswell-Miller Collection
62 (2) British Museum
64 (1) Staatsbibliothek, Berlin (2) *John R. Freeman*
65 (1) *Geoff Goode* (2) *Radio Times Hulton Picture Library*
66 *Mansell Collection*
67 *Mansell Collection*
68 *Victor Kennett*
69 (1) Museum of America, Madrid: *Joseph Martin/Scala* (2) *Jean Tandel/A.A.A. Photo*
70 (1) *Mansell Collection* (2) *Mary Evans Picture Library*
71 *Mary Evans Picture Library*
72 *Mansell Collection*
73 National Portrait Gallery, London
74 (1, 2) *Mansell Collection* (3) Courtesy of John Murray Publishers: *Derrick Witty*
75 (1, 2) *Mansell Collection*
76 (1) National Portrait Gallery, London (2) Walker Art Gallery, Liverpool
77 (1) Musée des Beaux Arts, Bordeaux: *Giraudon* (2) Louvre: *Giraudon* (3) Trinity College, Cambridge: *Mansell Collection*
78 Reproduced by gracious permission of Her Majesty The Queen: *Phoebus Picture Library*
79 Reproduced by gracious permission of Her Majesty The Queen: *Phoebus Picture Library*
80 (1) National Portrait Gallery, London (2) Alan G. Thomas Collection: *John R. Freeman*
81 (1) Louvre: *Giraudon* (2) Museum der Bildenden Kunste, Leipzig: *Tate Gallery*
82 Ladies Hermitage Association, Hermitage, Tennessee
83 Ladies Hermitage Association, Hermitage, Tennessee
84 (1) Smithsonian Institution (2) *Radio Times Hulton Picture Library*
85 (1) *Mansell Collection* (2) Smithsonian Institution
86 British Museum
87 Smithsonian Institution
88 (2) *Novosti Press Agency* (3) *Mary Evans Picture Library*
89 (1, 2) *Mary Evans Picture Library* (3) *Mansell Collection*
91 National Portrait Gallery, London
92 (1) Science Museum (2) *Mary Evans Picture Library* (3) National Portrait Gallery, London (4) *Mary Evans Picture Library* (5) National Portrait Gallery, London
93 Science Museum
94 (1) National Gallery, London (2) Royal Holloway College, London
95 (1) British Railways Board, London (2) Tate Gallery, London
96 (1, 2) Science Museum
97 (1, 2) *Mansell Collection*
98 (1) National Portrait Gallery, London (2) *Mansell Collection*
99 (1) French Government Tourist Office, London (2) National Portrait Gallery, London
100 International Harvester Company of Great Britain Ltd
101 International Harvester Company of Great Britain Ltd
102 International Harvester Company of Great Britain Ltd
103 (1, 2) Science Museum
104 Science Museum
105 International Harvester Company of Great Britain Ltd
106 (1) F. Krupp, Essen (2) British Museum: *R. B. Fleming*
107 (1) British Museum: *R. B. Fleming* (2, 3) *Radio Times Hulton Picture Library*
108 Everett L. DeGolyer, Jr. Collection
109 British Museum
110 (1) *Western Americana Picture Library* (2) San Antonio Museum Association, Texas
111 *Western Americana Picture Library*
112 *Western Americana Picture Library*
113 *Mary Evans Picture Library*
114 (1) Texas State Library: *B. Malone* (2) John Judkyn Memorial, Bath: *Derek Balmer*
115 *Mary Evans Picture Library*
116 (1) *Radio Times Hulton Picture Library* (2) *Mansell Collection*
117 (1) *Roger-Viollet* (2) *Radio Times Hulton Picture Library*
118 *Camera Press*
119 Staatsbibliothek, Berlin: *Camera Press*
120 Karl Marx Memorial Library, London
121 (1) *Mansell Collection* (2) *Giraudon*
122 (1, 2) *Mansell Collection* (3) British Museum: *John R. Freeman*
123 (1) Musée Carnavalet, Paris (2) *Novosti Press Agency*
124 (1) *Ullstein Bilderdienst* (2) *Mansell Collection*
125 (1) *Western Americana Picture Library* (2, 3) *Mansell Collection*
126 National Portrait Gallery of America, Smithsonian Institution
127 *Radio Times Hulton Picture Library*
129 American Museum in Britain, Bath: *Phoebus Picture Library*
130 *Western Americana Picture Library*
131 (1) National Portrait Gallery of America, Smithsonian Institution (2) *Mary Evans Picture Library*
132 (1) National Cotton Council of America, Memphis (2) National Portrait Gallery of America, Smithsonian Institution
133 (1) National Portrait Gallery of America, Smithsonian Institution (2) American Museum in Britain: *Phoebus Picture Library*
134 (1) *Ronan Picture Library* (2) National Portrait Gallery, London
135 (1) Science Museum (2, 3) National Portrait Gallery, London
136 Victoria and Albert Museum: *A. C. Cooper*
137 Victoria and Albert Museum
138 Victoria and Albert Museum
139 Victoria and Albert Museum: *A. C. Cooper*
140 (1) De La Rue Company, London: *Cooper-Bridgeman Library* (2) *Cooper-Bridgeman Library*
141 Victoria and Albert Museum: *A. C. Cooper*
142 Victoria and Albert Museum
143 (1) Victoria and Albert Museum (2) Guildhall Museum: *Su Gooders*
144 (1, 2) *Mansell Collection*
145 (1, 2, 3) *Mansell Collection* (4) Victoria and Albert Museum
146 British Museum: *John R. Freeman*
147 *Mansell Collection*
148 (1) *Radio Times Hulton Picture Library* (2) *Mansell Collection*
149 Victoria and Albert Museum
150 (1) Victoria and Albert Museum: *John R. Freeman* (2) British Museum: *John R. Freeman*
151 (1, 2) British Museum: *John R. Freeman*
152 (1) *Mansell Collection* (2) Smithsonian Institution
153 (1, 2) Smithsonian Institution

Managing Editor *Adrian Brink*
Assistant Editors *Geoffrey Chesler*, *Francesca Ronan*
Picture Editor *Julia Brown*
Consultant Designer *Tim Higgins*
Art Director *Anthony Cohen*